The BCG Genealogical Standards Manual

© 2000, Board for Certification of Genealogists®

Post Office Box 14291
Washington, DC 20044
www.bcgcertification.org

The BCG genealogical standards manual.
  p. cm.
 Includes index.
 ISBN 0-916489-92-2
  1. Genealogists—Certification. 2. Board for Certification of Genealogists (Washington, D.C.)—
Handbooks, manuals, etc. I. Board for Certification of Genealogists
 (Washington, D.C.)

CS8.5 .B38 2000
929'.1--dc21

                00-023694

Published by Ancestry® Publishing,
an imprint of MyFamily.com, Inc.

P.O. Box 990
Orem, Utah 84059
www.ancestry.com

First Printing 2000
10 9 8 7 6 5 4 3

Printed in the United States of America

CONTENTS

* This example illustrates the typographic style normally used in the *National Genealogical Society Quarterly*.

† This example illustrates the typographic style normally used in the *New England Historical and Genealogical Register*.

Introduction

When Standards Apply

Genealogists adhere to principles of competence, regardless of whether the results of their studies are communicated orally (in lectures and courses) or in writing (published in print or electronic format, privately circulated among family members or correspondents, reported to clients or employers, or placed in one's own research files). These standards of competence extend to all phases of a research project:

- Collecting the information;
- Evaluating the evidence; and
- Compiling the results.

They also apply to all phases of teaching activities:

- Lecturing;
- Presenting classroom sessions; and
- Preparing written instructional materials.

They apply, also, to participation in the kinds of continuing education that raises the skill levels of individuals and of the field as a whole.

The BCG Genealogical Standards Manual

Since its foundation in 1964, the Board for Certification of Genealogists (BCG) has promulgated—in lectures and publications—attainable, uniform standards of competence and ethics that have become generally accepted throughout the field. The present publication is designed to clarify, codify, and organize the standards and make them readily accessible to all. It is organized in four sections, the first three of which address standards for researchers, teachers, and ongoing skill development. The fourth section consists of a series of appendixes that provide information about the Board and example reports and compilations. The last section is a subject index to the text and to concepts illustrated in the examples.

The *Manual,* which originated as a proposal brought to the trustees by Thomas Jones and a series of drafts submitted by Helen Leary, is the result of more than three years of concentrated work by trustees, officers, and associates of BCG. Their names are listed below—in recognition of their heroic dedication to the realization of this manual and their unwavering support of the standards it reflects.

> Mary McCampbell Bell, CALS [now CLS*], CGL
> Bettie Cummings Cook, CG
> Joan Ferris Curran, CG
> Donn Devine, CG, CGI
> Kay Haviland Freilich, CG
> George B. Handran, CG
> Marty Hiatt, CGRS
> Kathleen W. Hinckley, CGRS
> Henry B. Hoff, CG, FASG†
> Kay Germain Ingalls, CGRS
> Thomas W. Jones, CG, CGL
>   President, 1999–
> Lynn C. McMillion, CAILS [now CLS]
> Brenda Dougall Merriman, CGRS, CGL
> Elizabeth Shown Mills, CG, CGL, FASG
> Joy Reisinger, CG
> William Bart Saxbe, CG, FASG
> Elisabeth Whitman Schmidt, CALS [now CLS]
> Kip Sperry, CG, FASG
> Beth A. Stahr, CGRS

Additional information about the Board is provided in Appendix A. Its code of ethics is included in Appendix B.

> Helen F. M. Leary, CG, CGL, FASG
> Editor
> February 2000

---

* CALS (Certified American Lineage Specialist) and CAILS (Certified American Indian Lineage Specialist) are certification categories that have been discontinued in favor of the general category, CLS^SM (Certified Lineage Specialist^SM). The other categories represented here by their short-form identifiers are: Certified Genealogist^SM (CG^SM), Certified Genealogical Records Specialist^SM (CGRS^SM), Certified Genealogical Lecturer^SM (CGL^SM) and Certified Genealogical Instructor^SM (CGI^SM). All are service marks of the Board for Certification of Genealogists derived from its program of competence testing and are used under licenses granted to its associates.

† FASG is Fellow, American Society of Genealogists.

Research Standards

The Genealogical Proof Standard

The ultimate goal for all genealogists is to assemble (and perhaps share with others) a reconstructed family history that is as close to the truth as possible. In order to achieve that goal, we adhere to an overall standard by which we measure the credibility of the statements we make about ancestral identities, relationships, life events, and biographical details.

This credibility standard is called the Genealogical Proof Standard (GPS). We use the GPS, also, to assess the reliability of genealogical statements other people make, whether they relate to our families or to their own.

Meeting the Genealogical Proof Standard is a five-step process:

(*a*) We conduct a reasonably exhaustive search in reliable sources for all information that is or may be pertinent to the identity, relationship, event, or situation in question;

(*b*) We collect and include in our compilation a complete, accurate citation to the source or sources of each item of information we use;

(*c*) We analyze and correlate the collected information to assess its quality as evidence;

(*d*) We resolve any conflicts caused by items of evidence that contradict each other or are contrary to a proposed (hypothetical) solution to the question; and

(e)   We arrive at a soundly reasoned, coherently written conclusion.

Meeting the GPS does not require—or ensure—proof beyond the shadow of a doubt, but an objection that "something else *could* have happened" is insufficient to discredit our own or another person's conclusions. Genealogists recognize, however, that any statement about ancestors, even if it meets the GPS, is not absolute or everlasting. When new evidence surfaces or flaws in the conclusion are found, we re-examine the statement to determine if it remains valid.

Data-Collection Standards

Genealogists collect information from a variety of sources, and about widely diverse subjects, in order to understand the intricate history of a particular family or group. Although some sources are people from whom we collect oral data and some are physical objects from which we collect visual information, the vast majority are written and printed records—fragile, one-of-a-kind originals, exact-image reproductions (photocopies, microfilm, and the like), or published volumes. Because the information we collect is the foundation of everything else we do, we adhere to the following standards:

1. **Materials (published, unpublished, microfilmed, photographic, and original) are handled with careful regard** for their preservation and availability for future researchers.

2. **Custodians of records are treated with courtesy**, recognizing their role in preserving and making available for research the records within their jurisdiction.

3. **Authors, editors, compilers, lecturers, and electronic publishers are respected** for their contributions to the genealogical literature, and their rights in their work *are not infringed*.

4. **Other people's work products are reused prudently**, a standard that includes

    • *full citation to them and their work product,* regardless of how it is used;

    • *meticulous observance of copyright,* fair-use principles, and ethical constraints—that is, appropriate permission is obtained before significant portions of their work are reused or incorporated in any way within our own print or electronic publications or widely distributed materials;

    • *faithful adherence* to the work product's overall concept as well as to its details; and

- *honest, impartial judgment* of the nature and significance of the contribution.

5.   **Information is collected efficiently** by

- *carefully analyzing and defining* the question an investigation is intended to answer;

- *identifying sources for the data* that may be needed to answer that question; and

- *designing an intelligent plan* for accessing and examining those sources.

6.   **Information is collected accurately** by

- *reading correctly* the handwriting in the record;

- *understanding fully* the words and phrases in the record;

- *rendering precisely* all names, dates, places, and circumstances that are mentioned in the record; and

- *collecting completely* all data about the record that places the names, dates, localities, and situations in context. EXAMPLES: column headings in a list, notations on the back of or appended to a document, indications that the record is an incomplete copy or significantly damaged, and so forth.

7.   **Information is collected dispassionately** by

- *setting aside* any bias, preference, or preconception that might color what is collected from the record; and

- *suspending judgment* about the information's effect on the research question until after it has been collected from the record, analyzed, and correlated with other findings.

8.   **Information's source is scrupulously acknowledged**, regardless of its form or the method we use to collect the data (handwritten notes, photocopies, microfilm printouts, scanned images, e-mail, Internet downloads, and so on). Source acknowledgment (its "citation")[1] includes

- *recording all pertinent details about the specific record* being examined, whether or not it is the "best" or most authoritative source. Such details might include the following kinds of data, depending on the nature and location of the record:

---

1.   Source citation models can be found in footnotes and endnotes used in scholarly genealogical journals and in such genealogy-specific manuals as Elizabeth Shown Mills, CG, CGL, FASG, *Evidence! Citation and Analysis for the Family Historian* (Baltimore: Genealogical Publishing Company, 1997).

(*a*) its form (original document; official record-book; published abstract, summary, or compilation; CD; online transmission; oral interview; and so forth);

(*b*) who created it and, if applicable, who edited, abstracted, compiled, or otherwise manipulated or rearranged the information. If an interview, the name of the person who spoke *and* of the person to whom he or she was speaking are included;

(*c*) when it was created (or the interview given) and, if applicable, when the data were edited, abstracted, or compiled; and

(*d*) where it was created (or the interview given) and, if applicable, where the edition, abstract, summary, or compilation was created or published.

- *recording the record's present location* (identified by full titles), including

  (*a*) the volume, and if applicable, the series of which the volume is a part; or

  (*b*) the folder or bundle of papers, as well as (1) the record group of which the folder or bundle is a part, (2) the collection of which the record group is part, and (3) the institution or private residence (identified by address) where the collection is housed.

- *recording the specific location* within the record from which an item of information was taken. EXAMPLES: page number in the book, page and line or family-and-dwelling numbers in a census schedule, item number in a list, and so forth; and

- *attaching the record's source citation* to every item of information collected from it. The citation may immediately precede or follow the item or be connected to it as a footnote or endnote.

9.   **Photocopies and microfilm printouts include the entire record or item of interest**[2] **and are appropriate collection methods when**

- *the appearance of the record* (handwriting, page layout, or damaged portion) is needed for analysis, or the image is needed as evidence of the record's content;

---

2.   The entire record or item of interest includes notations on the back of an original document (typical of wills, writs, and pre-printed vital records forms); introductory matter that prefaces a compilation (typical of published abstracts); endnotes that supply source citations for or explanations of the data (typical of books and journal articles); and headings, subheadings, and explanatory data not immediately adjacent to the data of interest (typical of government documents, church records, and genealogical research reports).

- *information in the record* is confusing or subject to misunderstanding;

- *the record includes too much* information for accurate use of another collection technique; or

- *time for note taking* at the research facility is limited; and

- *provided that the source is cited on the copy*

   (*a*) by writing the citation neatly, typing it, or including it in a permanent label (on the front unless doing so interferes with the image); or,

   (*b*) when made from a published record, by attaching the title and copyright pages; or

   (*c*) when copies of multiple pages from the same source are made for the same purpose, by securely fastening all of them to the title and copyright pages, or by individually source-citing *each* of the copied pages.

10. **Scanned images of photographs, graphics, or text include the entire document or item of interest.**[3] Researchers who use scanners or scanned images

   - *store the full source citation* within or attached to the file and include it whenever the image is printed or transmitted to another person or file; and

   - *safeguard* at all times the integrity of the original image by taking care that no significant or misleading change is made.

11. **Transcriptions extend to the entire record**, including headings, insertions, and endorsements or notations on its reverse. Transcriptions are appropriate for data collection when photocopying or printing from microfilm is prohibited or impractical, or when the required equipment is unavailable. Transcribing is also useful as a preliminary step in learning how to abstract or summarize effectively a group of unfamiliar records. Researchers who transcribe

   - *include, exactly as given in the record*, the names, dates, spelling, capitalization, punctuation, and grammar;

   - *record obsolete letter forms* with their modern equivalents rather than their modern look-alikes. EXAMPLES: the long *s*, which looks like a modern *f*, is transcribed *s;* the *thorn*, which stood for the sound made by *th* but looks like a *y* is transcribed with the modern letters *th;* the form for capital F, which looks like but is not *ff*, is transcribed F; and an archaic *w* may look like *no* but is transcribed *w;*

3. See Note 2 (p. 4).

- *use good judgment* about including the same page layout and line lengths that appear in the record;

- *make appropriate notations* when passages in the record are illegible, crossed out, or inserted; or are missing because of damage to the document;

- *identify appropriate notations and other one- or two-word comments* by enclosing them within square brackets ([ ]); and

- *place longer comments* within indented and/or italicized paragraphs, or attach them as footnotes or endnotes.

12. **Extracts extend to identified portions of the record** and are appropriate when transcribing the entire document is impractical. EXAMPLE: the household of interest, along with neighboring households, is *extracted* from a census schedule. (A transcription, depending on its title, must include the entire state/province, county/parish, township, city, and so forth.) Extracts

- *follow the rules* of transcription; and

- *include source citations* that incorporate appropriate details about the whole record as well as the extracted portion.

13. **Quotations extend to selected words or passages in the record**, and are appropriate for capturing definitive, confusing, or colorful phrases. Quotations

- *are enclosed within quotation marks* or otherwise distinguished in the research note[4] to indicate which words came from the document and which are the researcher's;

- *need not include all words in the passage—provided that* omissions are replaced by ellipsis points (three spaced dots), and that the remaining text does not misrepresent the content of the passage or of the record as a whole.

14. **Abstracts include all data related to the event or circumstance that is the subject of the record** and are appropriate when a series of records of the same type are examined or a preliminary or overview search is conducted. Researchers who abstract

- *omit only* redundant, repetitive, or formula wording but retain all the "who, what, where, when, how, and why" data.

---

4. When quotations are used in compilations, however, they follow the rules of written English. A few words or sentences are enclosed within quotation marks; but a paragraph or more is set out in an indented block without marks unless taken from a letter, in which case, each paragraph opens with quotation marks and the *last* paragraph closes with them. Ellipsis points "hold the place" of omitted words. Words are enclosed in square brackets if inserted to conform short quotations grammatically with surrounding text.

- *quote passages* whose meaning is unclear or that are unusual for the record type;

- *refrain from "correcting"* names and dates, leaving them in the abstract exactly as they appear in the record;

- *may use moderate standardization* of the sequence of data in the record, taking care to ensure that the rearrangement does not distort the information's significance or confuse its meaning;

- *include notations* in the abstract when the source document is damaged or illegible or when data normally included in records of the same type are absent from this one; and

- *identify their notations and comments* by using square brackets for those within the abstract and placing longer comments in footnotes, endnotes, or separate indented and/or italicized paragraphs.

15. **Summaries include all data considered at the time to be relevant to the research project** and are appropriate collection techniques when large numbers of records of the same type are examined. Researchers who summarize

    - *follow the rules of abstracting except that* an extended series of complex details may be omitted and replaced with an appropriate notation. EXAMPLES: (1) A deed abstract includes the full land description; a deed summary includes instead a notation such as "metes and bounds description included" to act as a reminder that returning to the record will likely result in finding enough information to plat (make a map of) or locate the tract. (2) A will abstract includes the list of items bequeathed to each heir; a will summary includes instead a notation such as "itemized household goods" or "itemized livestock."

    - *return to the record* as needed to collect the rest of the data.

16. **Brief "nutshells" or "snapshots" of the general contents of records are fully cited** and are appropriately used for notation that the records were examined only briefly. If used, instead, to record that no relevant data were found in the records, at least enough information is included to make clear the researcher's reason for concluding that the remainder is irrelevant to the project.

17. **Research logs, pedigree charts, and family group sheets are dated and source-cited** and are best used only to track the progress of an investigation, not as a medium for data collection.

18. **Agents are provided with clear, coherent instructions about the work requested.** Whether they are professional or volunteer researchers, family members, or people with whom one exchanges research time, agents are asked to supply

- *document copies,* transcriptions, and/or detailed abstracts, along with full source citations; and

- *sufficient interpretive commentary* to ensure that there is no misunderstanding of the meaning of each record.

Evidence-Evaluation Standards

The Genealogical Proof Standard requires that we base our genealogical statements on evidence. Evidence is the information that we conclude—after careful evaluation—supports or contradicts the statement we would like to make, or are about to make, about an ancestor. The soundness of the underlying conclusion rests not only on our ability to reason but also on how closely our evaluation methods reflect the following standards:

19. **Reasonably extensive research is prerequisite**—regardless of whether the problem is simple or complex—and includes appropriately broadening the search beyond the person, family, event, or record of most-direct impact on the project. The search effort extends to discovery of information that does or might illuminate (or conflict with) the other items of collected data.

20. **Evidence is derived from appropriate, effective data analysis and correlation,** which are defined as

- *analysis:* the process of scrutinizing each information item to determine its details, meaning, nature, context, and impact on the research project.

- *correlation:* the process of comparing information items to identify connections and contradictions.

21. **Data analysis includes distinguishing between original and derivative sources,**[5] which are defined as

- *original source:* the person or record whose information *did not* come from data already spoken or written. The original

---

5.   A third category of sources whose quality affects the accuracy of our conclusions, albeit indirectly, are the research guides, methodology manuals, dictionaries, and similar materials (and oral presentations that have the same purpose) by which we direct our research. The standards for judging their value are the same ones writers and teachers use when producing them, and are addressed, therefore, in the "Teaching Standards" section of this manual, pp. 21–25

is the most authoritative source. Often, however, it no longer survives or its preservation dictates that it be examined only as an image copy (microfilm, digitized image, and so on).

- *derivative source:* a person or record that supplies information that is repeated, reproduced, transcribed, abstracted, or summarized from something already spoken or written. Because every repetition or recopying of data is an opportunity for error, the closer the derivative is to the original the more reliable the data are likely to be. EXAMPLE: John Doe's will found in the county record book is a first-generation derivative copied from his original testator-signed document; a photocopy of the record-book will is a second-generation derivative. Nevertheless, the photocopy is more complete and likely to be more accurate than a research note (fourth-generation-derivative) taken from a published abstract (third-generation-derivative) of the record-book copy.

22.   **Data analysis includes distinguishing between primary and secondary information,** which are defined as

- *primary information:* data contributed by a knowledgeable eyewitness to or participant in the event that is the subject of the record or by an official whose duties included making a full, accurate record of it. Primary information is further evaluated by *(a)* how close in time and place to the event the record was created, *(b)* how involved in the event the eyewitness was (participant versus bystander, for example), *(c)* the age and sanity of the eyewitness and consequent extent of his/her understanding of the event's significance and details, and *(d)* any bias on the official's or eyewitness's part that might have affected the account.

- *secondary information:* data supplied by a person who recorded it after hearing of the event or its details from someone else. It is judged according to *(a)* the probable number of times the story was passed along orally before it was written down, *(b)* the reputation of the secondary informant for reliability, and *(c)* the existence of any potential for bias on the part of the secondary informant.[6]

23.   **The significance of inconsistencies within the information item is taken into account,** regardless of whether the data's source is original or derivative or the information is primary or

---

6.   Many records supply *both* primary and secondary data. For example, the death information on a death certificate is primary, but the birth information is secondary; and the life-event details and relationships of the writer of a genealogical compilation are primary, but data about the early ancestors are secondary.

secondary. EXAMPLE: John's sale deed, which is primary information from the county deed book (a derivative source) is signed "William," an inconsistency that casts suspicion on the rest of that deed-book entry's reliability.

24. **The data's background context is considered**, including

- *changes in the geographic boundaries of the political subdivision,* its formation date and geopolitical origins, and the migration patterns and travel ways into and out of the area;

- *types of records created* (or not created) during the relevant time periods, and whether and where they survive at present;

- *characteristics of records* common to the area, time period, and record type, including: spelling, punctuation, and capitalization practices; handwriting forms; and usage of standard words and phrases;

- *terminology* used to express a relationship, occupation, civil status (married, single, or minor, for example), legal concept, military or church rank, socioeconomic class, and so on; and

- *the literature, laws, regulations, customs, and history* of the area, time period, population group, and government or military jurisdiction.

25. **The data's relevance to our research project is assessed.** Relevant information

- *links a person*—whether or not the name is given, and not necessarily the ancestor—to a life event (birth, death, land sale, military enlistment, or civil election, for instance), to a relationship (with kinsman, neighbor, enemy, prominent personage, religious leader,), to an on-going situation (literacy, poverty, military/public service, occupation, religion), or to a long-term status (minor, married woman, slave, felon);

- *may or may not be substantially reliable.* Unreliable data that establish the source of widely believed errors (in family tradition, perhaps) or readily available ones (in published abstracts, for instance) are relevant to the investigation, even though such data will not be used for any other purpose;

- *is not trimmed or tailored to fit* a preconception or bias, or to harmonize with the rest of the collected data; and

- *is not ignored* because the finding is inconvenient for the researcher's purposes.

26. **The sum of the evidence is the deciding factor** in arriving at a conclusion that will be expressed as an assertion (statement of "fact"), regardless of whether that assertion concerns a person's identity or relationships, an event or its details, or peripheral situations and circumstances.

27. **The evidence is correlated with earlier conclusions** about the same person, relationship, event, or situation, *provided that those conclusions also meet the Genealogical Proof Standard.*

28. **Previous assumptions (presumptions) brought to the correlation, often unconsciously, are recognized,** including

- *fundamental presumptions*—concepts generally accepted as *objectively true.* EXAMPLES: (1) People do not act after their deaths or before their births. (2) People cannot be in more than one place simultaneously (and travel-time between places is consistent with technology of the period). (3) Everybody has *one* biological mother and father. (4) A mother is present in the place and at the time her child is born and its father was with the mother roughly nine months earlier (present-day technology excepted). (5) No matter how temporary or rudimentary, everybody lives in a physical place.

- *valid presumptions*—concepts generally accepted as *true unless convincingly contradicted.* EXAMPLES: (1) A child is conceived when its mother was roughly twelve to forty-nine. (2) A person's behavior and life patterns are coherent. (3) People observed (at least in general) the legal, moral, and social standards of their place, era, and class. (4) Information in public and church records, contemporaneous family-Bible entries, and sworn court testimony is usually reliable. (5) The data in reputable encyclopedias, dictionaries, maps, and so forth are generally reliable depending on publication date.

- *unsound presumptions*—concepts that may be valid, *but cannot be accepted as true without supporting evidence.* EXAMPLES: (1) A man's widow was the mother of all (or any) of his children. (2) People died in their sixties (or fifties, or seventies). (3) People on the move followed the most popular migration routes. (4) A same-surname male and female who witnessed the same document were husband and wife. (5) A female with the same surname as her father was unmarried. (6) If exhaustive search does not discover the parents' marriage record, their child was illegitimate.

29. **Direct and indirect evidence is correlated with the question being investigated.** Direct and indirect distinctions are based on

two factors: *(a)* the information provided by a record and *(b)* our use of that information. Consequently, the definitions are

- *direct evidence:* an evidence item that is adequate by itself to answer the question. Direct evidence answers the question at hand but does not answer *every* question. EXAMPLES: (1) "Where and when was John born?" is answered by evidence from his birth certificate, but the certificate does not address "When did John's parents marry?" (2) John's land grant answers "Did John own land?" but not "Where did John live?"

- *indirect evidence:* an evidence item that is incomplete in itself and therefore inadequate to answer the question at hand. The inadequacy may stem from the fact that the item

  (a) fails to answer the whole question. EXAMPLES: (1) If John's tombstone inscription provides only his birth year, the evidence drawn from it does not fully answer "What was the *date* of John's birth?" Only if the question is "What *year* was John born?" is the tombstone information direct evidence.[7] (2) John's sale of his land grant answers the question "How long did John own the tract?" but it still does not address the question "Where did John live?"

  (b) is drawn from *circumstantial data* that contribute to the answer but require additional evidence items as well as judicious application of deductive reasoning. EXAMPLES: (1) From John's birth-certificate data, we deduce that, because his mother is termed "wife of" his father, the couple married before John was born. Additional evidence items are needed, possibly large numbers of them, to assemble a sufficient basis for the conclusion "John's parents married between X date and Y date." (2) The question of John's residence is partially answered by the land grant, partially by the tract's sale (which establishes the duration of his ownership). However, we cannot conclude that he ever lived on the tract unless his patterns of land ownership and interpersonal associations (identified by exhaustively examining additional records) justify such a conclusion.

30. **Each evidence item is carefully sifted for indirect evidence** that might be found in details surrounding the direct-evidence statement, no matter how insignificant those details may appear to be.

---

7. Note also that whether direct or indirect, the tombstone information is *secondary* unless provided by someone capable of supplying primary data about John's birth. (See Standard 22, p. 9.)

31. **Indirect evidence is assembled with care and caution** to ensure that all relevant evidence is included and all irrelevant evidence is excluded.

32. **The assembled indirect evidence is thoroughly tested** by reexamining the reasoning that led to each evidence item's inclusion, as well as by extending the research to answer relevant subsidiary questions. Doing so ensures that *any* evidence in support of or contradiction to the deduced answer has been found and considered.

33. **Greater or lesser weight is given to evidence items according to their degree of credibility**—not how often the information is repeated or the number of records in which it appears, but on whether the data are more probably reliable than not.

34. **Contradictions between evidence items are resolved** by demonstrating in a clear, logical, well-documented, written proof summary[8] that

   - *an item in conflict with the proposed answer* is substantially less credible than the item or items that support it; or

   - *the sum of the credible indirect evidence* outweighs a contradictory direct-evidence statement.[9]

Compilation Standards   Genealogists assemble the results of their data collection and evidence evaluation in the following types of compilations: *(a)* research reports; *(b)* proof summaries; *(c)* lineages, pedigrees, and descending genealogies; and *(d)* hereditary-society applications. All of them, in different ways, focus on the identities and relationships of the people within a family and to a greater or lesser degree include biographical information about those people. All compilations, therefore, meet the following standards:

35. **The writing is clear.** Grammar, spelling, usage, and punctuation follow the rules of standard English; organization is logical and comprehensible; and the writing style is straightforward, precise, and reasonably free from unintelligible abbreviations, undefined jargon, malapropisms, casual chitchat, and typographical errors.

8. The standards for proof-summary compilations are discussed on pp. 16–17. They are often written and published in the form of case studies that focus on the technique of evidence evaluation. Case studies are discussed on pp. 23–24.

9. For an extended discussion of evidence analysis, along with case studies that demonstrate the principles, see *Evidence: A Special Issue of the National Genealogical Society Quarterly*, 87 (September 1999). This issue is available for purchase by non-subscribers from the society at 4527 Seventeenth Street North, Arlington, Virginia 22207-2399.

36. **Sources for all genealogical and biographical fact statements are cited** in *The Chicago Manual of Style*'s "reference note" format in footnotes or endnotes.[10] The *Chicago Manual*'s in-text and reference-list styles, and formats used in other disciplines, such as the MLA (Modern Language Association), AP (Associated Press), or APA (American Psychological Association) styles, are not standard for genealogical writing.

Research Reports

Research Reports are written to record in permanent form the results of a genealogical investigation. To fulfill their purpose, the focus of a report is on *communicating* those results—to ourselves at some future date, or to someone else immediately (a for-pay, time-exchange, or *pro bono* client; or a correspondent, employer, patron, or society member). Consequently, research reports have the following qualities:

37. **Reports reflect efficiency.** Efficiency includes

   - *an intelligent research plan* for reaching the project goal, executed with suitable flexibility; and

   - *sufficient recapitulation* of earlier research to inform (or remind) the recipient of *this* investigation's goals and starting point.

38. **Reports are useful.** Utility extends to

   - *reporting both positive and negative findings* (sources examined with no useful result) in sufficient detail to avoid unnecessary future searches of the same records;

   - *transmitting information (a)* with thorough, clearly identifiable citation to its source; *(b)* in a manner that makes clear whether the data have been abstracted, extracted, quoted, summarized, or transcribed; and *(c)* with cross-references to and source citations for accompanying photocopies; and

   - *addressing the specifications of their intended recipients,* whether clients or employers, correspondents (postal or electronic), family members, or oneself in a "report to the file." To address recipients' specifications,

      (*a*) the underlying research conforms to the extent and focus of the project as it was explicitly or implicitly defined by the intended recipient. Explicit definitions, usually by a client or employer, may extend to

---

10. Models, using the *Chicago Manual* reference-note format as applied to the kinds of sources often used by genealogical researchers, are included in the publications mentioned in Note 1 (p. 3).

(1) the persons or events to be investigated; (2) the record or record groups to be examined; (3) the repository or repositories to be visited; (4) limits on time, travel, or expense to be observed; or (5) the extent of analysis and compilation to be included.

(*b*) the physical format conforms to their intended recipient's specifications (paper, diskette, e-mail, telephone) *and* to prudent standards of safety and permanence—those sent or stored in an ephemeral medium (telephonic or electronic) are accompanied by a good-quality paper copy.

39. **Reports are accurate.** Accuracy extends to providing within the report

- *a precise, itemized, source-cited account* of each relevant item of information found during the investigation;

- *the entire item of interest*, including headings and subheadings regardless of where they are located in the record; footnotes, end-notes, or explanatory text at the beginning or end of the record; and annotations, amendments, or superscriptions that are part of the item of interest; and

- *adequate notation* of the information's context within the record (for example: whether it is an afterthought addition or insertion, whether written in the same hand as the body of the record, and so forth).

40. **Reports are clear.** Clarity extends to

- *format*—The page layout, typeface, headings, and other elements of its physical appearance are designed for maximum intelligibility of the data, interpretations, analyses, and conclusions (see Appendix C for example report formats);

- *sequence*—The research findings are arranged by source, date, name, place, significance, or other scheme that is appropriate to the findings or to the research project; and statements within comments (about analyses, background, or conclusions) are arranged in logical progression; and

- *identification*—The report writer, recipient, preparation date, and subject are clearly stated on each (numbered) page.

41. **Reports include correct interpretation of the findings**—sufficient and accurate *pertinent* discussion of historical, geographic, social, religious, and/or legal concepts for the recipient to understand what a data item means as well as what it says.

42. **Reports include accurate analysis of the findings**—sufficient discussion of the information's reliability and its relevance to the objective of the research project for the recipient to understand the significance of each finding. Correlation of the data is included and the impact of the sum of the findings is explained.

43. **Reports provide well-reasoned conclusions** that include

    - *sufficient discussion* for the recipient to understand whether (and how) the goal of the research project was reached;

    - *correct placement* of individuals within their family or families when such placement is part of the project definition; and

    - *accurate reflection* of relevant background data.

Proof Summaries

Proof summaries are compilations that record in permanent, organized form our explanation of the evidence we used and how we used it to arrive at a particular genealogical conclusion. Depending on the nature of the evidence, proof summaries take one of the following forms:

- *a cover-sheet list*, used when the evidence is direct and unchallenged. The sheet is attached to the assembled photocopies and/or transcriptions of the evidentiary documents, and each is source-cited. (See Example 1 in Appendix D.)

- *source-cited text*, used when the evidence is indirect or the direct evidence conflicts. This kind of proof summary is published or widely distributed to invite challenge and solicit additional information about the subject of the argument. (See Example 2 in Appendix D.)

To fulfill their explanatory purpose, proof summaries meet the following standards:

44. **The genealogical question answered by the conclusion is clearly described**, including

    - *the principal*—person around whom the question revolves;

    - *the focus*—personal identity, or relationship, vital events, biographical details, and so on. (In a cover sheet, both the principal and the focus are usually identified in the title: "John Doe #34 — Son of William Doe #68 and Mary Roe #69," for example. Each record's role in the proof is normally stated in a label, such as "Birth," "Marriage," or "Relationship" placed before or after the source citation.)

- *the research background*—missing records, numerous "same name" people, an inaccurate prior compilation, and so on. (If such problems were encountered, a cover-sheet list is usually insufficient as a proof summary.)

45. **The evidence is presented in logical progression** by

- *sequencing the evidence* according to its place in developing the question's answer rather than the order in which the data were collected or subsidiary conclusions were reached;

- *providing a clear distinction* between major and minor points and using minor points to appropriately support major ones.

46. **The evidence is presented cleanly**, avoiding digressions, dead-end arguments, and extraneous details.

47. **Contrary or conflicting evidence is presented honestly.** Its significance is not underplayed or its details masked or distorted.

48. **The conclusions said to have been reached are based on the evidence presented within the compilation**, including any background or contextual information needed to clarify its meaning.

49. **Sources are fully cited**, regardless of whether source-cited document copies and/or transcriptions accompany the summary.

Lineage, Pedigree, and Genealogy Compilations

These types of compilations are written to make a permanent, orderly record of the sum of our conclusions about a family or designated part of a family. They include as much as is known at the time of writing about the family's history—its patterns and overall characteristics as well as the individual stories of family members.

Pedigree and descendancy charts, family group sheets, and genetic and relationship diagrams do not fulfill this purpose, although they may be helpful during the research phase, acting as overviews of the investigation's progress or the basis for organizing the project. They may be useful, also, as illustrations within the compilation.

- *Lineage* compilations trace the direct parent-to-child links in each generation between an identified individual and one of that person's ancestors or descendants;

- *Pedigree* compilations trace an identified individual's direct ancestors for a specified number of generations; and

- *Genealogy* compilations trace an identified individual's descendants for a specified number of generations.

To achieve their purpose, all three types of compilations exhibit the following qualities:

50.   **Each individual is placed accurately within the family**, based on reliable, source-cited evidence.

51.   **Descriptive biographical information is provided** for individuals in the lineage, pedigree, or genealogy. In addition to vital statistics, the compilation includes sufficient information about each person's activities, residences, circumstances, contributions, and lifestyle to place them within the context of their historical era, society, and geographic place. (For examples of this kind of biographical writing, see Appendixes E, F, and G of this manual.)

52.   **The compilation uses a clear, comprehensible format** that is generally accepted in the field and is *consistently* applied.[11] Generally accepted formats include

- *for lineages*, one of the genealogy formats, adapted to limit discussion of collateral lines; or a special-purpose format required by the recipient—the Bureau of Indian Affairs, for example, or a specific lineage society. (See Appendix E for examples of sound general-purpose lineage formats.)

- *for pedigrees*, the Sosa-Stradonitz System, which uses the ahnentafel numbering scheme found in pre-printed pedigree charts and computer programs; or the Multi-Surname System, which uses a numbering system based on compiled genealogies. (See Appendix F for an explanation and example of each format.)

- *for genealogies*, the *NGSQ* System and the *Register* System, both of which assign unique identification numbers to descendants of the ancestor or ancestral couple. (Appendix G includes explanation and examples of each of these formats.)

53.   **Sources are cited accurately and completely** for each fact included in the compilation except those that are "general knowledge" (battle dates and places, county formations, and so forth)

Hereditary-Society Application Papers

Hereditary-society application forms and their associated "proof documents" are special-purpose compilations. They are assembled

---

11.   For a detailed description (with illustrations) of genealogical formats, see Joan Ferris Curran, CG, Madilyn Coen Crane, and John H. Wray, Ph.D. *Numbering Your Genealogy: Basic Systems, Complex Families, and International Kin*, NGS Special Publication no. 64 (Washington: National Genealogical Society, 2000).

by (or for) someone who seeks membership in a particular society based on his or her descent from a qualifying ancestor. Such compilations, therefore, exhibit the following specific qualities:

54. **Meticulous adherence to instructions** of the society of interest, particularly as they relate to the types and presentation of acceptable evidence, qualifications for membership, and the format and timing of application papers.

55. **Independent verification of any data copied** from papers previously accepted by the society or from previously compiled lineages or genealogies (whether published or unpublished).

56. **In the underlying lineage, each individual is placed accurately within the family**, based on reliable, source-cited evidence.

Teaching Standards

Standards for Lecturers Lecturers are teachers whose instructional sessions, usually of about an hour in length, are given as stand-alone presentations at conferences and workshops or as a series of seminar talks all of which relate to a central theme. To achieve their educational purpose, lecturers meet the following standards:

57. **Presentations are accurately titled, coherent, reliable, and useful** for the intended audience.

58. **Handouts and visual aids prepared for each presentation are accurate, appropriate** to the topic, and enhance rather than detract from the lecture.

59. **Bibliographies included in lecture handouts are up-to-date, accurate, and suitably comprehensive** for the scope of the topic and space restrictions imposed by the lecture sponsors. Such bibliographies include materials referred to in the lectures and those recommended for further study of the topic, and are cited in *The Chicago Manual of Style* bibliographic format.[12]

60. **Lecturers do not reuse another speaker's overall presentation** or any part thereof (research, handouts, visual aids, case-study examples, or distinctively worded titles) without written permission *and* source

---

12. The publications mentioned in Note 1 (p. 3) also include models of bibliographic citation for materials often used in genealogical writing and lecturing.

acknowledgment in both the oral presentation and the written materials that accompany it.

Standards for Instructors

Instructors are teachers who present an extended series of interactive presentations that address genealogical methods and sources at the beginner, intermediate, or advanced level. Regardless of whether the sessions are presented in a formal academic setting or a less-formal, privately sponsored one, instructors meet the following standards:

61. **Courses are well organized, comprehensive, and sequential in nature**, and include student activities and projects related to the objectives of the course.

62. **Courses are designed to enable students** to develop knowledge and skills in at least the following areas:

     - *awareness of genealogical sources;*

     - *respect for historical and genealogical materials and their custodians;*

     - *ability to conduct creditable genealogical research;*

     - *ability to compile useful reports of the results;* and

     - *habitual, accurate citation of sources.*

63. **Lesson plans include a means for evaluating student outcomes**—a method for measuring the extent to which each student has attained the lesson objectives.

64. **Instructional materials used for each lesson are accurate, clear, up-to-date**, reasonably attractive, and appropriate to the lesson and the students' level of experience. Such instructional materials are directly related to the lesson topic, and may include such enhancements as handouts; written, oral, or visual examples; audio- and videotapes; computer-generated demonstrations; and dramatizations.

65. **Bibliographies included in instructional materials include citations in standard format** to materials mentioned during the class session and those recommended for further study of the lesson's subject. (See also Standard 59 above.)

66. **Classroom presentations are effective and varied, encourage student participation**, and foster interest in or enthusiasm for the subject of the lesson.

Standards for Writers

All genealogical writing is instructional in the sense that it imparts useful information to specific people (fellow descendants of the same person, for example). Some kinds of writing, however, are specifically designed to educate readers about genealogical methods, sources, or standards. Instructional writings may appear in print publication as books, articles, monographs, or newspaper and newsletter columns. They may also, or alternatively, appear in electronic publication as programs and their manuals, as CDs, and as website text. Regardless of their publication media, instructional writings can be generally divided by subject and purpose into the following categories:

- *source guides*, which describe published and/or unpublished materials related to a specified topic, giving citations, locations, access methods, and often some general advice about using the sources effectively.

- *methodology guides*, which describe a procedure in step-by-step detail. The procedure may have a general purpose (for example, how to begin the search for one's ancestors) or a narrowly circumscribed one (how to plat land tracts, for instance, or abstract wills).

- *case studies*, which illustrate the use of a technique, or several closely related techniques, *based on a single research-project example*. Case studies are sometimes used as summaries in methodology guides, but more often appear as stand-alone articles in journals and newsletters and their electronic counterparts.

- *publication and product reviews*, which offer advice (stated or implied) about the usefulness of newly available materials based on appraisal of their merits and, if applicable, their shortcomings.

- *database programs*, which, although generally viewed as computerized methods for storing, sorting, and assembling information, nevertheless instruct their users in certain kinds of genealogical techniques. For instance, the program's design for accepting research findings trains users (explicitly or by example) in a specific method of data collection; and its automatic formatting of names or source citations similarly affects its users' habits and sense of "right" and "wrong" practices.

To fulfill their educational purpose, the writers of such materials adhere to the following standards:

67. **The character of the writing meets general standards that apply throughout the genealogical field**—accuracy, clarity, coherence, and full citation of sources. (See "Compilation Standards" in the RESEARCH STANDARDS section of this manual.)

68. **Source guides provide sound directions to and information about materials** that

- *should be included* within a comprehensive treatment of the topic—and the guide's scope as defined in its title or introduction;

- *are readily available* in the form or edition cited; and

- *furnish the promised information* or type of information.

69. **Methodology guides provide lucid, explicit instructions** that

- *include all the steps needed to complete the process*, arranged in logical progression. Each step is built upon the one that preceded it, and no procedure learned near the beginning of the process will need to be unlearned or revised later;

- *include written and visual examples* that are precisely on point, clarify rather than obscure the process, and do not minimize or exaggerate the normal content of records used as illustrations; and

- *if followed precisely, will actually work.*

70. **Case studies provide an intelligent, honest illustration** of how the writer used a technique (or series of closely related techniques) to bring about the described result. Case-study writers

- *select for discussion* a research project whose outcome was based, in fact, on the focus technique or techniques;

- *include a brief, clear description of the problem* that generated the research project; and

- *present a logical, sure progression* from problem to solution, free of rambling explanations, extraneous characters and details, undue generalizations from the particular, and "surprise" solutions based on data not included within the compilation.

71. **Publication and product reviews provide a concise, balanced, impartial analysis** that is based on sufficient reading of the publication or use of the product—and sufficient background understanding of its subject or function—for a valid judgment of its utility. Reviews of electronic publications and products address the eviden-

tiary value of their contents (the data's reliability) as well as their functional dependability (minimal propensity to crash, for example, or full compatibility with commonly used programs or operating systems).

72. **Database programs accommodate sound data-collection, evidence-evaluation, and compilation standards** and do not force or encourage users to leap to premature conclusions about personal identities or relationships, or to tailor their research findings to the input interface.

GENEALOGICAL DEVELOPMENT STANDARDS

CONTINUING-EDUCATION STANDARDS   Genealogists never rest content with what they know at any given moment. They realize that there is always one more source or one more technique that might answer the unanswered question or solve the unsolved problem. Consequently,

73. **Genealogists regularly engage in development activities.** These activities include

    - *formal courses of study*;

    - *independent study programs* (formal or informal—including regular reading of major genealogical journals);

    - *attendance at conferences*, seminars, and workshops; and

    - *one-on-one consultations* with advanced practitioners in the field.

74. **Development activities are aimed at improving** and updating one's attainment of genealogical standards, expanding one's knowledge of sources, enhancing one's ability to interpret documents, and upgrading one's analytical techniques and compilation skills.

Appendixes

Appendix A — The Genealogist's Code

In 1964, the founding trustees of the Board for Certification of Genealogists developed and promulgated the first ethics code in the field. This code has stood the test of time, for it addresses the relationship that should prevail between genealogical practitioners and those who benefit from their work. The Genealogist's Code was updated in 1994 to reflect changes in copyright law and the impact of electronic media on research and reporting techniques, but its basic principles remain the same.

All genealogists certified by the Board sign a statement at the end of the code that says "I [name] do hereby acknowledge that I concur with the code of ethics set forth by the Board for Certification of Genealogists and that I shall follow its standards in all phases of my work as a genealogist." Regardless of whether or not we are certified, however, all of us, as reputable genealogists, abide by its provisions.

The code addresses the three major areas of genealogical enterprise in the following words:

To protect the public

- I will not publish or publicize as fact anything I know to be false, doubtful, or unproved; nor will I be a party, directly or indirectly, to such action by others.

- I will identify my sources for all information and cite only those documents I have personally used.

- I will quote documents precisely, avoiding any alterations that I do not clearly identify as editorial interpretations.

- I will present the purpose, practice, scope, and possibilities of genealogical research within a realistic framework.

- I will delineate my abilities, publications, and/or fees in a true and realistic fashion.

To protect the consumer (client, correspondent, or relative)

- I will keep confidential any personal or genealogical data given to me, unless I receive written consent to the contrary.

- I will reveal to the consumer any personal or financial interests that might compromise my professional obligations to him or her.

- I will undertake paid research commissions only after a clear agreement as to scope and fee.

- I will, to the best of my abilities, address my research to the issue raised by the consumer and report to that question.

- I will seek from the consumer all prior information and documentation related to the research and will not knowingly repeat the work, as billable hours, without explanation as to good cause.

- I will furnish only facts I can substantiate with adequate documentation and will not withhold any data necessary for the consumer's purpose.

- If the research question involves analysis of data in order to establish a genealogical relationship or identity, I will report that the conclusions are based on the weight of available evidence and that absolute proof of genealogical relationships is usually not possible.

- If I cannot resolve a research problem within the limitations of time or budget established by agreement or contract, I will explain the reasons why.

- If other feasible avenues are available, I will suggest them; but I will not misrepresent the possibilities of additional research.

- I will return any advance payment that exceeds the hours and expenses incurred.

- I will not publish or circulate research or reports to which the consumer has a proprietary right without prior written consent of the consumer; I will observe these rights whether my report was made directly to the consumer or to an employer or agent.

To protect the profession

- I will act, speak, and write in a manner consistent with the best interests and standards of both the profession and the scholarship of genealogy.

- I will assist legitimate efforts to expose genealogical charlatans; but I will not otherwise knowingly injure, or attempt to injure, the reputation, prospects, or practice of another genealogist.

- I will not attempt to supplant another genealogist already employed by a client or agency. I will substitute for another researcher only with specific written consent of and instructions provided by the client or agency.

- I will not represent as my own the work of another. This includes works that are copyrighted, in the public domain, or unpublished. This pledge includes reports, letters, lecture materials, audio/visual tapes, compiled records, and authored essays.

- I will not reproduce for public dissemination, in an oral or written fashion, the work of another genealogist, writer, or lecturer, without that person's written consent. In citing another's work, I will give proper credit.

Appendix B — The Board for Certification of Genealogists

The Board is an active and integral part of the genealogical community. Its mission is to promote the highest standards of competence and ethics among genealogical practitioners and thereby foster public confidence in genealogy as a respectable and respected branch of history.

Since its foundation by leading American genealogists in 1964, the Board has viewed genealogical study as a profession, vocation, and social science that requires training and advanced skills—regardless of whether the results of an investigation are shared orally, in writing, or online, or whether the practitioner accepts payment for services rendered.

Educational Activities

The Board does not offer a course of genealogical instruction. Its commitment to education is expressed in the following programs:

- *publications*, which include

   (*a*) *OnBoard*, an educational newsletter, every issue of which carries at least one article on the application of the Genealogical Proof Standard to a particular type of research. Other articles discuss sources (useful websites, for example) and issues that concern all researchers. *OnBoard* is distributed free-of-charge to certified associates and to potential associates who have filed a preliminary application. It is otherwise available by annual subscription.

   (*b*) *The BCG Certification Roster*, which lists the names, addresses, category designations, and other information about certified associates.

   (*c*) *The BCG Application Guide*, which sets out the requirements and procedures to be followed in applying for certification.

   (*d*) a pamphlet series that describes specific aspects of research or the process of applying for certification.

- *co-sponsorship of national-level institutes* such as the National Institute on Genealogical Research (P. O. Box 14274, Washington, DC 20044–4274) founded in 1950 and based at the National Archives; and the Institute for Genealogy and Historical Research (Samford University Library, 800 Lakeshore Dr., Birmingham, AL 35229), founded in 1964.

- *participation in national-level conferences* such as those sponsored annually by the National Genealogical Society and the Federation of Genealogical Societies, offering at those conferences workshops, panel discussions, lectures, and question-and-answer sessions.

- *sponsorship of lectures* by its representatives about standards and certification-related subjects at numerous regional and local seminars and meetings.

- *sponsorship of a website* (www.bcgcertification.org) that includes the current roster of certified persons and additional information about the Board's outreach to the genealogical community, as well as skill-building articles from *OnBoard*.

Organizational Structure

The Board for Certification of Genealogists is

- *an independent organization*, not affiliated with or part of any society or group;

- *a certifying body*, not a membership society; and

- *a nationally and internationally recognized organization*.

The Board consists of fifteen trustees, a professional executive director, and a panel of approximately forty-five judges. The associates elect five trustees each year to serve three-year terms; the officers (president, vice-president, secretary, and treasurer) are elected annually by the trustees. All trustees are certified, and all serve without compensation.

The scheduled annual meeting of the Board takes place in the fall, usually in October, at a site chosen at the previous annual meeting. Additional meetings are held throughout the year, often just before or after a national conference.

BCG's bylaws are a public document and may be obtained by writing the Executive Director at the office address, and enclosing a stamped, self-addressed envelope (SASE) with the request.

The Board's Addresses

- Post Office Box 14291, Washington, DC 20044
- bcg@megapipe.net
- www.bcgcertification.org

APPENDIX C — EXAMPLE REPORTS

The complexity of a research report depends on the complexity of the underlying research project. To meet the standards, however, all reports include the following elements—regardless of whether they are written for someone else or for one's own research files:

- *identification of the researcher* (full name and address);

- *identification of the intended recipient.* Reports to someone else include full name and address; reports to oneself include, also, their file designation (EXAMPLE: John Doe #6);

- *report date;*

- *project definition*, including *(a)* what the project was intended to accomplish and *(b)* limitations on time, scope, repository, subject matter, and so forth;

- *starting-point summary* of information that was known when the project began (and, if appropriate to the project, a preliminary analysis of the data);

- *results summary*, including correlation of findings and a conclusion about whether the project objectives were reached and whether the underlying genealogical question was answered;

- *itemized research results*, including *(a)* source citation; *(b)* summary, abstract, or transcription of each record; *(c)* notation of whether photocopies are attached; *(d)* interpretation of the data; and

- *suggestions, recommendations, or a complete plan* for continuing. If reporting to one's own file, this may be an informal "to do" list.

The examples that follow include reports from make-believe genealogists in letter and formal format to their fictitious clients,[13] and in memorandum format to a personal-research file. The families, source citations and explanatory data are also fictitious but represent the kinds of records and background information that genealogists often use. Typographic styles vary from genealogist to genealogist to demonstrate that such variations are acceptable. Readers seeking models for their own use should study all the examples and adapt them intelligently to their own purposes.

13. A "client" in the sense used here is someone else for whom one does research, regardless of whether that person: *(a)* pays a fee to the researcher, to the researcher's employer, or to an agency for which the researcher volunteers; *(b)* is engaged in an exchange of research time, or of work done on a mutual ancestral family; or *(c)* receives the benefit of the researcher's work *pro bono* (without fee or exchange).

1. Limited-project Client Report: Letter Format

identification of report writer and report date

Tradition L. Storey

92 Quick Street, #2A, Capital City, Research State 98765

16 Month 1999

Anny Other Researcher
1324 Any Street
Anytown, Any State 35468-4657

identification of intended recipient

identification of report subject & authorization

Dear Ms. Researcher:

Enclosed are photocopies of the two pension files you requested by e-mail, 22 Month 1999, from the Revolutionary War pension files at the National Archives. Both are taken from *Revolutionary War Pension and Bounty Land Warrant Application Files*; Record Group 15: Records of the Veterans Administration, microfilm publication M804 (Washington: National Archives), roll 828. Unfortunately, neither John Philip nor Joseph W. Doe mentioned the other in any connection whatsoever.

source citations to record group & file number

John Philip Doe (file #S1234) enlisted as a "six monthes soljer" in North County, Somewhere-Else, on 12 Month 1779 in Capt. Roe's company, 12th Regt., but kept re-enlisting and served with Roe to the end of the war. On 28 Month 1843, he stated that he was eighty-two [indicating a birth year of about 1761 and enlistment at age eighteen]. He was still living in North County when he died on 18 Month 1846.

findings — with interpretive comments in brackets

Joseph W. Doe, also called "Josey" (file #R5678), enlisted on 24 Month 1781 in Far-West County, Somewhere-Else, and was serving under Col. Goodtitle when wounded on 2 Month 1781. [Col. John Goodtitle commanded the 5th Somewhere-Else State regiment]. Joseph was living in New County, Far Away, in 1852 when he gave his age as ninety-one [indicating a birth year of about 1761 and enlistment at age twenty]. His pension application was rejected because of insufficient proof of service.

The files do not provide evidence, as you had hoped they would, that the two men were brothers. Quite the contrary. John and Joseph were born at about the same time and enlisted within two years of each other in places a great distance apart—North and Far-West counties are at opposite ends of the state.

statement of conclusion

I am sorry the search did not produce the hoped-for information, but perhaps there are clues in these papers that you, with your greater knowledge of the Does of Somewhere-Else and their neighbors, will find helpful.

There are three other pension-application files of Somewhere-Else soldiers that may be of interest to you if you do not already have copies of the papers:

William Dough, #S2468
Bentley Dough, #R1369, and
Thomas Dowe, #S2345.

responsible recommendation for continuing research

I do not know how voluminous the files are so cannot estimate the copying fee, but it would likely take two to three hours to order the files, examine them briefly for relevance, and make the appropriate copies. If there is specific information you want to be sure is included in each file before I copy it, I would probably need about four hours to complete the work.

enough data for informed client decision

Yours truly,

Tradition L. Storey

Tradition L. Storey

billing separated from report

Enc.   26 pp. photocopies; invoice for time and expenses

2. Limited-project Client Report: Letter Format

I. M. A. Goodfinder
3456 Hunter Street, Riverton, Research State 34567

report writer

9 Month 1999

report date and intended recipient

Martha A. Doe
890 Her Street
Hertown, Her State 98765

Dear Mrs. Doe:

statement of client commission and recapitulation of problem background

This replies to your letter of 1 Month 1999 requesting a copy of the Research County marriage record of Harold Doe to Sarah [surname not known], which you estimate occurred some time before the birth of their son Joseph Doe (your ancestor). Joseph, according to your letter, was born 12 Month 1837 in Research County, Research State.

source citations in report and on copies

1. The Research County Groom Index to Marriages, 1820–75, at the clerk's office in the courthouse at Riverton, R.S., shows no entry for marriage of a Harold or H. Doe to a lady named Sarah, Sally, or Sary. I did find record of "Harry" Doe's marriage to Malley Right on 22 Month 1832. After finding the record mentioned in paragraph #2, I obtained a photocopy (enclosed) of the Doe-Right marriage record. (Research County Marriages, 1820–35, p. 119). Note that one of the witnesses, Matthew Right, also witnessed the Harold Doe marriage, below.

2. Several published volumes of marriage records extracted from area church registers are also in the clerk's office. I am enclosing photocopies from Jane G. Genie, *Marriages of Research County, 1750–1900,* vol. 4, *1815–1845* (Northtown, NS: the compiler, 1982), 22–24, which include the Doe marriages during that period. Note the Harold Doe marriage to Sarah Notright at St. George [M.E.] Church, 5 Month 1843, with Jackson Notright, Matthew Right, and William Roe witnesses. It is probable that Jackson Notright was related to the bride Sarah. Matthew Right may have been Malley's kinsman but there were numerous Rights/Rites/Wrights (including several Matthews) mentioned in Ms. Genie's volumes.

analytical comments and statement of project conclusion

Your letter did not state the source of information that Sarah was Joseph's mother, but the marriage records indicate that Sarah Notright (if the same Sarah) was Harold's second or later wife and Joseph's stepmother—he was about eleven in 1843. Malley Right, however, was most likely the lady to whom Harold was married when Joseph was born. It is certainly possible, of course, that *none* of these records pertain to Joseph Doe's parents. If this is the case, my search of the Research County marriage records was unproductive, for these are the only two entries I found that relate to a Harold, Harry, or H. Doe.

If you decide you would like to pursue the Research County investigation further I will be happy to undertake it but would not be able to continue until after 1 Month due to other commitments.

Yours truly,

I. M. A. Goodfinder

I. M. A. Goodfinder

invoice separated from letter-format report

Enclosures: (1) photocopies of cited records, (2) statement of time and charges

3. Limited-project Client Report: Formal Format

I. M. A. Goodfinder
3456 Hunter Street, Riverton, Research State 34567

report writer

Compare with letter format. Note that the formal format, as a rule, allows greater flexibility in reporting research results, analyses, and suggestions for future work.

CLIENT   Martha A. Doe   *intended recipient*
890 Her Street
Hertown, Her State 98765

DATE   9 Month 1999   *report date*

SUBJECT   Marriage record of Harold and Sarah [–?–] Doe

CONTRACT   Two hours for research, analysis, and report authorized by letter of 1 Month 1999

PROBLEM   What was Sarah's surname and when did she marry Harold Doe? Their son, Joseph Doe, client's ancestor, was born 12 Month 1837 in Research County, Research State; married Jane Yourancestor, and was father of Joseph, Mary, Harold, and Jackson Doe. [Client's source for Harold and Sarah as parents of Joseph was not supplied.]

problem & starting-point data restatement

REMARKS   The research was done in the Research County courthouse, Riverton, R.S. (The county marriage records have not yet been transferred from the courthouse to the state archives.)

FINDINGS (SUMMARY)   Only two marriage records were found that might apply to the subject of this project. They indicate that Sarah was Harold's second wife, whom he married when Joseph was about eleven. Assuming that Joseph was Harold's legitimate son, Sarah was not the boy's mother—she was his stepmother. Joseph's mother was most probably Malley Right, who married Harold in 1832, five years before Joseph's birth. (It is possible, but unlikely, that Malley died between 1832 and early 1837 and Harold married *another* lady who is not represented in the records found to date).

FINDINGS (ITEMIZED)

full source citations

1.   Mountain County, Groom Index to Marriages, 1820–75, Clerk's Office, county courthouse, Riverton, R.S. No entry for Harold or H. Doe (or Dough, Dowe, or Daugh) was found. An entry for "Harry Doe" provided directions to record #2, below.

2.   Research County Marriages, 1820–35, p. 119, Clerk's Office, county courthouse, Riverton, R.S. (Photocopy enclosed). Groom: Harry Doe. Bride: Malley Right. Date: 22 Month 1832. Witnesses: James Fen, Matthew Right. Offficiant: John L. Bigwig, J.P.

3.   Jane G. Genie, *Marriages of Research County, 1750–1900*, vol. 4, *1815–1845* (North town, N.S.: the compiler, 1982), 22–24. (Photocopy enclosed, showing all Doe marriages for the period). Among them is that of Harold Doe to Sarah Notright, St. George [Methodist-Episcopal] Church, 5 Month 1843. Witnesses: Jackson Notright, Matthew Right, William Roe. Officiant: Rev. Walter Goodwill.

analytical comments

Comment: Matthew Right, who witnessed the marriage of Harry Doe to Malley Right <u>and</u> the later Harold Doe to Sarah Notright marriage, may have been Malley's kinsman (a clue to follow when researching her birth family). Also, Joseph Doe, client's ancestor, named his last known son Jackson, and a Jackson Notright, probably kin to stepmother Sarah, witnessed her marriage to Harold.

RECOMMENDATION   To determine whether Malley or a "hidden" wife was Joseph's mother, Harold's 1840 census household should be investigated to find out whether it included a wife-aged lady who could have been Malley. (If she died after the family was enumerated in 1840, she was still married to Harold when Joseph was born in 1837.) Land sales by Harold between 1832 and 1843 should be investigated, also, to see whether Malley or another wife was mentioned. (Wives in Research State during this period were required to release their "dower right" in land their husbands sold.)

END OF REPORT

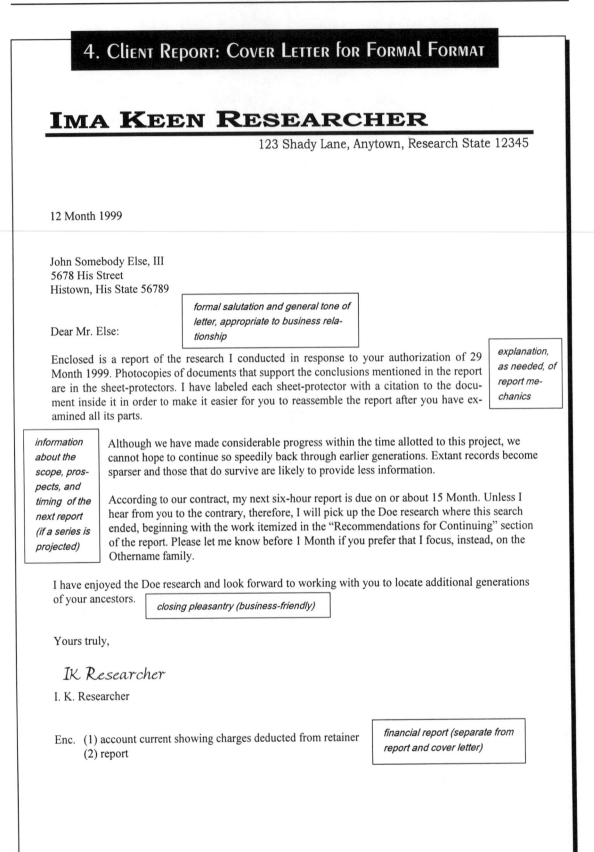

4. Client Report: Cover Letter for Formal Format

IMA KEEN RESEARCHER

123 Shady Lane, Anytown, Research State 12345

12 Month 1999

John Somebody Else, III
5678 His Street
Histown, His State 56789

formal salutation and general tone of letter, appropriate to business relationship

Dear Mr. Else:

Enclosed is a report of the research I conducted in response to your authorization of 29 Month 1999. Photocopies of documents that support the conclusions mentioned in the report are in the sheet-protectors. I have labeled each sheet-protector with a citation to the document inside it in order to make it easier for you to reassemble the report after you have examined all its parts.

explanation, as needed, of report mechanics

information about the scope, prospects, and timing of the next report (if a series is projected)

Although we have made considerable progress within the time allotted to this project, we cannot hope to continue so speedily back through earlier generations. Extant records become sparser and those that do survive are likely to provide less information.

According to our contract, my next six-hour report is due on or about 15 Month. Unless I hear from you to the contrary, therefore, I will pick up the Doe research where this search ended, beginning with the work itemized in the "Recommendations for Continuing" section of the report. Please let me know before 1 Month if you prefer that I focus, instead, on the Othername family.

I have enjoyed the Doe research and look forward to working with you to locate additional generations of your ancestors.

closing pleasantry (business-friendly)

Yours truly,

IK Researcher

I. K. Researcher

Enc. (1) account current showing charges deducted from retainer
(2) report

financial report (separate from report and cover letter)

5. Research-agent Client Report: Formal Format

IMA KEAN RESEARCHER

report writer

123 Shady Lane, Anytown, Research State 12345

report title

DOE REPORT #1

DATE: 12 Month 1999

ADDRESSED TO: John Somebody Else III   report date and
                     5678 His Street   intended recipient
                     Histown, His State 56789

SUBJECT: Parentage of client's ancestor, James P. Doe

STARTING POINT: James P. Doe was born 21 Month 1823[1] in Research State,[2] the county or town
                     not known. He married Mary Othername on 12 Month 1851[3] in Oakton, Oak

recapitulation of   County, R.S.,[4] and was father of four children, whose names and birth dates were
problem and of   entered in his family Bible (published 1854): *i. James P. Doe, Jr.,* born 8 Month
client-supplied   1853; *ii. William W. O. Doe,* born 10 Month 1855; *iii. Janet Amanda Doe,* born 2
data   Month 1858; and *ii. Zachary P. Doe,* born 30 Month 1861. James P. Doe [Sr.],
                     while serving in Othername's Company,[5] Oak County militia, was killed in a bi-
                     zarre rifle-training accident in May 1861.[6]

                     Client previously examined all Doe wills for Oak County on microfilm and re-
                     ports that none of the testators mentioned a son or brother James P., James, or J.P.
                     From his examination of the 1840 Oak County census, client has identified three
                     possible fathers for James P.: John Doe, Henry Doe, and James Doe—all of
                     whom had in their households white males the right age to have been the ances-
                     tor.[7] Henry's will, however, mentioned *only* wife Milly and sons John, "Zack,"
                     and Henry. No wills were found for John or James Doe.[8]

NOTE: Oak County was formed in 1837 from Pine, Elm, and Maple Counties (i.e., even
                     if James P. was born in the place where he married, it was not Oak County at the
background that does (or   time). A fire in 1882 destroyed the Pine County courthouse and most of its rec-
might) affect research   ords. Elm and Maple county records, however, are fairly complete.

AUTHORIZATION: Six hours for research, analysis, and report.   project limitations

SUMMARY OF FINDINGS: James P. Doe's father was Walter Doe, who was married by 1831 to Martha [–?–]
                     Doe.[9] Walter died in Elm County, R.S., between signing his will on 22 Month
                     1831 and its probate at the Month Court later that year.[9] We do not yet know his
                     birth date but estimate it at c1795–1805.

citations to sources the
report writer examined

---

[1] Doe Family Bible entry. Photocopy of family register pages supplied by client.
[2] 1850 U.S. census of South County, South State, population schedule, p. 38, dwelling 123, family 115.
[3] Doe Family Bible entry.
[4] Jane G. Genie, *Marriages of Oak County, 1750–1900,* vol. 5, *1846–1870* (Northtown, N.S.: the compiler, 1984), 108.
Photocopy supplied by client.
[5] The company commander, Capt. William W. Othername, was Mary's brother (will of Jasper Othername, Oak County,
Research State, Will Book 3: 32, cited in letter to I. K. Researcher from client, 6 Month 1999).
[6] Else to Researcher, 6 Month 1999, citing an unidentified newspaper clipping found in the Doe Family Bible.
[7] Photocopies of census schedules received from client; the information from them, however, is not repeated here.
[8] Will of Henry Doe, 16 Month 1855, probated 8 Month 1855, Oak County Will Book 2: 65. Photocopy supplied by
client.
[9] Will of Walter Doe, Elm County Will Book 11: 356–358.

ʌʌʌʌʌʌʌʌʌʌʌʌʌ *[Reference notes continue but are not included in this example]* ʌʌʌʌʌʌʌʌʌʌʌʌ

Walter Doe's father was the John Doe client found enumerated in the 1840 census of Oak County.[10] The young man in his household was very probably client's ancestor James P., who was still living near his grandfather in 1850.[11] John Doe was born about 1769 in R.S.,[12] and died in Oak County about Month 1857.[12] Detailed findings follow.

ITEMIZED RESEARCH FINDINGS:

> full identification of repository

1. Oak County Estate Files, Probate Office, county courthouse, Oakton, R.S.

> findings arranged for clarity (in date-of-death order, in this case)

a. Bundle #E-37: Estate of William Doe, 1848. The inventory was filed 17 Month 1848 by Ellen Doe, widow of deceased. The final settlement does not list the heirs; and, although the inventory mentions 245 acres of land, the file does not contain a record of its division.

Comment: The absence of a land-division record is unusual for Research State during this period and may indicate that the property was sold before being divided.

b. Bundle #E-92: Estate of Henry Doe, 1855. The inventory was filed 19 Month 1855 by John Doe, "executor." The division document merely states: "land and other property of deceased div[ide]d according to will" and provides the date, 22 Month 1861. The heirs are not mentioned [*but see the copy of Henry's will in client's files*].

c. Bundle #E-87: Estate of John Doe, 1857. (Photocopies attached; summarized here for reference). The inventory was filed 22 Month 1857 by Zachary L. Doe, "administrator." The division document, dated 4 Month 1857, shows that John's land, 300 acres "lying and being on the main rode from Oakton to Elmton," was apportioned as follows:

> Lot #1, 75 acres, to Amanda Davinchi
> Lot #2, 75 acres, to Zachary L. Doe
> Lot #3, 37 ½ acres to James P. Doe "Junr. [Jr.]"
> Lot #4, 75 acres to James P. Doe "Sinr. [Sr.]"
> Lot #5, 37 ½ acres to Janet Doe

> comments identified by label and typeface

Comment: Research State law from 1832 to 1960 provided that the land of a person who died intestate was to be divided equally among the heirs in the following manner: to children first and if there were none, to siblings; and if there were none, to siblings of deceased's father; and if there were none, to siblings of deceased's mother; and if there were none, to the state by "escheat." Further, if any heir was dead, his or her children would divide their parent's share between/among them. With the law in mind, if we can find evidence of the relationship between John Doe and <u>any</u> of the people to whom his land descended, we can identify the relationships of all the rest of the heirs.

James P. Jr. and Janet Doe were undoubtedly brother and sister and children of an unnamed heir who was dead by 1857 (their 37 ½ acre tracts together amount to another 75 acres). Despite the names, therefore, James P. Sr. and Jr. were not father and son.

> nutshell note for future reference

We noted the marked similarity of names between John Doe's heirs and the children of client's ancestor—and that John's land lay in the part of Oak County formed from Elm.

d. Other bundles in the file, not examined: Zachary L. Doe, 1891; Milly Doe, 1899; Jacob Doe, 1907; John A. Doe, 1929; John W. Doe, 1958; Jacob H. Doe, 1976.

2. Oak County Cross-Index to Deeds, vol. D–F, Office of County Clerk, Oakton, R.S. The index shows a large number of Doe deeds for land bought and sold. The only deed from or to a James,

DOE REPORT #1, 12 Month 1999   page 3 of 4
Addressed to: John Somebody Else III, 5678 His Street, Histown, His State 56789
From: I. K. Researcher, 123 Shady Lane, Anytown, Research State 12345

James P., or J. P. Doe was the following (photocopy attached, summarized here for reference):

citation to specific book and page (in report and on photocopy)

Oak County Deeds, Book 19: 14–16. James P. Doe of Bigtown, New State, to Jasper Othername of Oak County, Research State, 25 Month 1867. For $357.85, a tract of 75 acres
(by survey) on the "mane road" from Elmton to Oaktown, being Lot #4 in the division of
lands that belonged to John Doe, deceased, father of the said James P. Doe [*metes and
bounds tract description included*]. Signed ℙ as his mark. Witnessed by William W. Othername (signed W.W.), Benjamin Othername (signed), Elizabeth Othername (X her mark).

> *Comment: The seller was clearly James P. Doe Sr. of the 1857 land division—
> and he was a son of the deceased John Doe. That being the case, the two other
> 75-acre heirs were also John's children and the two 37 ½-acre heirs (including
> James P. Jr.) were John's grandchildren.*
>
> *It is significant, also, that the man who bought this Doe tract from James P. Sr.
> was Mary (Othername) Doe's father (or a man of the same name, of course)—
> and that one of the witnesses appears to have been her brother, the careless
> militia captain in whose company client's ancestor so briefly served.*

3.   1850 U.S. census, Oak County, R.S., NARA microfilm copy 000, reel 000. Examined at the Research State Genealogical Society Library, Treeton, R.S. [*Re-examined to compare the neighbor-
hoods of client's ancestor, the heirs of the John Doe, and Mary's Othername family.*]

reason for repeating work already done by client

∧∧∧∧∧∧∧∧∧∧∧∧∧∧∧∧[*And so forth. Report continues onto page 4*] ∧∧∧∧∧∧∧∧∧∧∧∧∧∧∧∧

6.   Elm County Wills, Book 11: 356–8, microfilm #085.302.11, Probate Office, courthouse annex,
Elmton, R.S. (Photocopy attached; summarized here for reference).

insertion in brackets

puzzling passage quoted precisely

Will of Walter Doe, 22 Month 1831. I, Walter Doe, carpenter, of Elm County, being very
sick and weak, [*standard provisions for payment of debts and burial expenses follow*]. To
beloved wife Martha, my entire estate to raise my children, "but if she should dye or re-
marrie to be devided equally between her and my said children." To my son James, $25
given him when he arrives at age twenty-one. To my daughters Janet and Elizabeth, $10 to
be given them when each arrives at age eighteen or marries. Wife Martha and brother
Zachary L. Doe to be executors. Signed WD. Witnessed by Jasper Othername, Zachary L.
Doe (signed Z), Harold G. Clerke. Probated at Month court, 1831.

> *Comment: Although the son James's middle initial was not stated in Walter's
> will, there is no reasonable doubt that the boy was James P. Doe—and no doubt
> that he was the same James P. called "Jr." in John Doe's 1857 estate division.
> (Walter's daughter Janet was the other 37 ½-acre heir and his brother Zachary
> L. was one of the 75-acre heirs). Walter, therefore, was John's son, represented
> in the land division by his own two children, James P. Jr. and Janet.*
>
> *Walter's daughter Elizabeth died without issue 1831–57. If she had been alive
> when the land was divided, she would have inherited a third of Walter's share;
> had she left surviving children, they would have inherited her third.*

RECOMMENDATIONS FOR CONTINUING:

A.   The three-county marriage records (and others if necessary) should be searched for documentation
of Walter Doe's union with Martha. Depending on its date, Martha may or may not have been
James P. Doe's mother.

B.   The 1830 and earlier censuses for ∧∧∧∧∧∧∧∧∧∧[*And so forth to end of report*] ∧∧∧∧∧∧∧∧∧

6. Continuation-project Client Report: Formal Format

Ima Keen Researcher

123 Shady Lane, Anytown, Research State 12345

DOE REPORT #2 | title of this report |

DATE: 28 Month 1999

ADDRESSED TO: John Somebody Else III
                       5678 His Street
                       Histown, His State 56789

SUBJECT: Ancestry of James P. Doe.

STARTING POINT:

> A. James P. Doe's father was Walter Doe, who had married Martha [–?–] Doe by
> 1831. Walter died in Elm County, R.S., between signing his will on 22 Month
> 1831 and its probate at the Month Court later that year.[1] He was father of at least
> the following three children[2] (their birth order not known): *i. James P. Doe
> "Jr.,"* client's ancestor, born 21 Month 1823 in Research State; married Mary
> Othername 12 Month 1851 in Oakton, Oak County, R.S.;[3] died [*data not sup-
> plied by client*]; *ii. Janet Doe*, under eighteen in 1831,[4] unmarried (or widow of
> another Doe) in 1857 when her grandfather's land was divided; and *iii. Eliza-
> beth Doe*, under eighteen in 1831,[5] died without surviving issue 1831–57.[6]

*recapitulation of
status of project
as of previously
reported findings*

> *We had estimated Walter's approximate birth date thus: He married James
> P. Jr.'s mother before 1823. If of normal age for the era and place, he was
> about eighteen to twenty-eight at marriage, or born c1795–1805.*

> B. Walter Doe's father was John Doe,[7] who was head of an 1840 census household
> in Oak County that appears to have included his grandson James P. Doe Jr.
> John's 1850 census age indicates a 1769 birth in R.S.;[8] he died in Oak County
> about Month 1857, intestate,[9] father of at least the following children (their birth
> order not known): *i. Walter Doe* (see above); *ii. Zachary L. Doe,* birth date un-
> known, died after 1857; *iii. James P. Doe "Sr.,"* birth date not known, died after
> 1857; *iv. Amanda (Doe) Davinchi,* birth date not known, died after 1857, mar-
> ried [–?–] Davinchi and apparently a widow by 1857.

*The text of the
reference notes is
omitted in this
example.*

> *NOTE: Amanda inherited in her own name a fourth of John's land in 1857.
> Because of the marital property laws in effect in Research State prior to
> 1869, had Amanda's husband been alive, the division would have named
> him as John's heir "in right of his wife, Amanda." Similarly, Janet Doe
> (daughter of Walter) who also inherited in her own name, was either single
> or a widow.*

NOTE: Elm County was formed in 1779 from Maple County; Maple was formed in
                       1727 from Willow County, one of the four jurisdictions into which Research
                       State was divided when founded as an English colony in 1697. If John was born
                       in what became Elm, his birthplace was Maple County.

AUTHORIZATION: Twelve hours for research, analysis, and report (extended from six hours),
                       authorized by telephone and confirmed by letter 31 Month 1999).

updated limits on authorization

SUMMARY OF FINDINGS:

A. Walter Doe, son of John Doe, was born about 1790–95 in Elm County, R.S.,[10] and died in Elm between 22 Month 1831 and Month 1831.[11] He married first, shortly after 19 Month 1816, Janet Planet,[12] daughter of Neptune Planet.[13] Janet (Planet) Doe died, probably in childbirth, between 8 Month 1818 when Neptune signed his will and 3 Month 1818 when he added a codicil in favor of grand-daughter Janet Doe, stating that the child's mother, "my daughter," was "re-cently deceased." Walter remarried almost immediately, by bond dated 12 Month 1818,[14] Martha (Brant) Yourancestor, widow of A.N. Yourancestor,[15] daughter of Rem Brant, sister of Sheriff Rem Brant,[16] and mother of Rem B. Yourancestor, Walter Doe's stepson.[17] Martha's death date and place have not been determined, but because her Doe son, James P. Jr., was living with his grandfather in 1840, we suspect she had died or remarried between 1831 and 1840. Walter, who styled himself "carpenter,"[18] never owned land in Elm County.[19] The placement of his census households in 1820 and 1830, however, indicates that he lived on his father's property but in a separate dwelling.[20]

    The only child of Walter and Janet (Planet) Doe was *Janet Doe,* born about Month 1818 and married first to Thomas Doe [*sic*] on 25 Month 1837 in Oak County, R.S.[21] She was a widow in 1857, when her grandfather's land was di-vided, but married second Lance A. Lott in Oak County on 10 Month 1858.[22] She has not been traced further.

    The children of Walter and Martha (Brant) Yourancestor Doe were: *James P. Doe,* client's ancestor; and *Elizabeth Doe,* born 1820–25, died without surviv-ing issue 1831–57, probably unmarried.

B. John Doe (Walter's father) was the oldest son of James Doe[21] and was born 1769–70 in Maple County, R.S.[21] He married Della Robbia about 1788[22] in [*And so forth*] ᴧᴧᴧᴧᴧᴧᴧᴧᴧᴧᴧᴧᴧᴧᴧᴧᴧᴧᴧᴧᴧᴧᴧᴧᴧᴧᴧᴧᴧᴧᴧᴧᴧᴧᴧᴧᴧᴧᴧ

ITEMIZED RESEARCH FINDINGS:

1. Elm County Original Marriage Bonds, basement vault files, "Loose Papers, 1815–25: Box 3," county courthouse, Riverton, R.S.

    Note: In 1820 the Research State legislature passed a marriage registration law that changed the types of records generated by a couple's decision to wed.[22] Until that date, the groom took out a bond with the clerk of court in the bride's county of residence, obligating himself (or in his de-fault, his sureties) to pay a penal sum if it later was discovered that he had not been legally free to marry. A license was issued to the groom, who surrendered it to the minister or magistrate who [*And so forth, rest of explanation*] ᴧᴧᴧᴧᴧᴧᴧᴧᴧᴧᴧᴧᴧᴧᴧᴧᴧᴧᴧᴧᴧᴧᴧᴧᴧᴧᴧᴧᴧᴧᴧᴧᴧᴧᴧᴧ

    a. Bond dated 19 Month 1816 for marriage of Walter Doe to Janet Planet. Sureties: John Doe (signed), Henry Doe (signed). Walter signed the bond WD. Photocopy enclosed.

    b. Bond dated 12 Month 1818 for marriage of Walter Doe to Martha Yourancestor. Sure-ties John Doe (signed "Ɨ" [*the old letter "J"*]) and Frª Yourancestor (signed X). Walter signed the bond WD. Photocopy enclosed.

    c. Bond dated 31 Month 1817 for marriage of Henry Doe to Mildred Pierce. Sureties: John Doe (signed "Ɨ"), Walter Doe (signed WD). Photocopy enclosed.

    d. Bond dated 28 Month 1815 for marriage of Amanda Doe to Leonard Davinchi "Senʳ." Sureties: John Doe (signed), Rem Brant (signed).

e.   Many other papers are in the file box. I examined them briefly, but the majority
     are writs issued to the sheriff by the court authorizing him to take some specific
     action. See enclosed photocopies of one that appears to be pertinent to this inves-
     tigation. It shows that on 22 Month 1818, Sheriff Rem Brant was ordered to "take
     the body" of John Doe to appear in court to answer the complaint of Martin V.
     Buren, to whom John owed $102.34 [*a considerable sum, roughly equivalent to
     the price of 75 acres of good land*]. Brant's endorsement on the back of the writ
     indicates that as of 13 Month, Doe was "not found ~ GW" [*The notation "GW"
     was often used to designate somebody who had "Gone West."*]

interpolations by researcher placed in square brackets and italics typeface

*Comment on the writ: The three-month delay in executing it was highly unusual.
Normally, the sheriff did whatever a writ ordered him to do within a week or so
of receiving it. It is likely that Brant deliberately delayed execution (of the writ,
not John) in order to give him enough time to get away, indicating kinship with—
or at least sympathy for—the debtor.*

*Comment on bonds: The Walter Doe involved in bonds a, b, and c, above,
was the 1831 testator, father of James P. Doe Jr. Judging by the signatures,
two John Does were involved in the four Doe bonds. The one who signed ł as
surety for Walter in 1818 and Amanda in 1815 was their father (see Research
Item #11, below). The John Doe who signed his name as surety for Walter in
1816 and for Henry in 1817 was most probably the man who had "Gone
West" by 13 Month 1818. We do not know yet who this John Doe was but we
suspect that he was the son of the 1855 testator, Henry Doe. (The wording of
Henry's will indicates that his son John was not in Research at the time.) Shf.
Brant's reluctance to imprison John for debt, and the use of "Zachary" in
both families, strengthens, but does not prove, an hypothesis that Henry Doe
was related to client's Doe ancestors.*

2.   1830 U.S. census, Elm County, R.S., NARA microfilm copy 111, reel 111. Examined at the Re-
     search State Genealogical Society Library, Treeton, R.S.

p. 211	line 12	Jackson B. Pollock		
	13	Rem Brant, S. [*Sheriff*]		
	14	James Brant		
	15	Phillip Brant		
	16	Winslow A. Homer		
	17	Michael Angelo		
	18	Leonard Davinchi	1 white male under 5	
			1 white male 15–20	
			1 white female 15–20	
			1 white female 30–40 [*possibly Amanda, widowed by 1830, living with her son*]	
			no slaves	
	19	Henry Doe	1 white male under 5 [*born 1825–30*]	
			2 white male 5–10 [*born 1820–25*]	
			1 white male 30–40 [*born 1790–1800*]	
			1 white female 20–30 [*born 1800–1810*]	
			no slaves	
	20	Thomas Angelo		
	21	Byrd O. Passage		
	22	William Brant		
	23	Grant C. Wood [*last name on the page*]		

sufficient information collected from record for analysis of its significance

extract of household data

for clarity, sets of household statistics are distinguished from each other by indentation (or extra line space)

analytical comments in brackets

p. 212   line 1   Rem Brant Junr.

            2   John Doe   2 white males under 5 [*born 1825–30*]

                                      2 white males 5–10 [*born 1820–30*]

                                    1 white male 50–60 [*born 1770–80*]

                                    1 white female 30–40 [*born 1790–1800*]

                                    1 white female 50–60 [*born 1770–80*]

                                    no slaves

            3   Walter Doe   2 white males 5–10 [*born 1820–25, one uniden-
tified (probaby stepson Rem Yourancestor); the other, James P., born 1823*]

                                    1 white male 30–40 [*born 1790–1800*]

                                    1 white female 5–10 [*born 1820–25*]

                                    1 white female 10–15 [*born 1815–20*]

                                    1 white female 20–30 [*born 1800–10*]

                                    no slaves

            4   Albrect Johann Durer

            5   Johann Peter Durer

            6   Green Hill

            7   River Jordan

            8   Willie Brant

            9   Alexander Roe

^^^^^^^^^^^^^ [*And so forth. Census reports continue through page 9*] ^^^^^^^^^^^^^^^

7.   A. Comp Eyeler, *Abstracts of Maple County Wills: 1779–1830* (Capital City: privately published, 1990).

    a.   Page 21: will of Luke D. Robbia, 1812. Among the named legatees were son Luke and daughter Della Doe, wife of John. [See enclosed photocopy of record-book copy of entire will, River County Will Book B: 301–3, made at probate office, courthouse, Elmton. The photocopy of Eyeler's abstract is also enclosed.]

citation in report and on photocopy

        NOTE: The Robbias were a prominent Research State family. The findings (reported below) provide ample evidence that Della was Walter Doe's mother, so even if Martha Brant's line cannot be proved to the early Johann Brant, your descent from the first Luke Robbia can be. Either lineage should produce ancestors with ample public and/or military service for your (and/or your children's) membership in several hereditary societies.

    b.   No other Doe (or Dough, Dowe, Deaux, or other variant) found in the index.

^^^^^^^^^^^^^^^^^^^^^^^^^^^^^[*And so forth*] ^^^^^^^^^^^^^^^^^^^^^^^^^^^^^^

RECOMMENDATION FOR CONTINUING: The published abstracts of Maple and Early county records examined for this report indicate that John Doe's father, James, was a son of Zachary Doe (who may have been a son of the first Willow County Doe, Henry). Before proceeding with the search for evidence of Zachary's possible relationship to Henry, however, I strongly advise that the rest of the original records be investigated and collected. As I remarked in the body of the report, most of these abstracts were done by the same compiler and, in my experience, they are often incomplete and sometimes erroneous, although useful as finding aids to the original records. They should not be relied upon as proof that James was, in fact, the son of Zachary.

END OF REPORT

candid, but impartial, evaluation (needed for client's understanding of findings and of the recommendation for continuing)

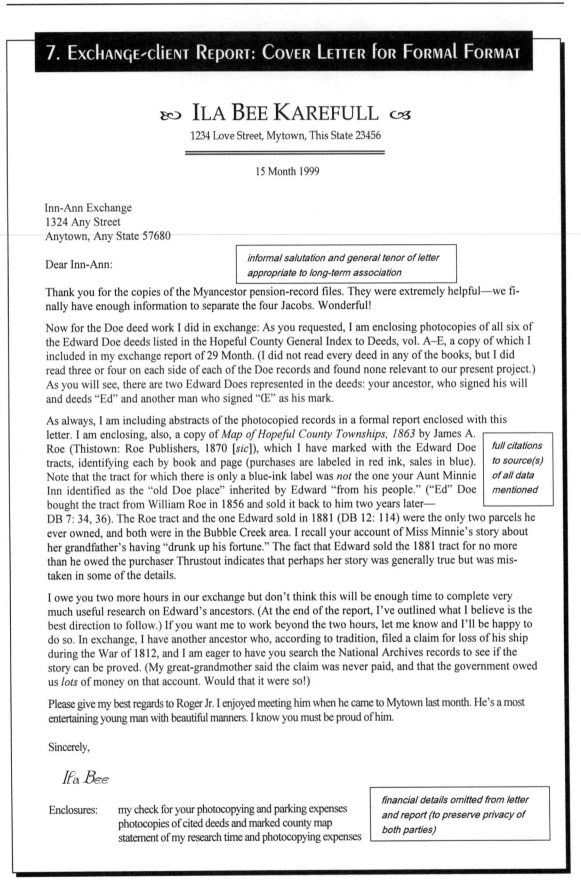

7. Exchange-client Report: Cover Letter for Formal Format

໒ ILA BEE KAREFULL ໕

1234 Love Street, Mytown, This State 23456

15 Month 1999

Inn-Ann Exchange
1324 Any Street
Anytown, Any State 57680

Dear Inn-Ann:

> *informal salutation and general tenor of letter appropriate to long-term association*

Thank you for the copies of the Myancestor pension-record files. They were extremely helpful—we finally have enough information to separate the four Jacobs. Wonderful!

Now for the Doe deed work I did in exchange: As you requested, I am enclosing photocopies of all six of the Edward Doe deeds listed in the Hopeful County General Index to Deeds, vol. A–E, a copy of which I included in my exchange report of 29 Month. (I did not read every deed in any of the books, but I did read three or four on each side of each of the Doe records and found none relevant to our present project.) As you will see, there are two Edward Does represented in the deeds: your ancestor, who signed his will and deeds "Ed" and another man who signed "Œ" as his mark.

As always, I am including abstracts of the photocopied records in a formal report enclosed with this letter. I am enclosing, also, a copy of *Map of Hopeful County Townships, 1863* by James A. Roe (Thistown: Roe Publishers, 1870 [*sic*]), which I have marked with the Edward Doe tracts, identifying each by book and page (purchases are labeled in red ink, sales in blue). Note that the tract for which there is only a blue-ink label was *not* the one your Aunt Minnie Inn identified as the "old Doe place" inherited by Edward "from his people." ("Ed" Doe bought the tract from William Roe in 1856 and sold it back to him two years later—DB 7: 34, 36). The Roe tract and the one Edward sold in 1881 (DB 12: 114) were the only two parcels he ever owned, and both were in the Bubble Creek area. I recall your account of Miss Minnie's story about her grandfather's having "drunk up his fortune." The fact that Edward sold the 1881 tract for no more than he owed the purchaser Thrustout indicates that perhaps her story was generally true but was mistaken in some of the details.

> *full citations to source(s) of all data mentioned*

I owe you two more hours in our exchange but don't think this will be enough time to complete very much useful research on Edward's ancestors. (At the end of the report, I've outlined what I believe is the best direction to follow.) If you want me to work beyond the two hours, let me know and I'll be happy to do so. In exchange, I have another ancestor who, according to tradition, filed a claim for loss of his ship during the War of 1812, and I am eager to have you search the National Archives records to see if the story can be proved. (My great-grandmother said the claim was never paid, and that the government owed us *lots* of money on that account. Would that it were so!)

Please give my best regards to Roger Jr. I enjoyed meeting him when he came to Mytown last month. He's a most entertaining young man with beautiful manners. I know you must be proud of him.

Sincerely,

Ila Bee

Enclosures: my check for your photocopying and parking expenses
              photocopies of cited deeds and marked county map
              statement of my research time and photocopying expenses

> *financial details omitted from letter and report (to preserve privacy of both parties)*

8. Exchange-client Report: Formal Format

❧ ILA BEE KAREFULL ☙ | report writer |

1234 Love Street, Mytown, This State 23456

15 Month 1999 | report date |

| report title |

DOE REPORT #4 TO: Inn-Ann Exchange | intended recipient |
1324 Any Street
Anytown, Any State 57680

| identification of research facility |

REPORT SUBJECT: Abstracts of Doe deeds, Hopeful County, T.S. Records examined on microfilm at the
This State Archives, Mytown, T.S, 12 and 13 Month 1999. Photocopies enclosed. (The
| explanatory remarks | microfilm reel number is enclosed in parentheses. The "S," "T," and "R" used in tract de-
scriptions stand for Section, Township, and Range.)

1.   Hopeful County, T.S., Deed Book 4: 34–35 (C.HO.101). | source citation includes repository microfilm designations |
10 Month 1834.
| abstracts (not summaries) of cited records | Edward Doe of Hopeful from Thomas Roe Sr. of same, for $120.00, 160 acres, n ½ of nw ¼, S12,
T2, R20. Signed: Th° Roe. Witnesses: Wm Fen, James Fen (X his mark), Eliza Fen (θ his mark [*sic*]).
[*Registration date not given.*]

2.   Hopeful County, T.S., Deed Book 4: 12 (C.HO.101)
3 Month 1835
Edward Doe of Hopeful from William Fen and his wife Mary of same, for $275.00, 160 acres, s ½ of nw
¼, S12, T2, R20. Signed: Wm Fen, Mary Fen (∅ her mark). Witnesses: James (X his mark) Fen, Henry
Goodtitle, Martin Den. Registered 12 Month 1835.

3.   Hopeful County, T.S., Deed Book 7: 34 (C.HO.102) | moderate rearrangement of data to standardize placement of date |
5 Month 1856
Edward Doe of Hopeful from William Roe and Jane Roe his wife of same, for $25.00, 50 acres, se ¼ of
se ¼, S18, T10, R11 and part in ne ¼ of se ¼, S18, T10, R11. Signed: William Roe, Jane Roe. Witnesses:
Walter Roe, William Roe Jr., Westfield Roe. Registered 6 Month 1856.

4.   Hopeful County, T.S., Deed Book 7: 36 (C.HO.102)
18 Month 1858
Edward Doe of Hopeful and Wilhelmina his wife to William Roe of same, for $8.00, 50 acres, part in se
¼ of se ¼, S18, T10, R11 and part in ne ¼ of se ¼, S18, T10, R11. Signed: Ed Doe, "Willameena" Doe.
Witnesses: Willy Roe Jr., Westy Roe, Wally Roe. Registered 1 Month 1858.

| interpretive comments based on relevant background | *Comment: This is the same tract Edward/Ed had bought from Roe two years earlier. I know of
no local events or circumstances that would account for the $17 difference between the purchase
and sale prices (no recession, for example), so if this was an investment tract it was an unprofit-
able one. Although $20 was low for 50 acres, the transaction does not appear to have been a gift
from Roe to Doe—the price is commensurate with the fact that this section of Hopeful County
(south of Bubble Creek) is chiefly swampland and is, even today, of little agricultural value.*

5.   Hopeful County, T.S., Deed Book 10: 154 (C.HO.103)
30 Month 1874
Edward Doe and Emily his wife "formerly of Hopeful County in the State of This but now residing in
Docktown in the State of Somewhere-Else" to Ben Goodtitle of Doubtful County, T.S., "for the sum of
five Hundred dollars and thirty two cents dully [*sic*] received by the said Edward Doe of the said Ben

Ila Bee Karefull to Inn-Ann Exchange, 15 Month 1999 | report identification on each (numbered) page | DOE REPORT #4, p. 2

| complex passage quoted | Gooditle's agent The Doubtful Bank and Surety Company," two tracts of land totaling 320 acres in Hopeful, one tract of 160 acres being the n ½ of nw ¼, S12, T2, R20, and one tract of 160 acres being the s ½ of nw ¼, S12, T2, R20. Signed: Edward Doe (Œ his mark), Emily Doe (X her mark). Witnesses: Jefferson Goodtitle, Westfield Doe (WD his mark), Emily Goodtitle (ED her mark). |

| data irrelevant to subject of project well identified, and reasons for conclusion that it is irrelevant explained | *Comment: This deed provides a great many hints about family relationships among the Does, Roes, and Goodtitles, but— unfortunately—this is the wrong Edward Doe. Not only did your ancestor sign his name (as this Edward did not), but this Edward's wife was Emily in 1874, while yours had married Wilhelmina Holdfast in 1848 and was still married to her when he died in Hopeful County on 31 Month 1902. (Also, the Westy who signed your Edward's deed as witness, was not the Westfield who signed this deed "WD") There may be some kind of family relationship between the two Doe groups, but their mere similarity of naming patterns is not a good enough reason to conclude that there was. I do not recommend abandoning our search for the "right" Edward's father in favor of pursuing the ancestry of this "wrong" one, even though he has provided us with more abundant clues to follow.* |

6.   Hopeful County, T.S., Deed Book 12: 114–5 (C.HO.104)
     2 Month 1881
     Edward Doe and Wilhelmina his wife of Hopeful to Frederick Thrustout [*residence not given*], in satisfaction of the sum of $128.44 owed by the said Edward Doe to the said Frederick Thrustout, a tract of fifty acres, it being all of ne ¼ of sw ¼, S18, T10, R11 and part of nw ¼ of sw ¼, S18, T10, R11. The tract is further described in the deed as "the land on which the said Edward now lives and include[es] the house barn fences orchards and plowed fields thereunto belonging." Signed: Ed Doe, "Willa" Doe. Witness: Fayette Doe, Benjamin F. Doe, George W. Doe.

     Comment: Note that there is no deed whereby Edward purchased this tract, although it was obviously the one on which he lived. We know from John Holdfast's 1884 will (Doe Report 2) that Ed and Willa were living with him by then. It is logical to conclude that Edward's loss of this tract (probably Miss Inn's "the old Doe place") caused the family's move.

ADDITIONAL RESEARCH:

A.   James A. Roe, *Name Index to Hopeful County Land Grants* (Thistown: Roe & Company Publishers, 1987). Roe listed twelve Doe/Dough/Dowe grants and gave the tract description and acreage for each. None was Edward's "extra" fifty acres. [Photocopy of p. 34 of Roe's book is enclosed.]

B.   Henry Local Historian, *A Complete History of Hopeful* (Capital City: privately published, 1913). The volume is not indexed, but I found no mention of a Thrustout in the chapter "Inns, Ordinaries, and Taverns." I did not read the rest of the book.

TO CONTINUE: The index to Hopeful County deeds includes eight pages of citations to Doe land purchases. Before searching all of these records for information about the origin of Edward's fifty-acre dwelling tract, I suggest that we examine the tax rolls. From the tax rolls we should be able to determine when Edward acquired the tract, and that year's list of "alienations" may include the name of the land's previous owner and whether Edward purchased or inherited it. Also, because tax assessments of the period included whiskey and "stock in trade," Thrustout might be identifiable as a tavern owner or barkeep—thereby supporting Miss Minnie's colorful story of Edward's having "drunk up his fortune."

— ☾ —

device signifying end of report

9. PERSONAL-RESEARCH REPORT: MEMORANDUM FORMAT

MEMO TO: Doe Files

JOHN DOE #36

BY: Your Own Name, 1234 Your Street, Yourtown, Your State 12345-6789

file identifier

DATE: 15 Month 1999

FOCUS: Parentage of John Doe #36

identification of report writer, date, and subject

SUMMARY OF KNOWN INFORMATION (as of 4 Month 1997): John Doe was born about 1821 in Old State and died in Your State between the taking of the 1850 and 1860 censuses.[1] He is said to have been a grandson of General John Doe, Revolutionary War hero of Old State,[2] but no evidence has been found of the relationship. John married Mary Elizabeth Fen on 25 December 1843 in Mournful Springs Church, Yourown County, YS.[3] The couple lived on their farm on Orchard Road (now State Route 33) about three miles south of present-day Happy Place. (More about the farm is in James Name #8's file.) John Doe's chief occupation was the breeding and raising of racehorses, said to have been among the swiftest in the state.[4] He apparently left a will but no copy of it has been found in the Yourown County will books and no original is on file at the YS State Archives. A series of exchange deeds between Solomon Doe (#18) and his brothers Malcolm and Conrad, however, quote from the will: "and to my sons [*unnamed*] equally divided . . . all my lands wherever situate."[5]

Mary Elizabeth Fen was the daughter of Henry and Davidene (Roe) Fen and a descendant of Frederick Fen I of Old State, the immigrant ancestor.[6] She was born 1 Month 1825 in Oldville, OS.[7] As her second husband, she married ____ Badtitle between September 1860 when the census was taken and 18 Month 1866 when she wrote her will, mentioning four surviving Doe children (Solomon; Malcolm; Conrad; and Elizabeth Den, wife of Joseph) and "my husband's son Philip Badtitle."[8] According to Doe family tradition, a Badtitle (possibly M. E.'s husband or son) "quarreled bitterly" with either Solomon or James Doe and "there has been bad blood between Does and Badtitles ever since."[9] Mary Elizabeth (Fen) Doe Badtitle died in YS on 19 Month 1867 and is buried at Mournful Springs Cemetery.[10] An unmarked grave in the plot is said to be that of her first husband, John Doe.[11]

TO-DO PLAN (from file Solomon Doe #18) updated 5 Month 1999:

"to-do" notes are temporary so may be in less formal writing style

1. **Source Unknown:** Find out where an "original paper writing purporting to be the will of . . ." would have been sent/filed if its probate was protested. A higher court? If John owned land in another county, would the will have been probated there? Or in another state? (Old State?)

2. **Census Research:**

    a. 1840 (searched for John Doe with no luck). Look for Doe households in & near YS with a white male about 40 or so (probable minimum age of John's father), with a white male aged 15–20 in the household (or perhaps 20–30 if John was not entirely candid about his age when he gave it to the 1850 enumerator).

source citations (and directions to document copies)

1. John Doe Household, 1850 U.S. census, Your State, Yourown County population schedule, Mournful Springs Township, page 138, dwelling 201, family 204, YS State Archives microfilm no. Cen.US.50; and household of M. E. Doe, 1860 U.S. census of Your State, Yourown County population schedule, Mournful Springs Township, page 388, dwelling 34, family 34, YS State Archives microfilm no. Cen.US.60. (Docs. 13 & 14, Solomon Doe #18 file.)

2. Calvin W. Roe, *Reminiscences of Yourown County People, Places and Events: A Full Account of the History of the County from Its Earliest Days to the Present Time and Including Lists of Her Gallant Fighting Men in the Great Wars of Independence* (1879; reprint, Thatplace: ABCD Publishers, 1974), 277. (Doc. 7, this file.)

3. "Three Local Marriages on Christmas Day," *Your* [Capital City] *Weekly Gazette*, 26 December 1843, p. 8, col. 3. A copy of the page was found tucked within Barbara Name's family Bible and reproduced in "Name is the Name" newsletter, 12 August 1983, p. 1. (Doc. 7, James Name #8 file.)

4. Roe, *Reminiscences*, 278.

5. Yourown County Deed Book G: 58, 61; and Deed Book H: 1, 109. (Docs. 22–25, Solomon Doe #18 file.)

6. Fine Genealogist, *Descendants of Frederick Fen (1634–1721) of Old State* (Oldville: privately published, 1987). (Doc. 1, Mary Elizabeth (Fen) Doe #37 file.)

^^^^^^^^^^^^ [*Reference notes continue but are not included in this example*] ^^^^^^^^^^^^

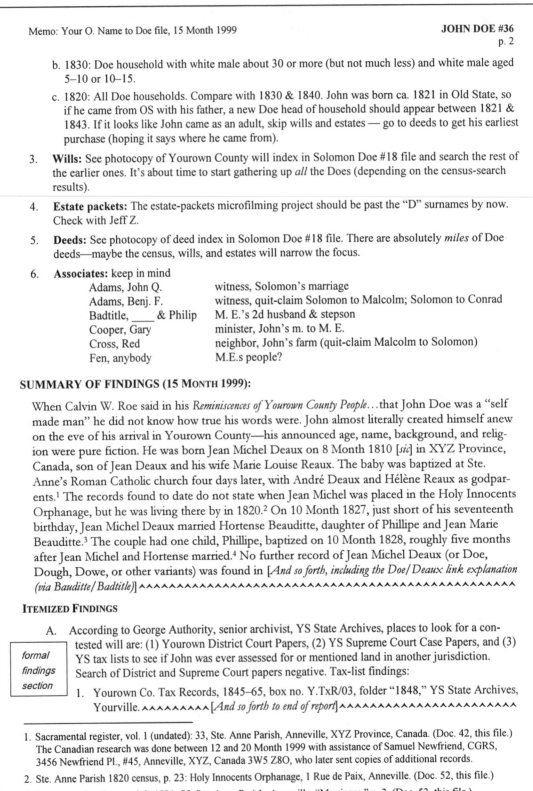

  b. 1830: Doe household with white male about 30 or more (but not much less) and white male aged 5–10 or 10–15.

  c. 1820: All Doe households. Compare with 1830 & 1840. John was born ca. 1821 in Old State, so if he came from OS with his father, a new Doe head of household should appear between 1821 & 1843. If it looks like John came as an adult, skip wills and estates — go to deeds to get his earliest purchase (hoping it says where he came from).

3. **Wills:** See photocopy of Yourown County will index in Solomon Doe #18 file and search the rest of the earlier ones. It's about time to start gathering up *all* the Does (depending on the census-search results).

4. **Estate packets:** The estate-packets microfilming project should be past the "D" surnames by now. Check with Jeff Z.

5. **Deeds:** See photocopy of deed index in Solomon Doe #18 file. There are absolutely *miles* of Doe deeds—maybe the census, wills, and estates will narrow the focus.

6. **Associates:** keep in mind

Adams, John Q.	witness, Solomon's marriage
Adams, Benj. F.	witness, quit-claim Solomon to Malcolm; Solomon to Conrad
Badtitle, ____ & Philip	M. E.'s 2d husband & stepson
Cooper, Gary	minister, John's m. to M. E.
Cross, Red	neighbor, John's farm (quit-claim Malcolm to Solomon)
Fen, anybody	M.E.s people?

SUMMARY OF FINDINGS (15 MONTH 1999):

When Calvin W. Roe said in his *Reminiscences of Yourown County People*…that John Doe was a "self made man" he did not know how true his words were. John almost literally created himself anew on the eve of his arrival in Yourown County—his announced age, name, background, and religion were pure fiction. He was born Jean Michel Deaux on 8 Month 1810 [*sic*] in XYZ Province, Canada, son of Jean Deaux and his wife Marie Louise Reaux. The baby was baptized at Ste. Anne's Roman Catholic church four days later, with André Deaux and Hélène Reaux as godparents.[1] The records found to date do not state when Jean Michel was placed in the Holy Innocents Orphanage, but he was living there by in 1820.[2] On 10 Month 1827, just short of his seventeenth birthday, Jean Michel Deaux married Hortense Beauditte, daughter of Phillipe and Jean Marie Beauditte.[3] The couple had one child, Phillipe, baptized on 10 Month 1828, roughly five months after Jean Michel and Hortense married.[4] No further record of Jean Michel Deaux (or Doe, Dough, Dowe, or other variants) was found in [*And so forth, including the Doe/Deaux link explanation (via Bauditte/Badtitle)*] ᴧᴧᴧ

ITEMIZED FINDINGS

A. According to George Authority, senior archivist, YS State Archives, places to look for a contested will are: (1) Yourown District Court Papers, (2) YS Supreme Court Case Papers, and (3) YS tax lists to see if John was ever assessed for or mentioned land in another jurisdiction. Search of District and Supreme Court papers negative. Tax-list findings:

formal findings section

  1. Yourown Co. Tax Records, 1845–65, box no. Y.TxR/03, folder "1848," YS State Archives, Yourville. ᴧᴧᴧᴧᴧᴧᴧᴧᴧ[*And so forth to end of report*]ᴧᴧᴧᴧᴧᴧᴧᴧᴧᴧᴧᴧᴧᴧᴧᴧᴧᴧᴧᴧᴧᴧᴧ

---

1. Sacramental register, vol. 1 (undated): 33, Ste. Anne Parish, Anneville, XYZ Province, Canada. (Doc. 42, this file.) The Canadian research was done between 12 and 20 Month 1999 with assistance of Samuel Newfriend, CGRS, 3456 Newfriend Pl., #45, Anneville, XYZ, Canada 3W5 Z8O, who later sent copies of additional records.

2. Ste. Anne Parish 1820 census, p. 23: Holy Innocents Orphanage, 1 Rue de Paix, Anneville. (Doc. 52, this file.)

3. Sacramental register, vol. 2: 1821–75, Ste. Anne Parish, Anneville, "Marriages," p. 3. (Doc. 53, this file.)

4. Ibid., "Baptisms," p. 19. (Doc. 54, this file.)

Appendix D — Example Proof Summaries

The purpose of a proof summary is to record in permanent form a succinct, coherent, convincing account of the evidence on which a genealogical conclusion is based. The compiler of a proof summary, therefore, exercises

- *suitable selectivity* in the choice of evidence. A great deal of research and analysis may have preceded the conclusion, but once reached, the underlying evidence is then reviewed and distilled. Biographical details and subsidiary conclusions that have no contribution to make are omitted—provided that no significant contradictions are suppressed.

  Proof summaries are severely tailored, precisely directed explanations that focus on the *specific* evidence that supports the *specific* conclusion that is the subject of the summary.

- *logical arrangement* of the selected evidence. Normally, the most useful arrangement is: *(a)* a brief statement of the problem and its background; *(b)* an introduction to the chief characters in the proof argument; *(c)* the main points in the proof, each point followed by subsidiary explanations that support it (but if merely peripheral to the point, such remarks are omitted or moved into explanatory footnotes).

  The main points are ordered in a sequence that develops the proof "from the problem to its solution." Constructing a well thought-out writing outline, therefore, is a wise preliminary step—one cannot say *everything* in the first paragraph.

- *thorough documentation* of every fact mentioned, individually cited to its source or sources. If several sources were needed to establish a fact, all are included in the citation.

  Most genealogical compilers now use footnotes rather than endnotes for source citation as well as for explanations that are necessary but would interrupt the flow of the text if included within it.

Two formats for proof summaries are generally accepted:

- *a cover-sheet list,* which is used only if the evidence is direct and complete in itself—that is, it derives from a limited series of records that require only assembly and brief explanation. The list, with full source citations and brief analytical comments, is attached to the document copies or transcriptions (not abstracts, summaries, or nutshell notes). The records are assembled and listed in logical order, and comments are clearly identified as distinct from the records' contents.

- *source-cited text* is used if items of direct evidence contradict each other, or if an item of direct evidence conflicts with persuasive but indirect evidence, or if proof can be established only by correlating all the indirect evidence. In these cases, extended explanation is needed. Headings, subheadings, and bulleted or numbered paragraphs can be used to organize or emphasize primary and subsidiary points.

The fictitious Else and Parent families are the subjects of the two examples here. The reader may wish to compare the types of data in these examples with those in Appendixes E and F that use the same families. Different kinds of detail are included in a compilation that focuses on evidence as opposed to a biography that summarizes personal life events and relationships.

Example 2 is more complicated than most proof summaries need be— it is deliberately complex to demonstrate a variety of analytical and research techniques that might lead to sound genealogical conclusions.

1. PROOF SUMMARY: COVER-SHEET LIST FORMAT

Compiler: Jane Q. Else
1234 Somewhere St., Somewhere, Any State
12 Month 1999

John Somebody Else #8
b. 1 Mo. 1858, d. 8 Mo. 1930

PROOF OF RELATIONSHIP TO FATHER John S. Else Sr. [#16]

1. **Will of John S. Else**, written 4 Month 1883, probated 28 Month 1883 (Near County, Any State, Will Book 45, p. 209, Probate Office, courthouse, Nearton). —Summary of important points:

   > to **"my youngest son" Johnny** my blacksmith tools and my ½ of Lot 35 in the plan of Otherton, including the shop.
   >
   > **real estate in Distant and Any Counties, A.S.**, given to son Jason Else
   >
   > **other children mentioned:** Rafe [*Ralph*] "bachelor"; Fifi [*Fiona*] Myancestor wife of Lemuel; Sonny [*Jason*]; Elly [*Ellen*] Roe wife of Homer; Tommy [*Thomas*]; and Sweety [*Mary S.*] Key wife of Luck.
   >
   > **to wife Sally** [*Sarah*] "my dwelling tract," on Cabin Branch in Near County, & Lot 34 in Otherton for life or widowhood and then to son Johnny.
   >
   > **signed will with name** not a mark.

   - *Son Johnny given blacksmith shop (see John S. Else #8 "blacksmith," 1900 census; but no record of his sale of Otherton lots)*
   - *John S. Else [Sr.] owned land in Near, Distant, and Any Counties*

2. **Any County Marriage Registers, Book 4: 1876–1900**, p. 376, courthouse, Big Place, A.S. —Summary of important points:

   > **12 Month 1881:** [Groom] John S. Else Sr., 77, [son of] Jason and Ellen Else; [Bride] Sarah Jane Young, 22, [daughter of] Michael Young and Louise Old.

3. **1880 federal census.** No John Else/Alse/etc. household in A.S. or nearby states.

4. **1870 federal census, population schedule, Distant County, A.S.**taken 3 Month 1870, "South District, Thatplace P.O.," p. 33, dwelling 53, family 53 (duplicate original at Any State Historical Society, Bigtown, A.S.; also NARA microcopy M777, roll 333, which gives only initials). —Summary of important points:

   > **John S. Else**   65, farmer, [born] A.S., $3320, $1190, literate
   > **Polly S. "**   55, at home, [born] A.S., literate
   > **John S. "**   11, [born] A.S., literate, at school within the year
   > also in household: Ralph G., 32 (laborer); Thomas H. (laborer), 20, and Mary S., 17 (at home), all born in A.S.

   - *John not yet married to Sally/Sarah, his 1883 wife; wife-aged female was Polly [Mary] S. Else*
   - *John S. [Sr.] born about 1805; Polly born about 1815, died 1870–81*

5. **1860 federal census, population schedule, Near County, A.S.**, taken 28 Month 1860, p. 201, dwelling 298, family 296 (NARA microcopy M666, roll 333). *Whether literate or at school columns are blank.* —Summary of important points:

   > **John Else Sr.**   55, farmer, [born] A.S., $8500, $2000 [*b. ca. 1805*]
   > **Polly Else**   40, domestic, [born] A.S. [*b. ca. 1810*]
   > Rafe Else   21, laborer, [born] A.S., married within the year

[continued on page 2]

page 2: Proofs, John Somebody Else #8 to his parents

Lucy Else	17, domestic, [born] A.S., married within year
Fifi Else	18, female, teacher, [born] A.S., [*Fiona*]
Sonny Else	15, laborer, [born] A.S.
Tommy Else	10, [born] A.S.
Polly Else	7, [born] A.S.
Johnny Else	**2**, [born] A.S.

- *Age of son Johnny agrees with birth date of John Somebody Else #8 (1 Month 1858)*

PROOF OF RELATIONSHIP TO MOTHER Mary Sweet Harte [#17]

6. **1850 federal census, population schedule, Near County, A.S.**, taken 30 Month 1850, p. 59, dwelling 101, family 101 (NARA microcopy M555, roll 333). —Summary of important points:

John S. Else	**46**, farmer, [born] A.S., $1234, literate [*b. c1804*]
Mary S. Else	**35**, at home, [born] A.S., literate [*b. c1815*]
Ellen M. Else	17, at home, [born] A.S, literate
Jane S. Else	15, at home, [born] A.S., literate
Ralph G. Else	12, [born] A.S., at school within the year
Fiona B. Else	8, [born] A.S., at school within the year
Jason L. Else	5, [born] A.S.
Thomas S. Else	3/12, [born] A.S.

household adjoins dwelling 102, family 102: **Jason Else** and family

- *John S. born 1804–5; Mary S. "Polly" born 1815 (1860 census is the only record that disagrees)*

7. **Distant County Marriage Register, 1821–51,** unpaginated, unindexed, arranged by date (office of county clerk, Distant County courthouse, Thatplace). *Note: parent, witness, and officiant names not given before law change, 1851.* —Transcription:

1830, 9 Month: [Groom] John S. Else, 24; [Bride] Mary Sweet Harte, 15.

- *First wife of John S. Else Sr. & mother of all children (including John #8): Mary <u>Sweet</u> <u>Harte</u>*
- *John #8 had son <u>Harte</u> A.; daughter Ellen <u>Sweet</u>*

END

2. Proof Summary: Source-Cited Text Format

[Draft for article, submitted to *The Research State Journal*, 12 Month 1999 by Ima Kean Researcher, 123 Shady Lane, Anytown, R.S.]

A Father for Lemuel Parent Jr. (1775–1805)
of Mountain County, Essex

Generations of genealogists have assumed, chiefly because of his name and location, that Lemuel Parent Jr. descended from the well-known Essex pioneer, William Parent. William[1] Parent married late in life and had only one known child, Benjamin[2], who, as "only son and heir at law of Wm Parren," petitioned for regrant of his father's lapsed land-patent in 1689.[1] Benjamin died in 1719 having fathered twelve daughters by his first wife Judith and, unbeknown to him, a posthumous son, Benjamin W.[3] Parent, by his second wife Mary [—?—] Contrary, widow of Leonard.[2] Benjamin W.[3] Parent married Milly Bridge about 1740–41[3] and by her had six children: Henry[4], Thomas, Millicent, Lemuel, Mary, and Benjamin Parent.[4] If Lemuel Parent Jr., born in 1775, was part of this family, he had to have been a child of one of these six people. But which one?

In a recently published history of the Parent family, Lemuel Jr. (14 Month 1775–27 Month 1805[5]) is said to have been one of seven children born to Henry[4] and Priscilla [—?—] Parent of Mountain County, Essex. No evidence is offered in source citations or analytical notes to support this assertion.[6] However, our investigation of Parent records in Mountain and surrounding Essex and North State counties produced what appears to be direct contradiction to the alleged Henry-Lemuel relationship.

---

1. J. Early Historian, *William Parent, Pioneer*, 3 vols. (Capitalsville: Essex Historical Society, 1967). Reproduction of William Parent's patent is at 1: 110, figure 5; Benjamin's regrant at 3: 18, figure 3.

2. "Mary Parent *vs.* Heirs of Benjamin Parent, 1720," Court of Chancery records, Essex State Archives, Capitalsville. Mary's suit to have her husband's will set aside was based on the birth on 27 Month 1719 "after the death of his father," of Benjamin's "only son" who, by law, could not be deprived of inheriting his father's land. The file includes Benjamin's original will and three depositions concerning Mary's marriage to him on 26 Month 1719.

3. Tole Bridge will, 17 Month 1746, probated 4 Month 1747, Ridge County Wills and Estates, Book B[1]: 33-5, Clerk's Office, Topton. Tole mentioned three Parent grandchildren: Henry, Thomas, and "Little Milly."

4. Benjamin W. Parent will, 1 Month 1772, probated 10 Month 1773, Ridge County Wills and Estates, Book B[2]: 191–203. Benjamin, with unusual attention to detail, specified the birth order of all but one of his children (the deceased daughter Millicent). It should be noted here that "Lemuel" appears as "Samuel" in James G. Wrong's *Abstracts of Essex Wills, 1673–1800* (1926: reprint, Riverton: The Press, 1976), 201.

5. Lemuel Parent grave marker, as recorded in "Peak City Cemetery," Essex Works Progress Administration (WPA) Cemetery Project, 1935–37, typescript at Essex State Archives. Lemuel's stone was lost when the Wide River flooded in 1966 (letter from J.M. Official, overseer, to author, 22 Month 1988).

6. Skie Blue, *Parent and Related Families* (Riverton: Riverton Press, 1990), 98.

Henry[4] Parent, oldest son of Benjamin W.[3] and Milly (Bridge) Parent of Ridge, later Mountain County, died testate in Mountain between 10 and 25 Month 1811.[7] His will provided for wife Priscilla[8] and devised and bequeathed specified property to five named children (Benjamin, William, and Thomas Parent; Josephine McIntosh, wife of Appley; and Serenity Cloud, wife of Charles). Two grandchildren (Benjamin and Serenity Parent, children of "my son Henry") were to receive sufficient funds for their education. The estate's residue was to be divided among "all my children after the death or intermarriage of their mother and one share to those of Henry dec'd. [deceased]" When the executor, wife Priscilla, died before the estate was fully settled, the court appointed son Benjamin Parent to complete the process. Six months later, as "administrator *cum testamento annexo* [with the will annexed]," Benjamin filed his final account, including within it a notation of his equal distribution of all remaining funds among himself and the other legatees named in the will.[9] No additional heirs claimed inheritance under the "all my children" clause.

Lemuel Parent Jr. died in 1805 before Henry wrote his will, so his absence as a legatee is inconclusive. However, Henry also failed to mention Lemuel's children, although he did provide for those of deceased son Henry [Jr.]. Omission of a son—or a grandchild representing him—by testators of that era often signals that the son had already been deeded his inheritance and the grandchildren thereby provided for. Extensive search of Mountain County deed books, however, produced no Henry-to-Lemuel deed and no other land purchase by (or grant to) Lemuel Jr. that Henry might have financed.[10] Thorough research in the records of nearby counties in Essex and North State was equally unproductive.

Alternative Possibilities

If Henry[4] Parent was not Lemuel Jr.'s father, one might suppose that one of Henry's siblings was his father (or, perhaps, his unmarried mother). Such a supposition, however, is untenable in the face of overwhelming evidence to the contrary.

- The 1772 will of Henry's father closes the possibility of a "hidden" sibling.[11] With unusually meticulous attention to detail, Benjamin W. Parent's elaborate will leaves no room for doubt that he had six and only six children, whom he identified as Henry, "my first-born child"; Thomas, "my second son"; "my midway child Lemuel"; "my youngest

7. Henry Parent will, 1 Month 1811, probated 25 Month 1811, Mountain County Wills and Estates, Book 2: 104–5, Clerk's Office, Peak City.
8. Priscilla's birth family has not been identified at this writing.
9. Henry Parent estate, Mountain County Wills and Estates, Book 2: 287, 316, Clerk's Office, Peak City.
10. The Mountain County land records (deeds and grants) are complete and well indexed. Not entirely trusting indexes in so important a matter, however, we read the registration books for every grant and deed recorded in Mountain between 1796, when Lemuel married, and 1810, by which time his widow had remarried. (One can safely assume that her new husband would have taken care to register any unrecorded deed for land in which she had a one-third dower interest.) Only two records were found that referred to Lemuel "Jr.": he witnessed a purchase by Henry Parent in 1799 (Deed Book 3: 333), and a sale by Lemuel "Senr." in 1801 (Deed Book 3: 407). The minutes of the Mountain County court, which had oversight of land transactions, were searched, also, for registration of a deed that might have been accidentally left out of the official record books. None was found. (The original court minutes were examined at the county courthouse but have since been moved to the Essex State Archives.)
11. Benjamin W. Parent will, 1772.

son Benjamin"; "my daughter Mary Vane, wife of Wether"; and "my deceased child Millicent," whose gravestone was to be purchased by the executor, son Henry.

- The son Thomas died in 1809 without issue—his River County will left small bequests to my "faithful servant Silas" and "all the remainder of my property real and personal" to brothers Henry and Lemuel, who were also appointed executors.[12] Thomas did not mention or provide for a wife or child, and his 1790 and 1800 census enumerations support the thesis that he had no offspring. The only other person in the household both years was a man born 1755–74, presumably the faithful Silas.[13]

- The family Bible of son Lemuel [Sr.] survives and records the births of seven daughters between 1770 and 1784.[14] It is inconceivable, given the social values and inheritance practices of the era, that Lemuel simply "forgot" to record the birth of an only son, as was proposed by one compiler.[15] More convincing, however, is the fact that a bare fourteen months intervened between the births of daughters Josephine (22 Month 1774) and Frances (24 Month 1776), insufficient time for another pregnancy in the interim.

- The son Benjamin died at age eighteen, unmarried, the victim of an unspecified "fatal accident" on 23 Month 1774,[16] eleven months before Lemuel Jr.'s birth.

- The daughter Mary was safely married to Wether Vane by 1772 when Benjamin wrote his will. Lemuel Jr., born three years later, cannot have been her illegitimate child.

One Parent researcher has advanced the theory that a *sister* of Benjamin W. was Lemuel's mother without benefit of marriage.[17] This thesis, too, is untenable. The youngest of Judith Parent's twelve daughters, Helen, was born in 1715 and would have been sixty by 1775, a highly unlikely age for pregnancy—and Mary Parent, Benjamin's second wife, had no daughters. Her only Parent child was the testator Benjamin W.[18]

12. Thomas Parent will, 19 Month 1809, probated 2 Month 1809, River County Will Book A: 301, Clerk's Office, Swamp City.
13. Thomas Parent households: (1) 1790 census, from *Heads of Families at the First Census of the United States Taken in the Year 1790: Essex* (1908, reprint; Bigtown: Bigtown Publishing Co., 1979), 133, col. 1; (2) 1800 U.S. census, River County, p. 13, NARA microprint M000, reel 000.
14. Birth, Death, and Marriage Register pages, *The Holy Bible*, Authorized Version, published at New City, 1795. The pages only are in the folder "Genealogy" in the John Famous Person Papers, file P.C.10003, Manuscript Collection, Research State University, Learnedville, R.S. Senator Person, son of John and Elizabeth (Famous) Person, was a great-grandson of Lemuel Parent Sr.
15. Amelia F. Wrong, *Our Parents and Their Kin* (Firstman, Weststate: Wrong, 1959), 44–53.
16. "Death Notices," *Capitalsville Mercury* (weekly), 27 Month 1774, p. 3, col. 3. Essex State Archives microfilm CM/w.3.
17. A. Poor Sourse, "Another Look at the Parent Problem," *Mountain County Journal of History* 103 (Fall, 1996): 33–36. Sourse cites MCJH 31 (Spring, 1924): 32 as the "vital missing clue" that led her to conclude that Lemuel was the illegitimate offspring of one of the twelve daughters, the most likely being the youngest, Helen. On the cited page, however, is a query *asking whether* Helen was Lemuel's mother. Helen's birth date, marriage date and spouse, and a list of her children, however, were provided in an answer to the query—published in the next issue, MCJH 31 (Summer, 1924): 185.
18. "Mary Parent *vs.* Heirs of Benjamin Parent, 1720," Court of Chancery records, Essex State Archives. Mary also had a son Philip, born of her first husband Leonard Contrary (will of Leonard Contrary, 1718, Ridge County Wills and Estates, Book A^1: 243; and will of Mary Parent, 1742, Book A^2: 413).

More-Remote Possibilities

If, as the evidence seems to show, Lemuel Parent Jr. was not a grandson of Benjamin W. Parent, he must have been either *(a)* offspring of a more-distant American father, or *(b)* a new immigrant from outside the country. Our investigation, however, discounted both possibilities:

- An exhaustive, two-year search of print, CD, and electronic sources unearthed only one other Parent family on this side of the Atlantic during the period when Lemuel Jr. and/or his parents flourished.[19] These Parents, residents of Farplace, were investigated by A. Close Looke, a skilled professional genealogist, and found to be well documented in the Farplace records.[20] No Lemuel, or possible father for Lemuel, could be found.

- Lemuel Jr.'s records are discussed below. Although sparse, they indicate close associations with the resident Parents of Mountain and nearby counties, and exhibit none of the confusion often evident among new immigrants unfamiliar with local practices.

The Only Probability

Although no direct evidence proves Lemuel Jr.'s parentage, when all the *indirect* evidence is assembled, its sum points inexorably to Henry Parent, the 1811 testator. To set that evidence in context, however, we must recapitulate Lemuel's life events and identify his children—one of whom is the vital link between Henry and this missing son.

Born on 14 Month 1775,[21] Lemuel Parent Jr. married Caroline Neighbor on 22 Month 1796.[22] As was customary, issuance of the marriage license was preceded by Lemuel's bond indemnifying the county against future charges arising from a possibly illegal marriage. The bond, dated 20 Month 1796, was secured by Waldo Neighbor (Caroline's father) and Henry Parent.[23] This was Henry-the-testator, then the only adult of that name in the region. The fact that he was co-bondsman with the bride's father suggests that he may have been father of the groom.

Lemuel died, according to his tombstone, on 27 Month 1805,[24] and on the 18th of the following month Waldo Neighbor was appointed guardian "for the *children* of Lemuel Parence deceased [emphasis supplied]."[25] Because Waldo did not file reports of his guardianship, neither the number of children nor their names appear in the orphan records. Other records, however, when carefully analyzed, provide that information.

19. The author is indebted to the following, who contributed their time and invaluable suggestions to this search: Michael D. Myancestor, Leonard D. Vinci, A. Close Look, and Abner Researcher, Jr.
20. "Parent Report #1," by A. Close Look, CGRS, 3456 Look Street, Old City, Farplace, to the author, 29 Month 1994. Also, "Parent Report #2," 30 Month 1994, and "Parent Report #3," 1 Month 1995.
21. Lemuel Parent grave marker, WPA typescript. (See note 5, above.)
22. Lemuel Parent Jr. entry, Mountain County Marriage Registers, Book 1: 219, Clerk's Office, Peak City. The ages and parentage of bride and groom were not required in register entries before 1858. The ceremony was performed by W. W. Big, a justice of the county court representing the Lazy Run–Swift Creek area of Mountain.
23. Lemuel Parent Jr. bond, 1796, Mountain County Marriage Bonds (original), Essex State Archives, Capitalsville.
24. Lemuel Parent grave marker, WPA typescript. (See note 5, above.)
25. "Lem¹ Parent Orphans," Mountain County Orphans Book 2: 33.

- *Son Gregory Parent* was mentioned in the 1857 will of Benedict Dogood, who had married Lemuel's widow Caroline on 18 Month 1806.[26] Benedict bequeathed to "my wife's son Gregory Parent" one dollar, "pervided he come for it." (Some thirty years earlier, Gregory had "[run] away with N.P. from that Riverton house of plesure,"[27] thus incurring his stepfather's undying wrath.) A Gregery Parrent, most probably this man, was enumerated in Eighth County, Elsewhere, in 1850 as born in Essex and aged 49,[28] indicating a birth year of 1800–1801. In 1860, he was enumerated in a boardinghouse in Eighth City as aged 58,[29] indicating a birth year of 1801–2. He has not been found in later censuses, and Eighth County records failed to produce additional information.

- *Daughter Priscilla Parent* is identified as a child of Lemuel in the 1853 record of her second marriage. Priscilla was born 3 Month 1803 and died 12 Month 1882.[30] She married first Michael Myancestor on Christmas Day 1823, by a bond dated 15 Month, secured by Benedict Dogood (her stepfather) and Samuel Neighbor (her uncle).[31] After Michael's death in 1852,[32] Priscilla married Jonathan Oldman. The bond does not survive, but the Mountain County Marriage Register carries the following entry "Month 17th 1853, Prisilla Miancestor, 50, dau/Lemuel to Jonath. Oldman, 72, son/Jonath."[33] The only Lemuel Myancestor in or near Essex in 1853 was the eighteen-year-old son of Michael and Priscilla.[34] The man referred to in the register, therefore, was clearly Lemuel Parent, father of the 1803-born *widow* Myancestor.

  By pursuing the search for Priscilla under her second married name, we found not only her tombstone, but also confirmation of our analysis of her father's birthplace. In 1880, in distant Any State, seventy-eight-year-old Prisiller Oldman, was living with her widowed step-granddaughter, Bethany (Oldman) Holdfast—and both of Prisiller's parents were reported as born in Essex.[35]

---

26. Benedict Dogood entry, Mountain County Marriage Registers, Book 2: 30, entry no. 9 (no bond has been found); also, Benedict Dogood will, 27 Month 1857, probated 31 Month 1857, Mountain County Will Book 9: 299. Both records examined at Clerk's Office, Peak City.

27. Blue, *Parent and Related Families*, 99, figure 8, letter, Benedict Dogood to "My dear Ben [presumably son Benedict Jr.]," written at "Pleasant Hill, Sunday" but otherwise undated.

28. Willson Willson household, 1850 U.S. census, population schedule, Eighth County, Elsewhere, p. 25, dwelling 53, family 53, NARA microprint M155, reel 444. Gregery's occupation was "laborer."

29. Jolly Rodgers household, 1860 U.S. census, population schedule, Eighth County, Elsewhere, "Eighth City District," p. 12, dwelling 21, family 23, NARA microprint M166, reel 555. Gregory's surname was "Parrence" and his occupation "boarder."

30. Priscilla Oldman grave marker in the Holdfast family plot (#217), Littleville Cemetery, Any State.

31. Michael Myancestor bond, 1823, Mountain County Marriage Bonds (original), Essex State Archives. Samuel is identified in "Naybors Est[ate]," Mountain County Wills and Estates, Book 7: 21 and 86.

32. Michael Myancestor will, 24 Month 1852, probated 18 Month 1852, Mountain County Wills and Estates, Book 8: 22, Clerk's Office, Peak City.

33. Michael Miannsester entry, Mountain County Marriage Registers, Book 5: 200, Clerk's Office, Peak City.

34. Michael Myancestor household, 1850 U.S. census, population schedule, Mountain County, Essex, p. 225, dwelling 459, family 456, NARA microprint M555, reel 222.

35. Bethany O. Holdfast household, 1880 U.S. census, population schedule, Any County, Any State, ED 87, SD 22, p. 109, dwelling 210, family 212, NARA microprint M888, reel 777.

- *An unidentified "first-born" son* appears to have been present in the 1800 household of "Lemuel Parence Juner.," which consisted of Lemuel, aged 16–26, a white female also 16–26 (undoubtedly Caroline), and a boy under 10.[36] This boy should not have been Gregory, whose later census ages indicate birth about 1801. The presence in Lemuel's household of a boy born *before* the 1800 census day (the first Monday in August) suggests the probability that he and Caroline were parents of an additional son, one born between 1796 and mid-1800.

The 1810 configuration of Benedict and Caroline Dogood's census household[37] lends some weight to the "first-born" son thesis. The Dogood family included a white male aged 10–16, born too early to have been a child of the couple's 1806 marriage (Benedict's first[38]). The household also included three boys under ten and a girl also under ten, too many single births for a four-year period. The younger children were most probably nine-year-old Gregory Parent, seven-year-old Priscilla Parent, and the Dogood's own children, three-year-old Ben and infant daughter Stephanie.[39] It is not unreasonable to theorize that the older boy living within this family was also Caroline's child, the unnamed oldest son.

The evidence gleaned from Mountain County land and tax records, set out below, verifies the existence of another Parent son, and supplies his name, Thomas.

Although Lemuel Parent Jr. did not purchase and was not granted any land in Mountain County, triennial tax reports show that in 1798, 1801, and 1804 he paid assessments on a white poll (himself), a varying number of cattle and horses, and *a consistent fifty acres of land.*[40] Since he did not buy or patent the land, its next most-likely source was inheritance—by Lemuel or by his wife Caroline. Extensive investigation of the Neighbor family found no evidence at all that the fifty acres was Caroline's. That being the case, its source ought to lie among the Parents.

---

36. Lemuel Parence Juner. household, 1800 U.S. census, Mountain County, Essex, p. 178, NARA microprint M000, reel 222.

37. Benedict Dogood ("Dueggod") household, 1810 U.S. census, Mountain County, Essex, p. 333, NARA microprint M111, reel 222.

38. Other than the record of his marriage to Caroline Parent, no marriage-register entry or original bond was found for Benedict Dogood under any variant spellings in Mountain, River, or Ridge Counties. All the Dogood children mentioned in the division of his estate (Mountain County Wills and Estates, Book 8: 22 and 47) were born after 1806, according to their census ages or tombstone records.

39. The ages in 1810 of the two oldest Dogood children are deduced from their later census records (e.g., household of Benedic Dogwood [*sic*], 1850 U.S. census, River County, Essex, p. 333, dwelling 491, family 489, NARA microprint 555, reel 22; and household of Sherlock A. and Stefany Homes, 1850 U.S. census, Sandy County, Eaststate, p. 29, dwelling 32, family 32, NARA microprint 555, reel 22).

40. Treasurer's Tax Reports, 1789–1845, volumes numbered I–VIII, Essex State Archives, Capitalsville. Lemuel Parent entries are at I: 233, sheet 3; II: 35, sheet 4; and II: 109, sheet 4. Essex taxes were levied annually, but the counties filed reports to the state treasurer only every three years until 1835, after which annual reports were required. The reports (unpaginated) have been mounted in bound volumes *by year*. Each county's report, regardless of the number of sheets, is mounted on a separate page; and the counties arranged in alphabetical order by county name. In general (but not always) taxpayer's names are arranged within each county list in alphabetical order by the first letter of the surname. Insolvent and delinquent taxpayer names are given at the end of the individual lists.

Henry[4] Parent executed only two sale deeds in his lifetime. One was registered in Ridge County, from which Mountain was formed in 1778. Dated 15 Month 1769, it conveyed to Waldo Neighbor ("Nayber") forty-five acres on the south side of Lazy Run, part of a grant (acreage unspecified) to Henry Parent dated 8 Month 1768.[41] The other was an 1805 Mountain County deed of gift made to Thomas Parent for fifty-five acres on the north side of Lazy Run adjoining Waldo Neighbor, it being "the Remains of one Hundred akers [granted] by pattent to me dated 8 month 1768."[42] The significance of this second deed cannot be understated.

- It was dated 3 Month 1805, more than thirty-five years after the sale to Neighbor but less than two months after the death of Lemuel Parent Jr.

- It was not a gift to the Thomas who was Henry's brother *or* to the Thomas who was his son, as earlier family chroniclers have assumed.[43] An official survey of the brother Thomas's 234 acres, preparatory to its division between Henry and Lemuel Sr., shows that the land lay on Canoe Creek a considerable distance from Lazy Run.[44] Examination of the son Thomas's land transactions and tax assessments shows that he never owned land in Mountain County. The tract he was given in Henry's will lay on Foaming Creek in Ridge County, where Thomas married in 1801 and lived thereafter.[45] The 1805 Henry-to-Thomas gift, therefore, was made to a *third* Thomas Parent.

Henry Parent's gift to Thomas was for roughly half of the 1768 land grant. The fate of the other half is also crucial to the proof of Lemuel Jr.'s identity.

- Waldo Neighbor, father of Lemuel Jr.'s wife Caroline,[46] was the gentleman to whom Henry Parent had deeded the first half of the grant. Waldo conveyed it in 1831, for "one dollar and other valuable considerations [as a gift]," to Michael Myancestor, describing the tract as "part of a patent to Henry Parent dated [blank] 1768," and stating that it adjoined "the Fifty five *other* Acers now owned by the said Michael [emphasis supplied]."[47] The inescapable implication of Waldo's use of "other" is that by 1831, Michael had become owner of Henry Parent's fifty-five acre gift to the mysterious Thomas.

---

41. Henry Parent to Waldo Neighbor, Ridge County Deed Book 4: 344, Clerk's Office, Topton. Henry's land grant is at Secretary of State Patent Book 12: 266, entry no. 601, Essex State Archives. The tract is described as "lieing on both sides of Lasy Run about a mile above Matthew Lukes plantation," and the metes and bounds are specified. Henry, however, did not provide them in his deed to Waldo.

42. Henry Parent to Thos. Parent, Mountain County Deed Book 3: 27. Metes and bounds are not specified.

43. Historian, *William Parent, Pioneer*, 3: 386, note 187; Blue, *Parent and Related Families*, 299; and Wrong, *Our Parents and Their Kin*, 231.

44. Thomas Parent Land Division, River County Plat Book 7: 259, Land Office, Swamp City.

45. See, for example: Henry Parent deed from Francis Other, 325 acres on Foaming Creek, 25 Month 1771 (Ridge County Deed Book 4: 45); Henry Parent will (cited above) devising to son Thomas "my land on Foming [*sic*] Creek"; Thomas Parent tax listings, 1798–1845 (State Treasurer's Tax Reports, Ridge County); Thomas Parent to Henrietta Doolittle (Ridge County Marriage Registers, Book 3: 28); Thomas Parent census households 1810–60; and Thomas Parent will, 26 Month 1860, probated 2 Month 1861, (Ridge County Will Book 13: 200–203), which divided the Foaming Creek land among his two youngest sons Mark and Luke after the death or remarriage of wife Henrietta.

46. "Naybors Est[ate]," Mountain County Wills and Estates, Book 7: 21 and 86, Clerk's Office, Peak City. Among heirs who inherited shares in the estate-sale proceeds was "Bene. Dugood in right of his wife."

47. Mountain County Deed Book 5: 513. Metes and bounds are not specified. Because Waldo's own acreage was landlocked, we suspect that his purchase from Henry Parent in 1769 was a water outlet for

- Examination of the Mountain County land grants, deeds, and tax records provided no evidence that a Myancestor—under any variant of the name—owned land in the county prior to Waldo's 1831 conveyance. Michael, therefore had procured the Henry-to-Thomas gift parcel by some other means, the most likely of which was, again, inheritance. The county's triennial tax reports to the state treasurer provide clear evidence that it was Michael's wife Priscilla (daughter of Lemuel Parent Jr.), who inherited the tract from its gift-deed recipient, Thomas Parent.

1807–16	Waldo Neighbor tax-listed his own 432 acres, as well as the *entire* hundred-acre Lazy Run tract, which he itemized as: fifty acres [*sic*] on "n [side of] lazy" and fifty acres on "s [side of] lazy."[48]
1819	Waldo paid taxes on the north-side fifty acres as administrator of the estate of Thomas Parent, deceased ("ad^{mr} of Th^o Parrent dec^d es^{ts}"),[49] as well as on his own south-side fifty acres. (Note that this deceased Thomas could not have been Henry Parent's son, who died in 1861 in Ridge County,[50] or his brother Thomas, whose estate was closed in 1810 by executors Henry and Lemuel Sr.[51])
1822	Waldo's tax burden again included two tracts on Lazy Run, his own (now restored to forty-five acres) and an *additional twenty acres* listed separately.[52]
	Gregory Parent, by then of poll-tax age (21) was also assessed for *twenty five acres* on Lazy Run (without having bought or patented it), but was noted as "insolvent [incapable of paying]."[53]
	Michael Myancestor (the first appearance of a Myancestor in the tax reports) was listed for a poll (himself) and two horses but no land.[54]
1825	Waldo Neighbor paid on his own acreage, now reduced to 330 by a deed he'd made to son Samuel. In addition, he was listed for forty-five acres on Lazy, *but not the twenty acres* on which he'd paid in 1822.[55]
	Gregory Parent was not listed at all.[56]

---

transporting market crops downstream to Coast City, and that for this reason he always considered the tract as an entity separate from his farm acreage. By 1831 when he sold the tract to Myancestor, however, the Essex road systems were well developed and water-borne shipping was no longer needed.

48. Neighbor entries, Tax Reports II: 183, sheet 4; II: 258, sheet 4; III: 35, sheet 4; and VIII: 109, sheet 5.
49. Neighbor entries, Tax Reports III: 194, sheet 3.
50. Thomas Parent will, 26 Month 1860, probated 2 Month 1861, Ridge County Will Book 13: 200–203.
51. Thomas Parent estate, River County Will Book A: 461, Clerk's office, Swamp City.
52. Neighbor entries, Tax Reports, III: 280, sheet 4. Whether north- or south-side of Lazy Run is not noted.
53. Parent entry, Tax Reports III, 280, sheet 6. The Mountain County land records do not mention Gregory Parent as buyer, seller, or witness
54. Myancestor entry, Tax Reports III: 280, sheet 4.
55. Neighbor entries, Tax Reports, IV: 46, sheet 3; and deed: Waldo Neighbor to Samuel Neighbor "for love and affection for my son," 18 Month 1825 (Mountain County Deed Book 4: 498).
56. Treasurer's Tax Reports IV. All counties read.

Michael Myancestor, married to Priscilla Parent since 1823, listed himself, two horses, and *fifty-five acres "[on] Lazy."*[57]

1828	Waldo Neighbor was listed only on his forty-five Lazy Run acres, having disposed of the remainder of his lands by deed.[58]
	Michael Myancestor was again taxed on fifty-five Lazy Run acres.[59]
1831	Tax listings for Waldo's and Michael's land remained unchanged.[60]
1834	Waldo Neighbor died in 1833; by 1834 his estate was closed.[61]
	Michael Myancestor's land taxes, now increased by the 1831 deed from Waldo, were reported as one hundred acres on Lazy Run.[62]
1835–44	Michael's acreage remained unchanged. In 1844 he purchased an additional one hundred acres, taxed to him in 1845.[63]

Only one logical scenario explains the otherwise peculiar movement through the tax records of the fifty-five acres on north-side Lazy Run that Henry retained after his deed to Neighbor:

(a) Henry had "loaned" the land to son Lemuel Jr., probably about the time Lemuel married Caroline, daughter of the tract's adjoining landowner Waldo Neighbor. The tax reports show that Henry had done the same for sons Thomas (who began paying the tax on Henry's River County acreage in 1798[64]) and William (who listed Henry's half of his brother Thomas Parent's Canoe Creek tract in 1810[65]). Both loans were confirmed by devises in Henry's 1811 will.

(b) Henry's deed to Thomas Parent in 1805 was to his *grandson*, oldest son of the deceased Lemuel, Jr., thereby confirming to the widow Caroline and her young

---

57. Myancestor entry, Tax Reports, IV: 46, sheet 3.

58. Neighbor entries, Tax Reports, IV: 132, sheet 4; also, Waldo Neighbor to Henry Neighbor, gift deed, 21 Month 1827 (Mountain County Deeds, Book 5: 87–88); to Frederick Neighbor, gift deed, 21 Month 1827 (Book 5: 88); and to Waldo Neighbor Jr., gift "after my decease," 21 Month 1827 (Book 5: 93).

59. Myancestor entry, Tax Reports, IV: 132, sheet 3.

60. Myancestor and Neighbor entries, Tax Reports, IV: 221, sheet 4. Taxes were listed in the spring; Waldo's deed to Michael was made in late summer and is not reflected, therefore, in the tax reports.

61. Waldo Neighbor estate, Mountain County Will Book 7: 322, 376.

62. Myancestor entry, Tax Reports, V: 49, sheet 4. The reports for 1846–68 do not survive.

63. Myancestor entries, Tax Reports: V: 137, sheet 3 (1835); V: 225, sheet 3 (1836); VI: 49, sheet 2 (1837); VI: 137, sheet 3 (1838); VI: 225, sheet 3 (1839); VII: 49, sheet 3 (1840); VII: 137, sheet 3 (1841); VII: 225, sheet 3 (1842); VIII: 49, sheet 2 (1843); VIII: 137, sheet 3 (1844); and VIII: 230, sheet 4 (1845). See Isaiah Prayer deed to Michael Mieansetter, sale deed, 28 Month 1844, 132 acres, south side of Lazy Run adjoining said Mieansetter (Mountain County Deed Book 7: 433). The land description does not include enough details to make a plat of the tract.

64. Thomas Parent entry, Tax Reports, I: 244, sheet 4. Henry Parent paid tax on the tract (although he listed its acreage variously) from 1789 to 1798 (Treasurer's Tax Reports, I: 39, sheet 3, I: 104, sheet 3; and I: 175, sheet 4). Henry's pre-1798 Mountain County tax reports are similarly inconsistent and no amount of mathematical manipulation identifies with assurance any Lazy Run acreage that may have been deducted when Lemuel Jr. began tax-listing his "fifty" acres.

65. William Parent entry, Tax Reports, II: 258, sheet 3.

children continued possession of their home. By deeding the land to a grandson rather than to the widowed daughter-in-law, Henry ensured that it would inure to his descendants' benefit rather than to that of her second husband should she remarry. Caroline did remarry the following year.

(c) Young Thomas's other grandfather, Waldo, as guardian of Lemuel Parent Jr.'s children, managed the property during their minority.

(d) Thomas died intestate between the 1816 and 1819 tax reports, possibly still a minor, and his land was divided between his surviving siblings, Gregory and Priscilla, both still under age and unmarried. Because *equal* division was called for under the intestacy laws, one suspects that Priscilla's smaller acreage included her parents' dwelling house. (The fact that this was the only land the Myancestors owned during the first eight years of their marriage lends considerable support to this thesis.)

(e) Grandfather-guardian Waldo Neighbor continued to list the still-minor Priscilla's portion of her inheritance until she married in 1823. Gregory, having reached his majority by 1822, failed to pay the tax on his part and by 1825 had left the area.

(f) Stemming from his marriage to Priscilla, Michael Myancestor became putative owner of her twenty acres under then-prevailing marital property law. By 1825 he had also become owner, by default, of her absent brother Gregory's twenty-five acres.

(g) Michael's gift from his wife's grandfather, Waldo Neighbor, reunited the 1768 Henry Parent land grant.

Conclusion

The direct evidence from easily found records appears to argue against attributing to Henry[4] and Priscilla [—?—] Parent a seventh child, Lemuel[5]. Nevertheless, the sum of *all* the evidence, including that gleaned from more obscure records, amply supports the conclusion that this was, indeed, the case.

Appendix E — Example Compiled Lineages

A lineage compilation (as opposed to a chart or outline) is a comprehensive history of the people who link a specific person with one of his or her specific ancestors. Those links, arranged by generation in an unbroken chain, are the focus of the two general-purpose formatting systems most-often used: *(a)* an ascending system that begins with the recent descendant and "ascends" to the remote ancestor, and *(b)* a descending system that begins with the remote ancestor. Regardless of where the compilation begins, however, the keys to successfully formatting it are:

- *study the explanations and examples* given here and the Curran-Crane-Wray volume cited on page 18 (note 11), and use lineages published in scholarly journals as models.

- *choose one format and use it consistently* throughout the compilation.

- *test-print often*, whether applying the format manually or using a computer-generated template, to ensure that

    (*a*) the *right* people are attached to their spouses, children, parents, earlier ancestors, and biographies;

    (*b*) a uniform numbering system, typographic style, and page layout is maintained;

    (*c*) sources are cited coherently—that reference note numbers are assigned in unbroken ascending order and correspond precisely to the related citation;

    (*d*) the text is printing correctly. (Beware the genealogy program that substitutes "canned" text unless specifically instructed otherwise.)

Lineage formats emphasize three basic elements: *(a)* personal biographies, *(b)* a series of numbers that identify family members and organize their biographies, and *(c)* typographic style.

Biographies

The biographies included in family-history compilations, whether lineages, pedigrees, or genealogies, supply information that identifies each family member unerringly. They place each person within the context of family unit; life events; ancestral line; societal, religious, and ethnic group; geographic place; and historical era. They are efficiently organized, accurately stated, and impeccably documented.

A biography, however, is the story of a unique human life, not a detailed recitation of research findings—and not a collection of suppositions, exaggerations, or indecisive deliberations. Despite the need to include the "dull, dry facts" (vital statistics), the biographies need not be tedious to write and boring to read. Incidents and characteristics that the researcher finds interesting will usually interest the reader also, provided they are written in clear, expressive, positive language.

The biography text is generally divided into three parts:

- *Genealogical summary.* The first paragraph in the biography includes as much as is known of the subject's vital statistics and parent's names; and the name, vital statistics, and parentage of his or her spouse (or partner if the couple did not marry). Multiple unions are arranged in chronological order.

  The first time the subject's name is mentioned, it is emphasized by a change in typeface; the first mention of a spouse's or partner's name is similarly emphasized. In both case, the name also includes nicknames (enclosed in quotation marks), and a.k.a. [also known as] names or aliases. All of a widow's or divorcee's previous married surnames are included—and in these cases, her maiden surname is placed in parentheses. EXAMPLE 1: John "Jack" Doe, a.k.a. Goodtitle. EXAMPLE 2: Mary "Molly" (Den) Fen.

- *Life story.* Succeeding paragraphs discuss significant events in the subject's life, usually in approximate chronological order. If the biography's subject was prominent professionally, militarily, or socially, his or her achievements are often described first, followed by personal-life details. (Integrating the two may provide a more well-rounded view of the person but doing so can be confusing if not handled with skill.) Life stories cover, also, events in the spouses' lives, usually including information about their earlier or later marriages and personal- or professional-life details.

- *Child-list.* After an introductory sentence or sentence fragment, the subject's biological children are listed in birth order (if it is known), beginning with the oldest. If the subject of the sketch had more than one union, children are grouped accordingly, with the unions arranged in chronological sequence. Each group is introduced by a relevant sentence or sentence fragment.

  Child-lists also include the subject's adopted children, listed in birth order or the order in which they entered the nuclear family (provided that consistency is maintained throughout the compilation); and the subject's stepchildren. Each of these groups is also introduced by an appropriate statement EXAMPLES: Adopted child [children] of X and his wife Y; or Stepchild [children] of X born of his wife Y by her first husband Z.

Child-list biographies: Each child's entry in the list includes his or her full birth name plus nickname in quotation marks and a.k.a. name or alias (but not married surnames). A brief genealogical summary follows, including vital statistics and the date, place, and spouse-name (or partner-name) for each union.

Because lineage-compilation formatting allows full biographies only for persons in the direct line, a child-list is the place where life-story data can be included about the subject's other children. If desired, a child's children (the subject's grandchildren) can be listed, in birth order, within the life story.

- *Restatement of parentage.* In an ascending lineage system, the subject's parentage is restated in a final sentence that introduces the next biography in the series.

Numbering System

Regardless of how seemingly complex a lineage is or how often the same name is repeated, each person in the overall family has a distinct position within it. Two sets of numbers are used to designate that position clearly:

- *Identifying numbers.* Arabic numbers denote each person in the direct line. The numbers begin with "1" for the first person discussed (the remote ancestor or the recent descendant) and continue thereafter in sequence. Ancestral biographies are arranged according to these numbers.

  Identifying numbers are uniquely personal—with the exception of "1," each number appears twice within the compilation and in both cases it is associated with a specific direct-line individual. *(a)* It is written near the left margin preceding the person's name in a parental child-list. *(b)* It precedes the same person's name at the beginning of his or her genealogical summary.

- *Birth-order numbers.* Lower-case Roman numerals are assigned to each of the offspring mentioned in a child-list. The numerals begin with "i" for the person's first-born child and continue in sequence to his or her last-born. Birth-order numbers are not unique to any given person; *all* first-born children, for example, are "i." Because stepchildren and adoptees were not "born of" the direct-line person, they are not assigned birth-order numbers.

  Birth order numbers for grandchildren mentioned in a child's life story may be lower-case letters, Arabic numbers, or italicized Roman numerals.

Typographic Style

Typographic style refers to the way information appears on the page: indentation, typeface, paragraphing, and data placement.

Unless the lineage is compiled for a specific purpose (publication in a journal with its own requirements, for example) typography normally follows the style used in genealogy compilations, either the *NGSQ* System or the *Register* System. Both are described at length in Appendix G, pages 102–3.[14]

In the present appendix, the choice of typographic style was arbitrary—either style can be used with either lineage system, provided it is used consistently.

The examples that follow are based on fictitious families. Reference note numbers are included but the notes themselves are omitted. (For documentation examples see Appendixes C, D, and G and the models in Mills's volume cited in note 1, page 3.) The portions of biographies that are included in the examples are suggestions only, but follow the pattern described above: genealogical summary, life story, and child-list.

---

14.   These systems are used by the *National Genealogical Society Quarterly* and the *New England Historical and Genealogical Register*, respectively. The models in this manual reflect the typographic styles used by their current editors.

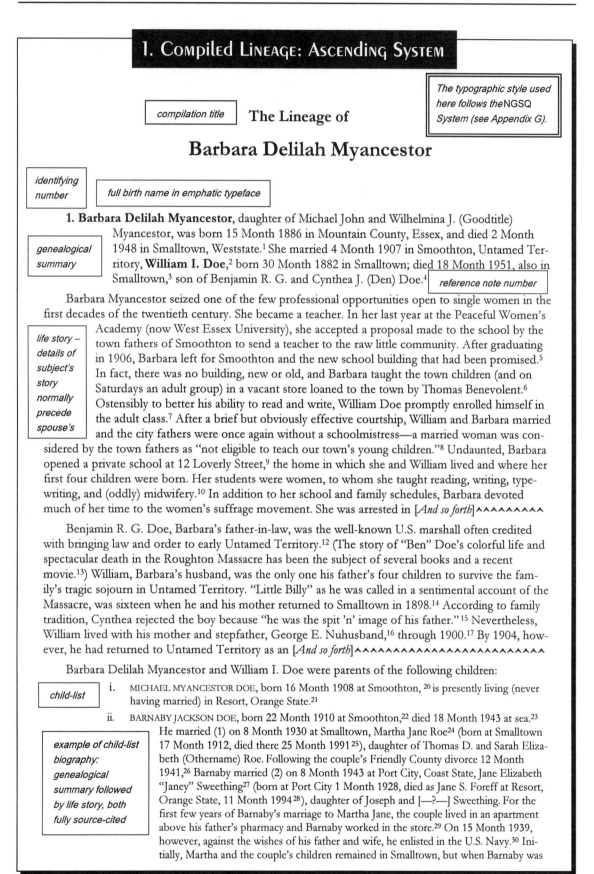

1. Compiled Lineage: Ascending System

The typographic style used here follows the NGSQ System (see Appendix G).

compilation title   **The Lineage of**

Barbara Delilah Myancestor

identifying number

full birth name in emphatic typeface

1. Barbara Delilah Myancestor, daughter of Michael John and Wilhelmina J. (Goodtitle) Myancestor, was born 15 Month 1886 in Mountain County, Essex, and died 2 Month 1948 in Smalltown, Weststate.[1] She married 4 Month 1907 in Smoothton, Untamed Territory, **William I. Doe**,[2] born 30 Month 1882 in Smalltown; died 18 Month 1951, also in Smalltown,[3] son of Benjamin R. G. and Cynthea J. (Den) Doe.[4]

genealogical summary

reference note number

Barbara Myancestor seized one of the few professional opportunities open to single women in the first decades of the twentieth century. She became a teacher. In her last year at the Peaceful Women's Academy (now West Essex University), she accepted a proposal made to the school by the town fathers of Smoothton to send a teacher to the raw little community. After graduating in 1906, Barbara left for Smoothton and the new school building that had been promised.[5] In fact, there was no building, new or old, and Barbara taught the town children (and on Saturdays an adult group) in a vacant store loaned to the town by Thomas Benevolent.[6] Ostensibly to better his ability to read and write, William Doe promptly enrolled himself in the adult class.[7] After a brief but obviously effective courtship, William and Barbara married and the city fathers were once again without a schoolmistress—a married woman was considered by the town fathers as "not eligible to teach our town's young children."[8] Undaunted, Barbara opened a private school at 12 Loverly Street,[9] the home in which she and William lived and where her first four children were born. Her students were women, to whom she taught reading, writing, typewriting, and (oddly) midwifery.[10] In addition to her school and family schedules, Barbara devoted much of her time to the women's suffrage movement. She was arrested in [*And so forth*]^^^^^^^^^^

life story – details of subject's story normally precede spouse's

Benjamin R. G. Doe, Barbara's father-in-law, was the well-known U.S. marshall often credited with bringing law and order to early Untamed Territory.[12] (The story of "Ben" Doe's colorful life and spectacular death in the Roughton Massacre has been the subject of several books and a recent movie.[13]) William, Barbara's husband, was the only one his father's four children to survive the family's tragic sojourn in Untamed Territory. "Little Billy" as he was called in a sentimental account of the Massacre, was sixteen when he and his mother returned to Smalltown in 1898.[14] According to family tradition, Cynthea rejected the boy because "he was the spit 'n' image of his father."[15] Nevertheless, William lived with his mother and stepfather, George E. Nuhusband,[16] through 1900.[17] By 1904, however, he had returned to Untamed Territory as an [*And so forth*]^^^^^^^^^^^^^^^^^^^^^^^^^^^

Barbara Delilah Myancestor and William I. Doe were parents of the following children:

child-list

   i.   MICHAEL MYANCESTOR DOE, born 16 Month 1908 at Smoothton,[20] is presently living (never having married) in Resort, Orange State.[21]

   ii.   BARNABY JACKSON DOE, born 22 Month 1910 at Smoothton,[22] died 18 Month 1943 at sea.[23] He married (1) on 8 Month 1930 at Smalltown, Martha Jane Roe[24] (born at Smalltown 17 Month 1912, died there 25 Month 1991[25]), daughter of Thomas D. and Sarah Elizabeth (Othername) Roe. Following the couple's Friendly County divorce 12 Month 1941,[26] Barnaby married (2) on 8 Month 1943 at Port City, Coast State, Jane Elizabeth "Janey" Sweething[27] (born at Port City 1 Month 1928, died as Jane S. Foreff at Resort, Orange State, 11 Month 1994[28]), daughter of Joseph and [—?—] Sweething. For the first few years of Barnaby's marriage to Martha Jane, the couple lived in an apartment above his father's pharmacy and Barnaby worked in the store.[29] On 15 Month 1939, however, against the wishes of his father and wife, he enlisted in the U.S. Navy.[30] Initially, Martha and the couple's children remained in Smalltown, but when Barnaby was

example of child-list biography: genealogical summary followed by life story, both fully source-cited

ordered to Southfork, Eaststate, they reluctantly moved into quarters there—temporarily. Martha and the girls returned to her Smalltown family after a year of what she termed "abject misery in this forlorn, friendless place." [31] Shortly after the outbreak of World War II, Barnaby transferred to the submarine service and was sent to Port City for training. Martha declined to join him there, and the couple divorced shortly thereafter. [32] Barnaby served in the Pacific aboard the *Gray Shark* from 1941 through Month 1942 and, after the submarine was damaged too severely to repair, was reassigned to Port City to await completion of the *White Shark*. [33] In Port City, Barnaby married Janey, a fifteen year-old high-school student. [34] The couple's marriage was tragically brief—Petty Officer Doe was lost at sea when the USS *White Shark* went down with all hands at an unidentified location in the Pacific. [35] Barnaby never knew [*And so forth*]

example of subject's grand-children listed in a child-list biography

The children of Barnaby Jackson and Martha Jane (Roe) Doe are: [39] *(a)* Barbara D. Doe, born 5 Month 1933 at Smalltown, living, married Big R. Better; and *(b)* Martha J. Doe, born 4 Month 1935, living, married I. M Happy. The children of Barnaby Jackson and Jane Elizabeth (Sweething) Doe were: *(c)* Barnaby Jackson Doe Jr. (twin), born 22 Month 1944 at Port City, died there 18 Month 1985, married Winona J. J. Winsome, 3 Month 1967; and *(d)* Joseph S. Doe (twin), born 22 Month 1944, died 16 Month 1949 at Port City.

iii.   BARBARA DELILAH DOE, born 3 Month 1912 at Smoothton, [40] died [*And so forth*] ^^^^^^^^

birth-order numbers

iv.   HERBERT VINCENT DOE (the last of the children born at Smoothton), born 5 Month 1915, died 7 Month 1921 after his parents' move to Smalltown. [48]

v.   CYNTHEA CHRYSTAL DOE, born 19 Month 1917 at Smalltown, [49] married Herman Munster 18 Month 1935, also in Smalltown. [50] She died [*And so forth*] ^^^^^^^^^^^^^^^^^^^^^^^^

vi.   BENJAMIN WILLIAM DOE, born 23 Month 1921 at Smalltown, [57] married [*And so forth*] ^^^^^^

Barbara Delilah Myancestor was the daughter of Michael John Myancestor and his only wife, Wilhelmina J. Goodtitle.

introduction of the next ancestor in the lineage

2. Michael John Myancestor, son of Lemuel Walter Myancestor and Fiona B. "Fifi" (Else) Fen, [62] was born 26 Month 1864 in Near County, Any State. [63] He died 16 Month 1902 in Mountain County, Essex [64] and is buried in Peak City Cemetery. [65] Michael married 16 Month 1884, in Mountain County, **Wilhelmina J. Goodtitle**, daughter of Eric Goodtitle and his first wife Sigrid [—?—]. [66] Wilhelmina, born about 1866 in Norway, died 27 Month 1926 at Peak City. [67]

Michael was raised on his father's large dairy farm in Any State. [68] He attended Any State University [69] but left in Month 1885 when his uncle Waldo Myancestor died having willed the young man half of the family farm in Mountain County. [70] Planning to sell his half to Waldo's adopted son Michael W. Myancestor (who had inherited the other half) and return to school in the fall, Michael went east to attend to the business but changed his mind and decided to stay. [71] (The charms of neighbor Wilhelmina Goodtitle undoubtedly influenced his decision—he married her within weeks of his arrival in Essex.) The two Michael Myancestors lived side by side for the next four decades, distinguishing themselves by meticulous use of their middle initials. [72] Michael J. added to his half of the tract in 1888, 1892, and 1895, [73] virtually surrounding the smaller acreage of Michael W. After Michael J. died in 1902, however, Wilhelmina sold the all the acreage to Michael W. [74] and moved into Peak City.

At the age of about eleven, Wilhelmina Goodtitle had immigrated from Norway with her father and stepmother Frieda, née Daughtername, arriving in Coast City on 18 Month 1875 aboard *Johnny One-Note*. [75] The Goodtitles moved immediately to Essex and leased a farm in the Myancestor neighborhood from relatives already settled nearby. [76] There Wilhelmina grew to adulthood. She was a pianist of at least local reputation. Turn-of-the-century issues of the *Peak City Observer* carried notices of concerts by "Miss Goodtitle" and later "Mrs. M. J. Myancestor" (always with the middle initial), although the paper's music critics failed to mention them. [77] According to family stories, Michael J. bought his wife a "very fine piano" while visiting Frenchville on business. [78] Wilhelmina taught music after her move to Smalltown—but "*always* on the *old* piano [emphasis in original]." The new one still has pride of place in the Myancestor family home in Peak City. [79]

The following children were born to Michael John and Wilhelmina J. (Goodtitle) Myancestor:

+ 1   i.   BARBARA DELILAH MYANCESTOR, born 15 Month 1886 in Mountain County, [80] died 2 Month 1948 at Smalltown, Weststate. [82] She married William I. Doe 4 Month 1907 at Smalltown. [83]

identifying number

ii.   MICHAEL JOHN MYANCESTOR JR., born in Month 1887 at Peak City;[84] died 25 Month 1942 at New City, New State;[85] and married at New City on 31 Month 1931, Rose O'Day.[86] Michael was a concert pianist of exceptional talent and considerable renown. (His death from pneumonia resulted from "chilly concert halls" according to family letters.[87]) In his teens, Michael was sent to the Bigname Conservatory in New City, where studied—and lived[88] until he married Rose, a soprano with the New City Opera Company.[89] By her he had the following children:[90] *(a)* Maureen Myancestor, born 17 Month 1934, New City; living, divorced, one child; *(b)* Coleen Myancestor, born 29 Month 1937, Frenchville; living, widowed, one child; and *(c)* Michael John Myancestor III, born 4 Month 1940, New City; believed to be married.

iii.   WILHELMINA GOODTITLE MYANCESTOR, born during Month 1889 in Mountain County, died after 1910.[91] Nothing further is known about her—no marriage record was filed in Mountain or nearby counties and no death notice or certificate was recorded in the area.

iv.   SIGRID D. MYANCESTOR, born in Month 1897, died before 1910.[92]

Michael John Myancestor was the son of Fiona B. "Fifi" Else and her second husband, Lemuel Walter Myancestor.

> the mother mentioned first when she is the direct-line ancestor

3. Fiona B. "Fifi" Else, daughter of John S. and Mary Sweet (Harte) Else,[93] was born 19 Month 1842 in Distant County, Any State,[94] and died 28 Month 1886 in Any County, Any State.[95] She married, first, **Jonathan Fen** on 5 Month 1860 in Near County, Any State;[96] and, second (1863–64), **Lemuel Walter Myancestor**, son of Michael Myancestor and Priscilla Parent.[97] Lemuel was born about 1835 in Mountain County, Essex,[98] and died 22 Month 1873 in Near County.[99]

Fiona, called Fifi in all but one census record,[100] was reputedly very beautiful. Her portrait, painted in 1867 by Pine Wood, is mentioned in the catalogue for his 1901 New City exhibition in glowing compliment to both artist and subject[101] (although her having posed for Wood was considered scandalous by the family[102]). Unfortunately, the painting was sold to a private collector and is not known to have been publicly displayed since the exhibition closed.[103]

Little is known of Fiona's first husband. When the 1860 census was taken a few months after the couple married, they were living in Nearton. Jonathan's occupation was given as "mill hand."[104] He appears to have died after a fire at the Great Flour Mill—his name was listed among those "seriously injured" on 12 Month 1863[105]—but no record of his death or burial has been found. Fiona remarried before the birth of son Michael John Myancestor on 26 Month 1864, however, and one assumes that Jonathan had died of his injuries in the meantime.

Fiona's second husband, Lemuel Walter Myancestor, was named for his two grandfathers, Lemuel Parent and Walter Myancestor.[106] He spent his early years in prosperous Mountain County, Essex,[107] but his father's death in 1852[108] and mother's remarriage the following year[109] had a significant impact on his later life—when his three step-siblings, a generation older than he, moved their families to Any State, eighteen-year-old Lemuel accompanied them. In 1860, he was a "laborer" living within stepbrother Jonathan Oldman's household,[110] but by 1870 Lemuel had married, fathered two children, and purchased a small farm in adjoining Distant County.[111] The following year, on 3 Month 1871, he bought a large farm on Babbling Brook in Near County[112] and moved the family there. In his 1873 will, he left both tracts to Fiona, specifying that their sons divide the Distant County land equally between them when the younger arrived at age twenty-one, and reserving the Near County property to Fiona for "life or widowhood."[113] She did not remarry, and died on the farm thirteen years later.

Fiona B. Else and her first husband, Jonathan Fen, were parents of one child:

i.   "JONNY" FEN, born about 1862 in Near County, died 22 Month 1870 while visiting his Fen grandparents in Distant County.[114]

By her second husband, Lemuel Walter Myancestor, Fiona B. Else was mother of three children:

+ 2   ii.   MICHAEL JOHN MYANCESTOR, born 26 Month 1864 in Near County,[115] died 16 Month 1902 in Mountain County, Essex.[116] He married there on 16 Month 1885, Wilhelmina J. Goodtitle.[117]

iii.   JASON SOMEBODY MYANCESTOR, born 9 Month 1867 in Near County,[118] married Polly Wanna Cracker 2 Month 1890, also in Near County.[119] He died after 1910, possibly without issue.[120] In 1910, Jason was living [*And so forth*]^^^^^^^^^^^^^^^^^^^^^^^^^^^^^^^^^^^^^^

> "+" in NGSQ style signals full biography elsewhere

       iv.   EVELYN FIONA MYANCESTOR, born 10 Month 1872 in Any County;[124] married 12 Month 1894, in Near Countym Philip Morris of Nearton. Evelyn's death [*And so forth*] ^^^^^^^^^^^^

Fiona B. "Fifi" Else was the daughter of John S. Else Sr. and his first wife, Mary Sweet Harte.

4. John S. Else Sr., son of Jason Else and his third wife, Ellen Somebody, was born 1804–5 in Any State[129] and died, presumably in Near County, between 24 Month 1883 when he signed his will and its probate at the Near County court on 18 Month 1883.[130] John married, first, on 9 Month 1830, **Mary Sweet Harte**,[131] daughter of Douglas and Fiona [—?—] Harte.[132] Mary was born about 1815[133] in Distant County and died (in Distant or Any County) between 1870 and 1881.[134] John's second wife, whom he married on 12 Month 1881 in Any County, was **Sarah Jane Young**, born about 1859 in Essex, daughter of Michael and Louise (Old) Young.[135]

John Else was an ordinary, law-abiding, quiet-living citizen of rural Any State. He lived in the part of the state where Near, Distant, and Any Counties come together, sometimes owning land in one jurisdiction, sometimes in another, and often in two or more counties simultaneously.[136] He is known primarily through the deeds whereby he bought and sold land. Many of his purchases appear to have been long-term investments in tracts he leased during his children's minority and deeded to them as the boys came of age and the girls married.[137] The deeds to them "read like" sales. They were "for and in consideration of [money amount]" rather than "for love and affection," but [*And so forth*]^^^^^^^

The children of John S. Else Sr. and his first wife Mary Sweet Harte were as follows:

       i.   ELLEN M. ELSE, born about 1833,[141] probably in Any County,[142] died after 1889.[143] She married 1850–54 in Near County,[144] Homer Roe, son of Shadrack "Shad" and Philadelphia Roe.[145] Homer was born about 1822 in Essex[146] and died after 1889.[147] Until her father's death in 1883, Ellen, Homer, and their children lived on the sixty-five acres on Troublesome Creek that John S. Else Sr. had given them in 1854.[148] The Roes moved to Uglytown, Other State, between 1870[149] and 9 Month 1885 when they sold the Troublesome Creek acreage and a tract on Crazy River in Distant County that Ellen inherited under John's will.[150] Apparently the family moved again—the 1889 Uglytown city directory does not [*And so forth*]^^^^^^^^

       ii.   JANE S. ELSE, born about 1835 (probably in Distant County[152]), died or married 1870–80.[153] Jane was active in church affairs throughout the [*And so forth*] ^^^^^^^^^^^^^^^^^^^

       iii.   RALPH G. "RAFE" ELSE, born about 1838 in Distant County,[160] died 19 Month 1892 at Nearton, Near County and is buried in the Somebody plot in Oak Grove Cemetery.[161] Although he was called "bachelor" in his father's will, Ralph had married Lucy Suit during the year before 28 Month 1860; but, according to his petition for divorce, Lucy had left him in Month 1864 taking with her their only child, son Grey.[162] Ralph lived with his parents through 1870[163] and, judging by the tone of his father's will, was still in the household as late as 1883. His own 1892 will left his estate to brother Jason in trust for Grey—specifying that if Grey did not claim it within seven years, the land was to be sold and the proceeds divided equally among "the children of my brothers and sisters."[164] Grey claimed the estate in 1899,[165] however. He was still in Near County when the 1900 census was taken,[166] but sold the property on 4 Month 1907 and had left Essex by 1910.[167] Efforts to trace him further have failed.[168]

  + 3   iv.   FIONA B. "FIFI" ELSE, born [*And so forth—rest of birth, death, and marriage data; no life story*]^^^^

       v.   JASON L. "SONNY" ELSE, born about 1845 in Near County. He lived with his parents through 1870[175] and was mentioned in his father's 1883 will. Jason sold his deeded and inherited land on 12 Month 1899[176] and advertised in the *Nearton News* on the nineteenth requesting that his friends "who have my books return them before 31 Month when it is my intention to leave for the west."[177] He has not been traced further, but was still unmarried in 1899.[178]

       vi.   THOMAS S. ELSE, born during Month 1850 in Near County,[180] also lived with his parents through 1870. He was nearby (probably on the seventy acres his father deeded him in 1881[175]) when John wrote his 1883 will. Thomas sold all his lands on 18 Month 1901[181] and is believed to have followed his brother Jason "west." If he married, it was after 1901.[182]

       vii.   MARY S. "SWEETY" ELSE, born about 1853–54 in Near County;[184] [*And so forth*] ^^^^^^^^^

       viii.   JOHN S. ELSE JR., born 1 Month 1858,[195] died 8 Month 1930 at [*And so forth*]^^^^^^^^^^^^

^^^^^^^^ [*And so forth, through the number of generations intended to be included in the compilation*]^^^^^^^^

2. Compiled Lineage: Descending System

compilation title

One Descendant of

The typographic style used here follows the Register System (see Appendix G).

John S. Else Sr. (1804/5–1883)

identifying number

full birth name in emphatic typeface

reference note number (bracketed in this style)

1. JOHN S. ELSE SR., son of Jason and Ellen (Somebody) Else,[1] was born in Any State about 1804–1805[2] and died in Near County, Any State, between 24 Month and 18 Month 1883.[3] He married (1) in Distant County, Any State, 9 Month 1830,[4] **MARY SWEET HARTE,** who was born in Distant County about 1815[5] and died (in Distant or Any County) 1870–1880,[6] daughter of Douglas and Fiona (____) Harte.[7] In Any County on 12 Month 1881, John married (2) **SARAH JANE YOUNG,** born about 1858, daughter of Michael and Louise (Old) Young.[8]

genealogical summary

John Else was an ordinary, law-abiding, quiet-living citizen of rural Any State. He lived in the part of the state where Near, Distant, and Any Counties come together, sometimes owning land in one place, sometimes in another, and often in two or more [*And so forth*]^^^^^^^^^^^^

life story

Children of John S. Else Sr. and his first wife, Mary Sweet Harte:

child-list with birth-order numbers

   i. ELLEN M. ELSE, b., probably in Any County,[12] ca. 1833;[13] d. after 1889;[14] m. in Near County, 1850–1854, HOMER ROE,[15] b. [*And so forth*]^^^^^^^^^^^^^^^^^^^^^^^^^^^^^
   ii. JANE S. ELSE, b., probably in Distant County, ca. 1835;[18] d. or m. 1870–1880 [*And so forth*]^^^^^
   iii. RALPH G. "RAFE" ELSE, b. in Distant County ca. 1838;[22] d. at Nearton 19 Month 1892 and was bur. in the Somebody plot, Oak Grove Cemetery;[23] m. in Distant County during the year before 28 Month 1860, LUCY SUIT.[24] According to Ralph's petition [*And so forth*]^^^^^^^^^^
2.   iv. FIONA B. 'FIFI" ELSE, b. in Near County 19 Month 1842, m. (1) JONATHAN FEN, m. (2) LEMUEL WALTER MYANCESTOR.

Fiona's identifying number in child-list

   v. JASON "SONNY" ELSE, b. in Near County ca. 1845;[28] [*And so forth*]^^^^^^^^^^^^^^^^^^^^^^
   vi. THOMAS S. ELSE, b. in Near County __ Month 1860;[33] [*And so forth*] ^^^^^^^^^^^^^^^^^^^
   vii. MARY S. "SWEETY" ELSE, b. in Near County ca. 1853–1854;[37] d. in Any County 15 Month 1911;[38] m. in Distant County 14 Month 1872, LUCK KEY.[39] Mary [*And so forth*]^^^^^^^^^^
   viii. JOHN S. ELSE JR., b. in Near County, 1 Month 1858; d. at Riverton, River State, 8 Month 1930;[43] m., probably at Riverton ca. 1879,[44] SILVER GOLD, b. at Riverton [*And so forth*]^^^^^^^^^

2. FIONA B. "FIFI" ELSE, daughter of John S. Else Sr. and Mary Sweet Harte, was born 19 Month 1842 in Distant County, Any State,[48] and died 28 Month 1886 in Any County.[49] She married (1) **JONATHAN FEN,** 5 Month 1860 in Near County.[50] After Jonathan's death (1863–1864), Fiona married (2) **LEMUEL WALTER MYANCESTOR,**[51] who was born in Mountain County, Essex, ca. 1835[52] and died in Near County 22 Month 1873,[53] son of Michael Myancestor and Priscilla Parent.[54] [*And so forth*]^^^^^^^^^^^^^^^^^^^^^^^^

Fiona's identifying number repeated

Fiona, called Fifi in all but one census record [*And so forth—life story*]^^^^^^^^^^^^^^^^^^^^^

Child of Fiona B. Else and her first husband, Jonathan Fen:

   i. "JONNY" FEN, b. in Near County ca. 1862, [65] d. in Any County 22 Month 1870 while visiting his Fen grandparents.[66]

Children of Fiona B. Else by her second husband, Lemuel Walter Myancestor:

3.   ii. MICHAEL JOHN MYANCESTOR, b. in Near County 26 Month 1864, m. WILHELMINA J. GOODTITLE.
   iii. JASON SOMEBODY MYANCESTOR, b. in Near County 9 Month 1867;[67] m. there 2 Month 1890, POLLY WANNA CRACKER;[68] d., possibly without issue, after 1910.[69] [*And so forth*]^^^^^^^^^
   iv. EVELYN FIONA MYANCESTOR, b. in Any County 10 Month 1872;[73] m. in Near County 12 Month 1894, PHILIP MORRIS of Nearton.[74] Evelyn is said to have died [*And so forth*]^^^^^^^^^^

3. MICHAEL JOHN MYANCESTOR, son of Fiona B. "Fifi" (Else) Fen and her second husband, Lemuel Walter Myancestor, was born in Near County, Any State,[85] 26 Month 1864.[86] He died in Mountain County, Essex, 16 Month 1902 and is buried in Peak City Cemetery among numerous Myancestor relatives.[87] Michael married in Mountain County, 16 Month 1885, **WILHELMINA J. GOODTITLE**,[88] who was born about 1866 in Norway and died at Peak City 27 Month 1926,[89] daughter of Eric and Sigrid (____) Goodtitle.[90]

Michael John was raised on his father's large dairy farm in Any State.[91] He attended Any State University but left in 1885[92] when [*And so forth*]^^^

Children of Michael John and Wilhelmina J. (Goodtitle) Myancestor, all born in Mountain County:

4.　i.　BARBARA DELILAH MYANCESTOR, b. in Mountain County 15 Month 1886, m. WILLIAM I. DOE.

　　ii.　MICHAEL JOHN MYANCESTOR JR., b. at Peak City in Month 1887;[100] d. at New City, New State, 25 Month 1942;[101] m. at New City 31 Month 1931, ROSE O'DAY.[102] Michael was a concert pianist [*And so forth*]^^^

　　iii.　WILHELMINA GOODTITLE MYANCESTOR, b. in Mountain County, Month 1889;[108] [*And so forth*]^^^

　　iv.　SIGRID D. MYANCESTOR, b. in Mountain County in Month 1897, d. there before 1910.[114]

4. BARBARA DELILAH MYANCESTOR, daughter of Michael John Myancestor and his wife, Wilhelmina J. Goodtitle,[115] was born in Mountain County, Essex, 15 Month 1886 and died at Smalltown, Weststate, 2 Month 1948.[116] On 4 Month 1907 in Smoothton, Untamed Territory,[117] Barbara married **WILLIAM I. DOE**,[118] who was born at Smalltown 30 Month 1882 and died there 18 Month 1951,[119] son of Benjamin R. G. and Cynthea J. (Den) Doe.[120]

Barbara Myancestor seized one of the few professional opportunities open to single women in the first decades of the twentieth century. She became a teacher. [*And so forth*]^^^^^^^^^^^^^^^^^^

William I. Doe, Barbara's husband, was a son of the well-known U.S. marshall often credited with bringing law and order to early Untamed Territory.[138] (The story of "Ben" Doe's colorful life and spectacular death in the Roughton Massacre has been the subject of several books and a recent movie.[139]) William was the only one of his father's four children to survive the family's tragic sojourn in Untamed Territory, and [*And so forth*]^^^

Children of Barbara Delilah Myancestor and her only husband, William I. Doe, all born at Smoothton:

　　i.　MICHAEL MYANCESTOR DOE, b. 16 Month 1908;[150] living in Resort, Orange State, unmarried.[151]

　　ii.　BARNABY JACKSON DOE, b. 22 Month 1910;[152] d. at sea 18 Month 1943;[153] m. (1) at Smalltown 8 Month 1930, MARTHA JANE ROE, who was b. at Smalltown 17 Month 1912 and d. there 25 Month 1991,[154] daughter of Thomas D. and Sarah Elizabeth (Othername) Roe.[155] Barnaby and Martha Jane divorced in Friendly County, Weststate, 12 Month 1941;[156] and he m. (2) at Port City, Coast State, 8 Month 1943, JANE ELIZABETH "JANEY" SWEETHING, who was b. at Port City 1 Month 1928 and d. as Jane S. Foreff at Resort, Orange State, 11 Month 1994,[157] daughter of Joseph and ____ Sweething.[158] For the first few years of Barnaby's marriage to Martha Jane, the couple lived in an apartment above his father's pharmacy, and [*And so forth*] ^^^^^^^^^^^ Children of Barnaby and Martha Jane, surname *Doe*:[168] 1. *Barbara Delilah*, b. at Smalltown 5 Month 1933; living; m. Big R. Better; two children. 2. *Martha Jane*, b. at Smalltown 4 Month 1935; living; m. I. M Happy, two children. Children of Barnaby and Janey, surname *Doe*: 3. *Barnaby Jackson* (twin), b. at Port City 22 Month 1944; d. there 18 Month 1985; m. 3 Month 1967, Winona J. J. Winsome; four children. 4. *Joseph Sweething* (twin), b. at Port City 22 Month 1944; d. at Port City 16 Month 1949.

> biographies of siblings are within the child-list; each biography fully source-cited

　　iii.　BARBARA DELILAH DOE, b. at Smoothton 3 Month 1912;[169] d. [*And so forth*]^^^^^^^^^^^^

　　iv.　HERBERT VINCENT DOE, b. at Smoothton 5 Month 1915, d. at Smalltown 7 Month 1921 after his parents' return from Untamed Territory.[173]

　　v.　CYNTHEA CHRYSTAL DOE, b. at Smalltown 19 Month 1917;[174] m. at Smalltown 18 Month 1935, HERMAN MUNSTER,[175] b.[*And so forth*]^^^^^^^^^^^^^^^^^^^^^^^^^^^^^^^^^^^^^^^

5.　vi.　BENJAMIN WILLIAM DOE, b. at Smalltown 23 Month 1921,[179] m. ANNIE BODIE WHATSERNAME.

^^^^^^^^^^[*And so forth, through the number of generations intended to be included in the compilation*] ^^^^^^

Appendix F — Example Compiled Pedigrees

A pedigree compilation (as opposed to a chart or outline) is a comprehensive history of all the direct ancestors of a specific person for an identifiable number of generations. It normally includes, also, a brief overview placing that ancestry in its social, geographic, and historical context. Its building blocks are well researched, thoroughly documented, soundly constructed lineages (discussed in Appendix E). Two formatting systems are generally accepted in the family-history field: *(a)* the Sosa-Stradonitz System, most-often used for articles and monographs; and *(b)* the Multi-Surname System, often used for longer works. Both are inherently logical; but they serve somewhat different purposes and their form, use, and final appearance are radically different. Consequently, each will be described separately and both will be illustrated in the examples that follow.

The choice and use of a system for formatting these compilations should adhere the guidelines discussed in detail on page 65. In brief, they are: *(a)* study the explanations and examples in this manual and the Curran-Crane-Wray volume mentioned on page 18 (note 11), and use scholarly published works as models; *(b)* choose one system and use it consistently; and *(c)* test-print often to ensure that consistency is, in fact, being maintained.

Sosa-Stradonitz System

This is an "ascending" system—that is, it proceeds from the recent descendant to the remote ancestors. It focuses on the *couples* who link the generations, and completes discussion of all couples in one generation before moving on to those in the next. In addition to its overall arrangement, this system is distinguished by its assignment of numbers to designate the place of each person in the compilation and the arrangement of data in its biographies.

- *Numbering system.* Two sets of numbers are assigned:

  (a) *Identifying numbers.* Arabic numbers denote each person in each direct line, beginning with "1" for the recent descendant. His or her father is "2" and mother "3," and thereafter each couple is numbered in sequence. All ancestral fathers have even numbers (twice their child's number). All ancestral mothers take the next-following odd number. This "ahnentafel" identifying method is also used on paper and computer-generated charts. For this reason, Sosa-Stradonitz is sometimes called the Ahnentafel System.

  Identifying numbers are uniquely personal—each number is used for only one ancestor. Each ancestor, however, can be assigned more than one identifying number. If a person in the direct line descends from the same couple through two of their children, or from one ancestral parent through two marriages, such "duplicate" ancestors take additional numbers—in ahnentafel sequence—to maintain the compilation's overall numbering scheme.

(b) *Birth-order numbers.* Lower-case Roman numerals are assigned to the offspring mentioned in a child-list, beginning with "i" for the first-born of the couple's children and continuing in sequence to their last-born. These numbers are not unique to any given person; "i" is used for all first-born children.

- *Biographies.* In this format, the recent descendant is the only person in the compilation who has a fully developed individual biography—all other biographies are joint father-mother discussions, which are arranged according to the father's identifying number. These biographies demonstrate the qualities described in Appendix E (see pages 65–68). They are divided into the same three sections, but with the following differences:

  (a) *Genealogical summaries* are broken into two parts, one for each parent.

  The father's part begins with his identifying number and full name. Nicknames are included (in quotation marks) as well as a.k.a. [also known as] names or aliases. EXAMPLE: John "Jack" Doe alias Roe. The father's part of the summary continues, giving the names of his parents (preceded by "son of") and his birth and death dates and places. It ends with the date and place of his union with the ancestral mother but not her name—and no final period.

  The mother's part, separated from the father's by paragraph spacing, begins with her identifying number and full name at the time of her union with the ancestral father. Her nickname, if any, is included (in quotation marks), as well as aliases or a.k.a. [also known as] name(s). If she was a widow or divorcee, her birth surname is placed within parentheses and is followed by the surname of each previous mate. The mother's name is followed by her birth and death dates and places, and her parents' names (preceded by "daughter of"). This part of the summary ends with the final period that marks the end of the paragraph.

Only the starting-point descendant's summary may be split further to accommodate additional spouses.

(b) *Life stories* may include, in addition to the father-mother discussion, information about unions other than the one through whom the line ascends. Children of these unions may be mentioned also, but within the text.

(c) *Child-lists* include the couple's biological and adopted children. Offspring are named and numbered in birth order, but children adopted by the couple are listed in a separate child-list group in birth order or the order in which they entered the nuclear family—provided that consistency is maintained throughout the compilation.

This format's focus is on ancestors *as a couple*, not on each partner as an individual. Consequently, any children of one parent but not the other are omitted from the couple's child-list. Stepchildren, if included in the compilation, therefore, are mentioned within the life-story text.

Cross-references between biographies are inserted as appropriate when a couple or individual has two or more identifying numbers. This occurs when the the recent descendant's ancestry includes: *(a)* two or more children born of the same couple; *(b)* children of the same ancestral father through two or more of his marriages, or *(c)* children of the the same ancestral mother through two or more of her marriages.

The Sosa-Stradonitz System is easy to use from the compiler's viewpoint and as more people do so, it will become familiar and therefore easier for readers to understand. It does have one awkward defect: if research has not yet identified a particular person or couple, those identifying numbers will not be used. As more and more numbers disappear from the compilation, it begins to take on an unfinished, lopsided appearance. The difficulty can be overcome by halting discussion of all ancestral lines in approximately the same generation, or by "reserving" the numbers for missing couples. Neither solution is entirely satisfactory, which is why the Sosa-Stradonitz System is usually chosen only for compilations of limited length. Longer compilations, particularly if one family line has been followed far beyond others, are better compiled in the formatting system described below.

Multi-Surname System

This is a "descending" system—that is, it begins with a series of remote ancestors, tracing them forward to a recent descendant that all of them have in common. It focuses on the direct ancestors (usually male) who carried their surname into the next more-recent generation. Each surname line is presented separately.

The compilation begins with a primary line, most-often that of the descendant's father. The lineages of associated families (those who married into the primary line) are thereafter discussed in individual chapters or, in shorter works, individual sections. In most cases, the surname chapters or sections are arranged in alphabetical order—and each is often preceded by a chart of the descendant line.

Each lineage, whether primary or associated, begins with the earliest known ancestor in that line and is brought forward to the recent descendant. Only one line, that of the descendant's father, can be carried that far forward, however, without becoming repetitive. Consequently, each surname chapter ends with the most-recent marriage of a direct-line female into the primary line—or into an associated family whose lineage is brought farther forward. A cross-index is used at that point, directing readers to the appropriate continuation chapter.

Other than by marriage, changes in a surname are handled within the chapter that addresses it. In the following circumstances, for example, the line, and therefore the chapter, continues when: *(a)* the surname of an immigrant family was translated into English or its spelling was dramatically altered; *(b)* a court authorized the surname change; *(c)* a European surname came to be used by (or when referring to) a Native American family; or *(d)* an African-American family was known by several surnames during and after slavery.

In addition to its overall arrangement, the Multi-Surname System is distinguished by its numbering scheme and biographical elements.

- *Numbering system.* Three sets of numbers are assigned to designate each direct ancestor: *(a)* identifying numbers, *(b)* birth-order numbers, and *(c)* generation indicators. (A fourth identifier, the parenthetical lineage list, is used when necessary.)

    (a) *Identifying numbers* are Arabic numbers that denote each person in each direct lineage, beginning with "1" for the earliest known ancestor in that line (its "progenitor"). Each surname line is numbered individually. EXAMPLE: 1. John Doe (the Doe line's progenitor); 1. Richard Fen (the Fen line's progenitor); 1. David Roe, and so forth. Thereafter, within each lineage, the numbers continue in sequence. If more than one child in a generation is in the direct line (by cousin marriages, for example), each is assigned an identifying number in proper sequence.

    Identifying numbers are uniquely personal. With the exception of "1," each number appears only twice within each line, and in both cases it directly relates to a specific member of that family. It is written (1) near the left margin before the person's name in a parental child-list; and (2) precedes the same person's name at the beginning of his or her biography.

(b) *Birth-order numbers* are lower-case Roman numerals assigned to each of the offspring in a child-list, beginning with "i" for the person's first-born and continuing in sequence through the last-born. These numbers are not unique to any given person; all first-born children, for example, are "i."

(c) *Generation indicators* are superscripted Arabic numbers or upper-case letters that denote the generation of descent from the line's progenitor. The direct-line person and all of his or her siblings are members of the same generation and share the same indicator. By tradition:

Arabic numbers are used if the compilation's progenitor was the immigrant ancestor or a descendant of the immigrant. He or she is generation "1," and thereafter the numbers continue in sequence through more-recent generations. EXAMPLE: progenitor^1, all children^2, all grandchildren^3 and so on.

Upper-case letters are used if the compilation begins in the country of origin. The indicator "A" is assigned to the immigrant's parent, and thereafter the letters continue in sequence through earlier generations. The immigrant ancestor continues with the indicator "1," and succeeding generation with Arabic numbers. EXAMPLE: progenitor^C, all children^B, all grandchildren^A, the immigrant great-grandchild^1, his or her children^2, and so on.

(If generation^1 included siblings who did not immigrate, the *NGSQ* System used for compiled genealogies provides a method for assigning indicators to that generation. It is discussed on pages 100–101; a graphic presentation of the system is on page 101.)

Generation indicators attach to a person's given name (or the last middle name or initial), and normally nothing—not even punctuation—comes between them.

(d) *Parenthetical lineage lists* that appear within genealogical summaries written for compiled genealogies are used if needed to identify, with absolute assurance, each descendant in each line. Because they are not normally an integral part of the Multi-

Surname System, they are not discussed at length here, but their form and use is explained on pages 99–100. If parenthetical lineage lists are used anywhere in the compilation, they must be used everywhere to maintain the format's continuity.

- *Biographies.* Biographies in compilations formatted with the Multi-Surname System demonstrate the qualities described in Appendix E (see pages 65–68) and are divided into the same three sections, but with the following differences:

    (a) *Genealogical summaries:* The first time the biography's subject is mentioned, his or her name includes the appropriate generation indicator. If his wife's ancestral line is followed elsewhere in the compilation, her name in the summary includes her generation indicator; and a cross-reference is inserted directing readers to the appropriate chapter or section.

    (b) *Life stories:* There is little difference between life stories written for lineage and pedigree compilations.

    (c) *Child-lists:* Because this formatting system focuses on individual surname carriers (rather than on couples as is true in the Sosa-Stradonitz System), all of the subject's children are listed. Children are grouped (in birth order, beginning with the oldest) according to the union from which they came, and each group is introduced by a sentence or sentence fragment that identifies their parents. Child-lists also include the subject's stepchildren and his or her adopted children, who are listed in birth order or the order in which they entered the nuclear family. Each of these groups is also introduced by an appropriate statement. EXAMPLES: Stepchild [children] of X born of his wife Y by her first husband Z; or Adopted child [children] of X and his wife Y.

    Child-list biographies: Each child's entry begins with his or her full birth name, nickname in quotation marks, and a.k.a. name or alias—but not married surnames. A brief genealogical summary follows, including vital statistics; and the date, place, and spouse- or partner-name for each marriage or liaison. A child-list is the place where life-story data can be included about children who are not in the direct line. If desired, those children's children (the subject's grandchildren) can be listed—in birth order—within their life story.

Child-list numbering: (a) Stepchildren and adoptees, because they were not "born of" the biography's subject, are not assigned birth-order numbers. *(b)* The generation indicator is included within the name of the first child in each list. It is "silent" in the names of his or her siblings.

Typographic Style

Unless the pedigree is compiled for a specific purpose, typography is normally based on one of the generally recognized compiled-genealogy formats (*NGSQ* or *Register*).[15] Both formats are described at length in Appendix G (see pages 102–3). Although compilations that use the Multi-Surname System most-often follow the *Register* System's typography, either style can be used for either pedigree system.

The examples that follow are based on fictitious families. Reference note numbers are included but the notes themselves are omitted. (Note that in the Multi-Surname System these numbers start again at "1" in each chapter.) For documentation examples see Appendixes C, D, and G and the extensive models in Mills's volume cited on page 3 (note 1).

---

15. These systems are used by the *National Genealogical Society Quarterly* and the *New England Historical and Genealogical Register*, respectively. The models in this manual reflect the typographic styles used by their current editors.

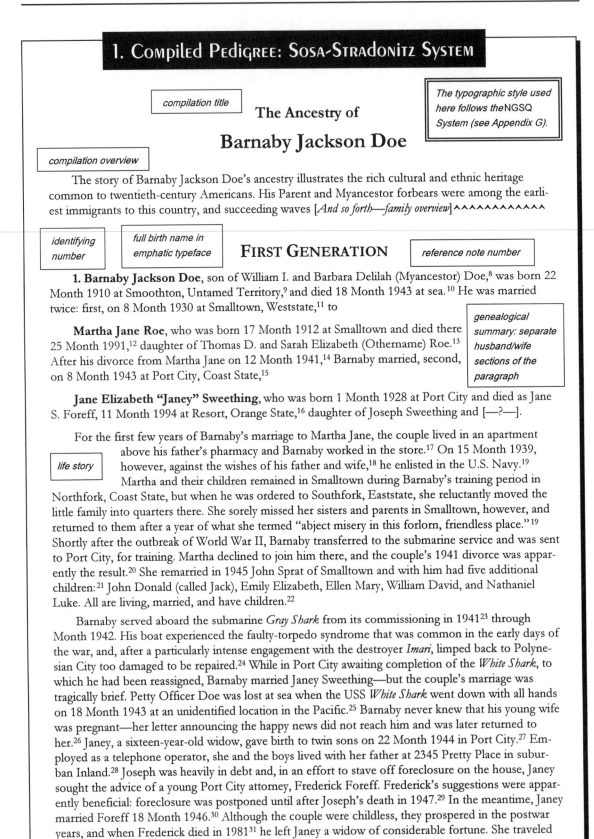

1. Compiled Pedigree: Sosa-Stradonitz System

compilation title

The Ancestry of

Barnaby Jackson Doe

The typographic style used here follows the NGSQ System (see Appendix G).

compilation overview

The story of Barnaby Jackson Doe's ancestry illustrates the rich cultural and ethnic heritage common to twentieth-century Americans. His Parent and Myancestor forbears were among the earliest immigrants to this country, and succeeding waves [*And so forth—family overview*] ∧∧∧∧∧∧∧∧∧∧∧∧

identifying number

full birth name in emphatic typeface

FIRST GENERATION

reference note number

1. Barnaby Jackson Doe, son of William I. and Barbara Delilah (Myancestor) Doe,[8] was born 22 Month 1910 at Smoothton, Untamed Territory,[9] and died 18 Month 1943 at sea.[10] He was married twice: first, on 8 Month 1930 at Smalltown, Weststate,[11] to

Martha Jane Roe, who was born 17 Month 1912 at Smalltown and died there 25 Month 1991,[12] daughter of Thomas D. and Sarah Elizabeth (Othername) Roe.[13] After his divorce from Martha Jane on 12 Month 1941,[14] Barnaby married, second, on 8 Month 1943 at Port City, Coast State,[15]

genealogical summary: separate husband/wife sections of the paragraph

Jane Elizabeth "Janey" Sweething, who was born 1 Month 1928 at Port City and died as Jane S. Foreff, 11 Month 1994 at Resort, Orange State,[16] daughter of Joseph Sweething and [—?—].

For the first few years of Barnaby's marriage to Martha Jane, the couple lived in an apartment above his father's pharmacy and Barnaby worked in the store.[17] On 15 Month 1939, however, against the wishes of his father and wife,[18] he enlisted in the U.S. Navy.[19]

life story

Martha and their children remained in Smalltown during Barnaby's training period in Northfork, Coast State, but when he was ordered to Southfork, Eaststate, she reluctantly moved the little family into quarters there. She sorely missed her sisters and parents in Smalltown, however, and returned to them after a year of what she termed "abject misery in this forlorn, friendless place."[19] Shortly after the outbreak of World War II, Barnaby transferred to the submarine service and was sent to Port City, for training. Martha declined to join him there, and the couple's 1941 divorce was apparently the result.[20] She remarried in 1945 John Sprat of Smalltown and with him had five additional children:[21] John Donald (called Jack), Emily Elizabeth, Ellen Mary, William David, and Nathaniel Luke. All are living, married, and have children.[22]

Barnaby served aboard the submarine *Gray Shark* from its commissioning in 1941[23] through Month 1942. His boat experienced the faulty-torpedo syndrome that was common in the early days of the war, and, after a particularly intense engagement with the destroyer *Imari*, limped back to Polynesian City too damaged to be repaired.[24] While in Port City awaiting completion of the *White Shark*, to which he had been reassigned, Barnaby married Janey Sweething—but the couple's marriage was tragically brief. Petty Officer Doe was lost at sea when the USS *White Shark* went down with all hands on 18 Month 1943 at an unidentified location in the Pacific.[25] Barnaby never knew that his young wife was pregnant—her letter announcing the happy news did not reach him and was later returned to her.[26] Janey, a sixteen-year-old widow, gave birth to twin sons on 22 Month 1944 in Port City.[27] Employed as a telephone operator, she and the boys lived with her father at 2345 Pretty Place in suburban Inland.[28] Joseph was heavily in debt and, in an effort to stave off foreclosure on the house, Janey sought the advice of a young Port City attorney, Frederick Foreff. Frederick's suggestions were apparently beneficial: foreclosure was postponed until after Joseph's death in 1947.[29] In the meantime, Janey married Foreff 18 Month 1946.[30] Although the couple were childless, they prospered in the postwar years, and when Frederick died in 1981[31] he left Janey a widow of considerable fortune. She traveled extensively, eventually settling in Resort, Orange State, and died there in 1994.[32]

The children of Barnaby Jackson Doe and his first wife, Martha Jane Roe, are as follows:

birth-order numbers

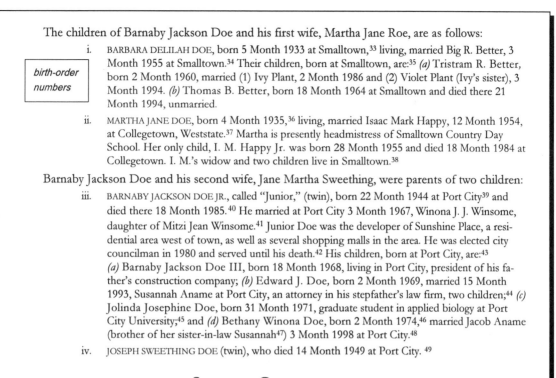

i. BARBARA DELILAH DOE, born 5 Month 1933 at Smalltown,[33] living, married Big R. Better, 3 Month 1955 at Smalltown.[34] Their children, born at Smalltown, are:[35] *(a)* Tristram R. Better, born 2 Month 1960, married (1) Ivy Plant, 2 Month 1986 and (2) Violet Plant (Ivy's sister), 3 Month 1994. *(b)* Thomas B. Better, born 18 Month 1964 at Smalltown and died there 21 Month 1994, unmarried.

ii. MARTHA JANE DOE, born 4 Month 1935,[36] living, married Isaac Mark Happy, 12 Month 1954, at Collegetown, Weststate.[37] Martha is presently headmistress of Smalltown Country Day School. Her only child, I. M. Happy Jr. was born 28 Month 1955 and died 18 Month 1984 at Collegetown. I. M.'s widow and two children live in Smalltown.[38]

Barnaby Jackson Doe and his second wife, Jane Martha Sweething, were parents of two children:

iii. BARNABY JACKSON DOE JR., called "Junior," (twin), born 22 Month 1944 at Port City[39] and died there 18 Month 1985.[40] He married at Port City 3 Month 1967, Winona J. J. Winsome, daughter of Mitzi Jean Winsome.[41] Junior Doe was the developer of Sunshine Place, a residential area west of town, as well as several shopping malls in the area. He was elected city councilman in 1980 and served until his death.[42] His children, born at Port City, are:[43] *(a)* Barnaby Jackson Doe III, born 18 Month 1968, living in Port City, president of his father's construction company; *(b)* Edward J. Doe, born 2 Month 1969, married 15 Month 1993, Susannah Aname at Port City, an attorney in his stepfather's law firm, two children;[44] *(c)* Jolinda Josephine Doe, born 31 Month 1971, graduate student in applied biology at Port City University;[45] and *(d)* Bethany Winona Doe, born 2 Month 1974,[46] married Jacob Aname (brother of her sister-in-law Susannah[47]) 3 Month 1998 at Port City.[48]

iv. JOSEPH SWEETHING DOE (twin), who died 14 Month 1949 at Port City. [49]

SECOND GENERATION

2. William I. Doe, son of Benjamin R. G. and Cynthea J. (Den) Doe, was born 30 Month 1882 at Smalltown, Weststate, and died 18 Month 1971 at Smalltown.[50] He married 4 Month 1907 at Smoothton, Untamed Territory,[51]

3. Barbara Delilah Myancestor, who was born 15 Month 1886 in Mountain County, Essex;[52] and died 2 Month 1948 at Smalltown,[53] daughter of Michael John and Wilhelmina J. (Goodtitle) Myancestor.[54]

William was the only one of his parents' four children to survive the family's sojourn in Untamed Territory—he was sixteen when his father was killed in what came to be called the Roughton Massacre.[55] According to family tradition, Cynthea rejected the boy after their return to Smalltown, "because he was the spit 'n' image of his father."[56] Nevertheless, William lived with his mother and stepfather, George E. Nuhusband, through 1900.[57] Surprisingly, he then returned to Untamed Territory (before its 1904 census).[58] There he married Barbara Delilah, a distant relative he always called "Cousin Babs."[59] Barbara had come to the territory in the fall of 1906 to accept a contract with the Smoothton city fathers to keep the new school.[60] Ostensibly to better his ability to read and write, William promptly enrolled himself as an adult student.[61] After a brief but obviously effective courtship, [*And so forth*] ^^

Barbara had graduated from [*And so forth*]^^^^^^^^^^^^^^^^^^^^^^^^^^^^^^^^^^^^^^^

William I. and Barbara Delilah (Myancestor) Doe were parents of the following children:[69]

i. MICHAEL MYANCESTOR DOE, born 16 Month 1908 at Smoothton, died there during Month 1909 of yellow fever.[70]

\+ 1. ii. BARNABY JACKSON DOE, born 22 Month 1910 at Smoothton,[71] died 18 Month 1943 at sea.[72] He married (1) Martha Jane Roe, 8 Month 1930, at Smalltown;[73] and (2) Jane Elizabeth Sweething 8 Month 1943 at Port City, Coast State.[74]

iii. BARBARA DELILAH DOE, born 3 Month 1912 at Smoothton,[75] [*And so forth*]^^^^^^^^^^^^

iv. HERBERT VINCENT DOE, born 5 Month 1915 [*And so forth*]^^^^^^^^^^^^^^^^^^^^^^

v. CYNTHEA CHRYSTAL DOE, born 19 Month 1917 [*And so forth*]^^^^^^^^^^^^^^^^^^^

vi. BENJAMIN WILLIAM DOE, born 23 Month 1921[95] at Smalltown, living, [*And so forth*]^^^^^^^

identifying number; "+" in this style signifies full biography earlier/later

Third Generation

4. Benjamin R. G. Doe, son of Robert G. Doe and Martha Chrystal (Myancestor) Martyr,[103] was born 17 Month 1854 at Light City, Farstate; and died 29 Month 1898 at Roughton, Untamed Territory.[104] On 30 Month 1875 in Friendly County, Weststate,[105] he married

5. Cynthea J. Den, who was born 19 Month 1860 in Friendly County[106] and died as Cynthea D. Lucky 22 Month 1919 at Smalltown;[107] daughter of Jackson B. W. and Roma Ann C. [—?—] Den.[108]

In 1867, Benjamin moved with his uncle and cousins (William I. Doe and his children) to Friendly County's remote Goodland Valley.[109] Like his father Robert, Benjamin was apparently uncomfortable with William's firmly-held views about the responsibilities and proper practices of farming[110]—he preferred a lawman's life, serving first as sheriff of Smalltown (1879–84) and then as United States marshall for [*And so forth*] ∧∧∧∧∧∧∧∧∧∧∧∧∧∧∧∧∧∧∧∧∧∧∧∧∧∧∧∧∧∧∧∧∧∧∧∧∧∧∧

Benjamin was killed [*And so forth*]∧∧∧∧∧∧∧∧∧∧∧∧∧∧∧∧∧∧∧∧∧∧∧∧∧∧∧∧∧∧∧∧∧∧∧∧∧

After her husband's death, Cynthea returned to Smalltown with her only surviving child, "Little Billy,"[116] and tried to manage the farm Benjamin's uncle William had given him on his twenty-first birthday.[117] She found the task beyond her and sought refuge with her parents in nearby Smalltown,[118] where she met George E. Nuhusband, the town's only barber, newly arrived from Germany.[119] They married on 21 Month 1899,[120] some five months after the traumatic events at Roughton. On her fortieth birthday, Cynthia gave birth to a daughter, Clarissa L.,[121] and two years later to a son, George Benjamin (born in Month 1902).[122] George E. was killed by a stray bullet [*And so forth*] ∧∧∧∧∧∧∧∧∧∧∧

The children of Benjamin R. G. and Cynthea J. (Den) Doe, all born at Smalltown,[125] were as follows:

- i.   JACKSON D. DOE, born 1 Month 1877,[126] died before 29 Month 1898 in Untamed Territory.[127]
- ii. BENJAMIN R. G. DOE JR., born 2 Month 1880,[128] died before 29 Month 1898 in Untamed Territory.
- + 2 iii. WILLIAM I. DOE, born 30 Month 1882;[129] died at Smalltown 18 Month 1971.[130] He married, 4 Month 1907 at Smoothton, Barbara Delilah Myancestor.[131]
- iv. DAUGHTER (name unknown), born 12 Month 1885[132] at Smalltown, died before 29 Month 1898 in Untamed Territory.

6. Michael John Myancestor, son of Lemuel Walter Myancestor and Fiona B. "Fifi" (Else) Fen,[133] was born 26 Month 1864[134] in Near County, Any State,[135] and died 16 Month 1902 in Mountain County, Essex.[136] He married 16 Month 1885 in Mountain County,[137]

7. Wilhelmina J. Goodtitle, who was born about 1856 in Norway and died 27 Month 1926 at Peak City, Essex,[138] daughter of Eric and Sigrid [—?—] Goodtitle.[139]

Michael was raised on his father's large dairy farm in Any State. He attended Any State University but left in 1885 [127] when his uncle Waldo Myancestor died and left him half the family farm in Mountain County.[128] Planning to sell it to Waldo's adopted son (Michael W. Myancestor, who had inherited the other half of the tract) and return to school in the fall,[129] Michael J. went east to attend to the business but changed his mind and decided to stay. (The charms of neighbor Wilhelmina Goodtitle may have had something to do with his decision—he married her within a few weeks of his arrival in Essex.) The two Michael Myancestors lived side by side for the next four decades, distinguishing themselves by meticulous use of their middle initials.[130] Michael J. added to his half of the tract in 1888, 1892 and 1895,[131] virtually surrounding the smaller acreage of Michael W. When Michael J. died in 1902, however, his widow Wilhelmina sold all the land to Michael W.[132] and moved into Peak City.[133]

At the age of about eleven, Wilhelmina Goodtitle had immigrated from Norway with her father and stepmother, arriving in Coast City on 18 Month 1875 aboard *Johnny One-Note*.[134] The Goodtitles [*And so forth*] ∧∧∧∧∧∧∧∧∧∧∧∧∧∧∧∧∧∧∧∧∧∧∧∧∧∧∧∧∧ After her move into town, Wilhelmina taught music but the lessons were given "*always* on the *old* piano!"[137] Turn-of-the-century issues of the

Peak City Observer carried occasional notices of Mrs. Myancestor's concerts, but the music critics did not mention them.[138]

The children of Michael John and Wilhelmina J. (Goodtitle) Myancestor, all born in Mountain County,[139] were as follows:

+ 3   i.   BARBARA DELILAH MYANCESTOR, born 15 Month 1886,[140] died [*And so forth—the rest of her birth, death, marriage data required by the* NGSQ *System's typographic style*]∧∧∧∧∧∧∧∧∧∧∧∧∧∧∧∧∧∧∧

      ii. MICHAEL JOHN MYANCESTOR JR.,[143] born 9 Month 1887, died 25 Month 1942 at New City.[144] He married, at New City [*And so forth*]∧∧∧∧∧∧∧∧∧∧∧∧∧∧∧∧∧∧∧∧∧∧∧∧∧∧∧∧∧∧∧∧∧

      iii. WILHELMINA GOODTITLE MYANCESTOR, born in Month 1889, died after 1910.[152] The Essex records reveal nothing more about her.[153]

      iv. SIGRID D. MYANCESTOR, born Month 1897, died before 1910.[154]

[box: birth-order numbers]

*[box: parent identifying numbers:
father's = child's number x 2
mother's = child's number x 2 +1]*

FOURTH GENERATION

8. Robert G. Doe, son of Tristram and Elizabeth (Holdfast) Doe,[155] was born 15 Month 1809[156] in Sandy County, Eaststate,[157] and died 15 Month 1909 (exactly one hundred years later) at Light City, Farstate.[158] Robert married (as her second husband) on 25 Month 1853 in Mountain County,[159]

9. Martha Chrystal (Myancestor) Martyr, a.k.a. Chrystal Knight, a.k.a. Lydia Chrystal, who was born 1832–33 in Mountain County[160] and died 12 Month 1857 at Light City, Farstate,[161] daughter of Michael Myancestor and Priscilla Parent.[162]

Like others in his family, Robert grew up attending Crane Creek Baptist Church, but his behavior (alcohol-related, apparently) led to [*And so forth*]∧∧

At the time Robert and Martha married, he was a struggling poet and she a struggling actress using the stage name Chrystal Knight.[175] She was also a widow with an infant son. Martha had met her first husband, St. Stephen Martyr in New City while playing Mrs. Mumble [*And so forth*]∧∧∧∧∧∧∧∧∧∧

Martha and St. Stephen had one child, Michael Martyr, a.k.a. Michael Waldo Myancestor, who was born 5 Month 1851 at New City[180] and adopted by his uncle Waldo N. and aunt Charity (Always) Myancestor after Martha's death.[181] Michael grew up on the Myancestor family farm in Mountain County and married Olivia Fruitful, daughter of Rev. Henry Fruitful of nearby Oak Grove Church.[182] If Michael resented Waldo's having willed half the farm to a distant cousin, he did not express his displeasure in any way that entered the public records. He lived quietly on his half of the property, raising his and Olivia's eighteen children.[183] Shortly after Michael W. purchased Michael J.'s holdings from the widow Wilhelmina in 1902,[184] he began deeding portions of the acreage to his sons and sons-in-law[185] and wrote his will (dated 7 Month 1903) devising "whatever lands remain" to the children who had "not yet received their inheritance."[186] He died 4 Month 1919 and, according to his testamentary instructions, lies buried in a private graveyard on the farm.[187]

Robert G. and Martha Chrystal (Myancestor) Doe were parents of two children:

+ 4   i.   BENJAMIN R. G. DOE, born 17 Month 1854 at Light City,[188] died 29 Month 1898 in Untamed Territory.[189] He married in Friendly County, Weststate, 30 March 1875, Cynthea J. Den.[190]

      ii. WALDO N. DOE, born 25 Month 1856 at Light City, died in Month 1866 of a "[fall] from that old oak on Willy's place," according to his father's *Private Book I*.[191] "Willy's place" was the home of Robert's brother William I. Doe, with whom the Doe boys had been left when he returned to Light City after a brief stay on William's Sandy County farm.

10. Jackson B. W. Den, son of Goodorum Adam and Leah (Jerusalem) Den,[192] was born about 1825–28,[193] probably at Pleasantville, North State,[194] and died 19 Month 1881 in Friendly County, Weststate.[195] He married about 1845–47 at Pleasantville,[196]

11. Roma Ann C. [—?—], who was born about 1832 in North State[197] and died 1862–70, possibly in Friendly County.[198]

At an early age, Jackson [*And so forth*]∧∧∧

The children of Jackson B. W. and Roma Ann C. [—?—] Den were as follows:

    i.   AMANDA ANN DEN, born 19 Month 1847 at Pleasantville,[209] [*And so forth*]^^^^^^^^^^^^

    ii.   through vi. [*Five more children*]

+ 5 vii. CYNTHEA J. DEN, born 19 Month 1860 in Friendly County, Westate,[231] died 22 Month 1919 at Smalltown as Cynthea D. Lucky.[232] She married (1) Benjamin R. G. Doe in Friendly County 30 Month 1875,[233] (2) George E Nuhusband[234] at Smalltown 21 Month 1899,[235] and (3) Harold Lucky on 29 Month 1916 at Smalltown.[236]

12. Lemuel Walter Myancestor, son of Michael Myancestor and Priscilla Parent,[237] was born about 1835 in Mountain County, Essex,[238] and died about 22 Month 1873[239] in Any County, Any State.[239] He married 1863–64,[240] probably at Nearton, Near County,[241]

13. Fiona B. "Fifi" (Else) Fen, who was born 19 Month 1842 in Distant County, Any State[242] and died 28 Month 1886 in Any County,[243] daughter of John Somebody Else Sr. and Mary Sweet Harte.[244]

Lemuel was named for his two grandfathers, Lemuel Parent and Walter Myancestor.[245] He spent his early years near Peak City in prosperous Mountain County[218] but his father's death in 1852[246] and mother Priscilla's remarriage to Jonathan Oldman the following year[247] [*And so forth*]^^^^^^^^^^^

Lemuel's wife, called Fifi in all but one census record,[261] was reputedly very beautiful. Her portrait, painted by Pine Wood, is mentioned in the catalogue for his 1901 New City show, in glowing compliment to both the artist and his subject[262] (although her having posed for Wood was considered scandalous by [*And so forth*]^^^^^^^By her first marriage, Fiona was the mother of [*And so forth*]^^^

Lemuel Walter Myancestor and his wife Fiona B. (Else) Fen were parents of the following children:

+ 6 i. MICHAEL JOHN MYANCESTOR, born in Near County 26 Month 1864,[269] died in Mountain County 16 Month 1902.[270] He married Wilhelmina J. Goodtitle 16 Month 1885 at Peak City, Essex.[171]

    ii. JOHN SOMEBODY MYANCESTOR, born [*And so forth*]^^^^^^^^^^^^^^^^^^^^^^^^^^

    iii. EVELYN FIONA MYANCESTOR, born 10 Month 1872 in Any County,[278] married Philip Morris of Nearton 12 Month 1894 in Near County.[279] [*And so forth*]^^^^^^^^^^^^^^^^^^^^

14. Eric Goodtitle was born about 1820 in Norway;[283] died 24 Month 1889 in Mountain County, Essex;[284] and married, first, about 1850 in Norway,[285]

15. Sigrid [—?—], who was born about 1827 in Norway[286] and died before 15 Month 1873, probably in Norway.[287]

Eric Goodtitle left Norway after [*And so forth—the rest of their biography and their child-list, which includes no. 7 Wilhelmina J. Goodtitle*]^^^

FIFTH GENERATION

[Of the sixteen identifying numbers set aside for fifth-generation ancestors, six must be blank or reserved, and two are for "duplicate" ancestors. In the Sixth Generation, the quantity of missing numbers multiplies.]

16. Tristram Doe was born in Wishful County, Essex, about 1780[301] [*And so forth*]^^^^^^^^^

17. Elizabeth Holdfast, who was born [*And so forth*]^^^^^^^^^^^^^^^^^^^^^^^^^^

Wishful County, where Tristram was born, and Sandy County, where he married and died, are a considerable distance from each other, a circumstance that might give rise to doubt that the *same* Tristram lived in both counties. Evidence of one man, however, [*And so forth*]^^^^^^^^^^^^^^^^^

The children of Tristram and Elizabeth (Holdfast) Doe were [*And so forth—their child-list with biographies of all but no. 8 Robert G. Doe*] ^^

18. Michael Myancestor, son of Walter and Crystal (Palace) Myancestor, was born 25 Month 1792 at Brownton, Thirdplace;[321] died 24 Month–18 Month 1852 in Mountain County;[322] having married 25 Month 1823 in Mountain County,[323]

19. Priscilla Parent, who was born 3 Month 1803 in Mountain County[324] and died as Priscilla Oldman on 12 Month 1882 in Any County, Any State.[325] She was the only daughter of Lemuel and Caroline (Neighbor) Parent.[326]

Michael Myancestor "read law" in Brownton under the guidance of his uncle, John Cooper.[327] At twenty-one, however, he left Cooper's law offices and moved to Capital City, Essex, to set up his own practice there. Waldo Neighbor,[328] then mayor of Peak City[329] met the young [*And so forth*]^^^^^^^

The children of [*And so forth, including no. 9 Martha Chrystal Myancestor and no. 12 Lemuel Walter Myancestor*] ^^

20. Goodorum Adam Den was born 1800–1810 (probably about 1800–1805),[342] place not known. He died 1849–50 at Pleasantville, North State,[343] and married 27 Month 1825 at Pleasantville,[344]

21. Leah Jerusalem, who was born about 1803–12 in North State[345] and died 12 Month 1872 in Friendly County, Weststate.[346]

Aside from the date of their marriage, little of the lives of Goodorum and Leah Den can be learned from the surviving North State and Weststate records. Apparently the Dens leased the land they lived on, for no records of land acquisition (by deed or land grant) document their [*And so forth*] ^^^

The children of Goodorum and Leah (Jerusalem) Den included several whose names have not been found at this writing:

     i.   SON, unidentified, born 1825–30,[346] probably at Pleasantville.[347] He had left the household by 1850 and has not been found thereafter in Weststate or nearby states.

+ 10   ii.   JACKSON B. W. DEN, born about 1825–28,[348] probably at Pleasantville; died in Friendly County 19 Month 1881.[349] He married about 1845–47 in Pleasantville[350] Roma Ann C. [—?—].[341]

    iii.   [*And so forth—the rest of the child-list*] ^^^^^^^^^^^^^^^^^^^^^^^^^^^^^^^^^^^^^^^

22. Reserved for the father of no. 11 Roma Ann C. [—?—].

23. Reserved for mother of no. 11 Roma Ann C. [—?—].

24. Michael Myancestor. (See no. 18.)

25. Priscilla Parent. (See no. 19.)

26. John Somebody Else Sr., son of Jason and Ellen (Somebody) Else, was born 1804–5[365] in Any State[366] and died between 4 and 28 Month 1883 in Near County.[367] He married 9 Month 1830 in Any County,[368]

27. Mary Sweet Harte, who was born during 1815[369] and died 1870–81 in Any or Distant County;[370] daughter of Douglas and Fiona [—?—] Harte.[371]

[*And so forth—the couple's life story and child-list, which includes no. 13 Fiona B. "Fifi" Else*] ^^^^^^^^^

28. Reserved for father of no. 14 Eric Goodtitle.

29. Reserved for mother of no. 14 Eric Goodtitle.

30. Reserved for father of no. 15 Sigrid [—?—].

31. Reserved for mother of no. 15 Sigrid [—?—].

^^^^^^[*And so forth, through the number of generations intended to be included in the compilation*] ^^^^^^^

2. COMPILED PEDIGREE: MULTI-SURNAME SYSTEM

compilation title

The Ancestry of

The typographic style used here follows the Register System (see Appendix G).

Barnaby Jackson Doe (1910–1943)

DOE FAMILY   primary line (father's)

explanatory chart, usually included in compilations that use this format

CHART OF DOE DESCENDANTS

Tristram Doe = Elizabeth Holdfast

Robert G. Doe = Martha Chrystal Myancestor

Benjamin R. G. Doe = Cynthea J. Doe

William I. Doe = Barbara Delilah Myancestor

Barnaby Jackson^5 Doe

identified descendant (the person whose ancestry is the subject of the compilation)

Does of the early generations identified to date were not "great men," socially, politically, militarily, or economically. Their achievements individually [*And so forth—introduction to the primary family*]∧∧∧∧∧∧∧

generation indicator   reference note number

1. TRISTRAM^1 DOE was born, probably in Wishful County, Eaststate,[10] about 1780 [11] and died in Sandy County, Eaststate, 25 Month 1844.[12] He married (1) in Sandy County about Month 1808, **ELIZABETH HOLDFAST**,[13] who was born 1784–1794[14] and died in 1823,[15] daughter of Thomas Holdfast and possibly Jane (____), Thomas's widow.[16] Tristram married (2) **LUCY GOODTITLE**, who died 7 Month 1825,[17] daughter of Harrison Goodtitle and his wife Flora (____). He married (3) in Sandy County 25 Month 1826, **JUDITH L. PLUTARCH**,[18] who was born [*And so forth*]∧∧∧∧∧∧∧∧∧∧

Tristram Doe's probable birthplace in Wishful County is distant from [*And so forth*]∧∧∧∧∧∧∧∧∧

Children of Tristram and Elizabeth (Holdfast) Doe, all born in Sandy County:[35]

2.   i.   ROBERT G.^{2} DOE, b. 15 Month 1809, m. MARTHA CHRYSTAL (MYANCSTOR) MARTYR.
     ii.   WILLIAM I. DOE, b. 30 Month 1810;[36] d. in Friendly County, Weststate, 2 Month 1883;[37] m. in Sandy County 1850–1851, LOUISA ABITLATE,[38] who was b. in [*And so forth*]∧∧∧∧∧∧∧∧∧

birth-order numbers

     iii.   JANE E. DOE, b. ca. 1818,[44] d. unmarried in Sandy County in 1877.[45] She was clearly the white female enumerated in Tristram's 1820–1840 census households,[46] [*And so forth*]∧∧∧∧∧∧∧

     iv.   ELIZABETH MARY DOE, b. 26 Month 1823;[49] [*And so forth*]∧∧∧∧∧∧∧∧∧∧∧∧∧∧∧∧∧∧∧

Child of Tristram and Judith (Plutarch) Doe, born in Sandy County:

v.   TRISTRAM A. P. DOE, b. ca. 1832;[56] d. [*And so forth*]∧∧∧∧∧∧∧∧∧∧∧∧∧∧∧∧∧∧∧∧∧∧∧∧∧

2. ROBERT G.[2] DOE (*Tristram[1]*) was born in Sandy County 15 Month 1809[61] and died at Light City,

genealogical summary — note cross references to other chapters

Farstate, 15 Month 1909, precisely one hundred years later.[62] He married at Light City 25 Month 1853, **MARTHA CHRYSTAL (MYANCESTOR) MARTYR**,[63] who was born in Mountain County about 1832–1833[64] and died at Light City 12 Month 1857,[65] widow of St. Stephen Martyr[66] and daughter of Michael[7] Myancestor and Priscilla[6] Parent. (See Myancestor and Parent Chapters.)

Like others in his family, Robert was a member of Crane Creek Baptist Church in Sandy County, but his behavior (alcohol related, apparently) led to his dismissal from fellowship in 1848.[67] He was still living with his stepmother Judith when the 1850 census [*And so forth*]∧∧∧∧∧∧∧∧∧∧∧∧∧∧∧∧∧∧∧∧

Children of Robert G. Doe and his wife Martha Chrystal (Myancestor) Martyr, born at Light City:

3.   i.   BENJAMIN R. G. DOE, b. 17 Month 1854, m. CYNTHEA J. DEN.

ii.   WALDO N. DOE, b. 25 Month 1856,[74] d. in Month 1866. He "fell from that old oak Willy's place,"

↑↓ identifying number

[*And so forth*] ∧∧

3. BENJAMIN R. G.[3] DOE (*Robert G.[2], Tristram[1]*) was born in Sandy County 17 Month 1854[76] and died in Untamed Territory 29 Month 1898.[77] He married in Friendly County, Weststate, 30 Month 1875, **CYNTHEA J. DEN**,[78] who was born in Friendly County, 19 Month 1860 and died at Smalltown, Weststate, as Cynthea D. Lucky, 22 Month 1919,[79] daughter of Jackson B. W. and Roma Ann C. (____) Den.[80]

[*And so forth—Benjamin's life story, followed by Cynthea's*]∧∧∧∧∧∧∧∧∧Nuhusband, Smalltown's only barber, newly arrived from Germany.[86] They married on 21 Month 1899,[87] some five months after the traumatic events in Roughton. By 1910, Cynthea and George were parents of two children,[88] whose stories are intertwined with those of their Doe half-siblings:

in this format, stepchildren are in text, not in child-list

a)   *Clarissa L. Nuhusband*, who was born 19 Month 1900[89] (Cynthea's fortieth birthday) and married at Smalltown on 19 Month 1923, Douglas D.[5] Gracious, son of Dennis Gracious and Goodness[4] Doe (*Tristram Plutarch[3], William I.[2], Tristram[1]*).[90]

b)   *George Benjamin Nuhusband*, who was born in Month 1902.[91] George wrote *Bloody Ben* (New City: Scandal Press, 1939), a highly fictionalized [*And so forth*] ∧∧∧∧∧∧∧∧

Children of Benjamin R. G. and Cynthea (Den) Doe, all born in Smalltown, presumably:[94]

child-list

i.   JACKSON D.[4] DOE, b. 1 Month 1877,[95] d. in Untamed Territory before 29 Month 1898.[96]

ii.   BENJAMIN R. G. DOE, b. 2 Month 1880,[97] d. in Unnamed Territory before 29 Month 1898.

4.   iii.   WILLIAM I. DOE, b. 30 Month 1882, m. BARBARA DELILAH MYANCESTOR.

iv.   DAUGHTER (name unknown), b. 12 Month 1885,[98] d. in Unnamed Territory before 29 Month 1898.

4. WILLIAM I.[4] DOE (*Benjamin R. G.[3], Robert B.[2], Tristram[1]*) was born at Smalltown 30 Month 1882[99] and died at Smalltown 18 Month 1951.[100] At Smalltown on 18 Month 1906, he married **BARBARA DELILAH[10] MYANCESTOR**,[101] who was born in Mountain County, Essex, 15 Month 1886 and died at Smalltown 2 Month 1948,[102] daughter of Michael John[9] Myancestor and Wilhelmina J. Goodtitle.[103] (See Myancestor Chapter.)

[*And so forth—William's life story followed by Barbara's*] ∧∧∧∧∧∧∧∧∧∧∧∧∧∧∧∧∧∧∧∧∧∧∧∧∧∧∧∧∧

Children of William I. and Barbara Delilah (Myancestor) Doe:

i.   MICHAEL MYANCESTOR[5] DOE, b. at Smoothton 16 Month 1908;[110] d. [*And so forth*]∧∧∧∧∧∧∧∧∧∧

5.   ii.   BARNABY JACKSON DOE, b. at Smoothton 22 Month 1910, m. MARTHA JANE ROE.

∧∧∧∧∧∧∧∧∧[*And so forth—four more children*] ∧∧∧∧∧∧∧∧∧∧∧∧∧∧∧∧∧∧∧∧∧∧∧∧∧∧∧∧∧∧∧∧∧∧

5. BARNABY JACKSON[5] DOE (*William I.[4], Benjamin R. G.[3], Robert B.[2], Tristram[1]*) was born at Smoothton, Untamed Territory 22 Month 1910 [*And so forth—his full biography*]∧∧∧∧∧∧∧∧∧∧∧∧∧∧∧∧∧∧∧∧∧∧∧

The chapter ends. Barnaby is the "identified descendant" whose ancestry is the compilation's subject.

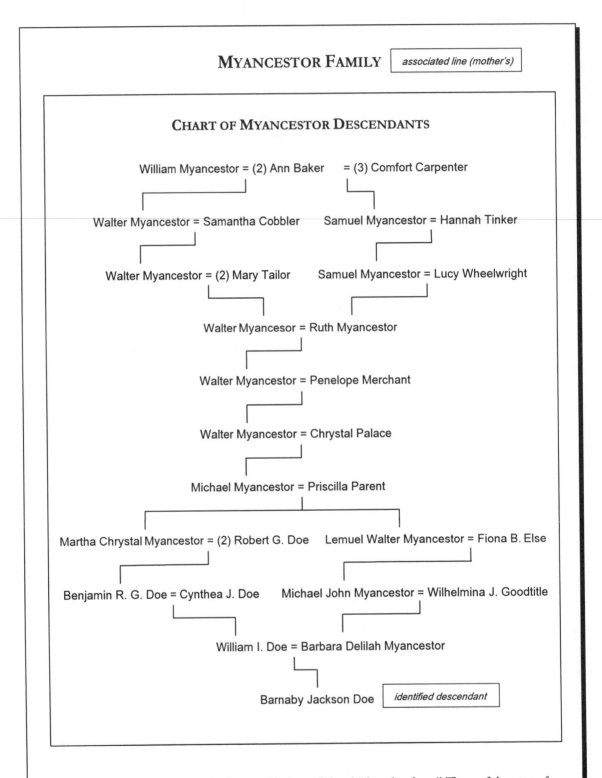

MYANCESTOR FAMILY   *associated line (mother's)*

CHART OF MYANCESTOR DESCENDANTS

William Myancestor = (2) Ann Baker   = (3) Comfort Carpenter

Walter Myancestor = Samantha Cobbler   Samuel Myancestor = Hannah Tinker

Walter Myancestor = (2) Mary Tailor   Samuel Myancestor = Lucy Wheelwright

Walter Myancesor = Ruth Myancestor

Walter Myancestor = Penelope Merchant

Walter Myancestor = Chrystal Palace

Michael Myancestor = Priscilla Parent

Martha Chrystal Myancestor = (2) Robert G. Doe   Lemuel Walter Myancestor = Fiona B. Else

Benjamin R. G. Doe = Cynthea J. Doe   Michael John Myancestor = Wilhelmina J. Goodtitle

William I. Doe = Barbara Delilah Myancestor

Barnaby Jackson Doe   *identified descendant*

The Myancestor family in America began with the traditional "three brothers." Three of the sons of Walter[A] Myancestor did, in fact, come to the colonies, although not together. The first was Charles, who arrived on the *Sweet Georgia Brown* in 1634;[1] the next to immigrate was Charles's older brother, William on the *Darling Clementine* in 1639;[2] and the third (and youngest) brother, Michael, crossed the

Atlantic at age sixteen in 1641 on the *Bobby McGee*.[3] The Myancestor brothers' uncle, also named William Myancestor, arrived in the colony about 1645.[4] All four Myancestors settled in Greenton, Oldplace.[5] Within a generation, however, they had begun to seek new [*And so forth*] ∧∧∧∧∧∧∧∧∧∧∧∧∧∧∧

1. MICHAEL[B] MYANCESTOR died before [*And so forth*] ∧∧∧∧∧∧∧∧∧∧∧∧∧∧∧∧∧∧∧∧∧∧∧∧∧∧∧∧∧

    The only known children of Michael Myancestor:

  2.   i.   WALTER[A] MYANCESTOR, b. in England in Month 1586, m. ANNE QUE.

        ii.   WILLIAM MYANCESTOR, b. in England ca. 1590; d. at Greenton [*And so forth*] ∧∧∧∧∧∧∧∧∧∧∧∧∧

2. WALTER[A] MYANCESTOR (*Michael[B]*) was born at Tree-on-Bank, Shandashire, England, in Month 1586[10] and died at Folkridge, Shandashire, 18 Month 1640.[11] He married [*And so forth*] ∧∧∧∧∧∧∧∧∧

3. WILLIAM[1] MYANCESTOR, (*Walter[A], Michael[B]*) was born at Folkridge, Shandashire, 29 Month 1608[16]

genealogical summary	and died at Greenton 17 Month 1648.[17] He married (1) at Folkridge 6 Month 1630, **MARY BUTCHER,**[18] who died at Folkridge; and (2) in England on 4 Month 1636, **ANN BAKER,** daughter of Joseph and Purity (____) Baker.[19] Ann died at sea in 1639

on the *Darling Clementine*; and William married (3) aboard ship, **COMFORT CARPENTER,**[20] who was born in England about 1616[21] and died at Blueton, Nextplace, 12 Month 1707,[22] daughter of Thomas and Charity (Cooper) Carpenter.[23]

	Before leaving his birthplace for the colonies, William Doe had been apprenticed (at age twelve)
life story	to James Fen to learn the art of blacksmithing.[24] Mary Butcher, James's niece [*And so*
	forth] ∧∧∧

    Children of William Myancestor by his first wife, Mary Butcher, all born in England:

child-list	i.	WALTER[2] MYANCESTOR, b. ca. 1631, d. at sea 1639.[36]
	ii.	CHARLES MYANCESTOR, b. ca. 1633; d. at Greenton, Oldplace, 27 Month 1671;[37] m. at Greenton, 18 Month 1661, PURITY INNKEEPER,[38] who was b. at Greenton, [*And so forth*]∧∧∧∧∧∧∧∧∧

        iii.   MARY MYANCESTOR, b. at Folkridge 6 Month 1635;[41] m. (1) at Greenton 8 Month 1631, JOHN[3] TAILOR. (See Tailor Chapter.) Mary m. (2) at Greenton 26 Month 1657, as his second wife, CALEB FARMER,[42] who was b. at Pinkton, Oldplace, 6 Month 1641 and d. at Pinkton, 5 Month 1711, son of Dudley Farmer and (____).[43] Caleb's first wife [*And so forth*]∧∧∧∧∧∧∧∧∧∧∧∧∧∧∧

cross-reference to spouse's surname chapter

    The only child of William and Ann (Baker) Myancestor, born at sea:

  4.   iv.   WALTER MYANCESTOR (second of the name), b. 12 Month 1639, m. SARAH COBBLER

    Children of William and Comfort (Carpenter) Myancestor, born at Greenton:

        v.   ANN BAKER MYANCESTOR, b. in 1642; d. at Blueton, Nextplace, in 1704;[47] m. at Greenton 3 Month 1663, JOSHUA[2] FISHERMAN,[48] who was b. at Blueton 5 Month 1635, son of Joshua[1] Fisherman and his third wife, Elizabeth Fortuneteller.[49] Ann and Joshua lived with his parents in Blueton until the elder Joshua, by then a widower, died in 1678.[50] (Joshua Jr.'s mother, Jerusha, née Jump, had died 17 Month 1674.[51]) The Fisherman heirs sold their parents' house and town lot on 16 Month 1678[52] and Joshua moved with his two youngest brothers, Jason and Joseph, to Blueton, where the three Fishermans [*And so forth*]∧∧∧∧∧∧∧

Walter & Samuel both in the direct line; both have identifying numbers

  5.   vi.   SAMUEL MYANCESTOR, b. 1 Month 1647, m. HANNAH TINKER.

4. WALTER[2] MYANCESTOR (*William[1], Walter[A], Michael[B]*) was born in England 12 Month 1642[59] and died at Blueton, Nextplace, 24 Month 1701.[60] He married 25 Month 1685, at Greenton,[61] **SARAH COBBLER**[62]), who was born about 1657,[63] and died after 25 Month 1690, probably at Blueton.[64]

    Walter and Sarah were active participants in the religious and political life of both Greenton and Blueton. Walter, a blacksmith like his father, was an elder [*And so forth*] ∧∧∧∧∧∧∧∧∧∧∧∧∧∧∧∧∧∧∧∧

    Children of Walter and Sarah (Cobbler) Myancestor:

        i.   WILLIAM[3] MYANCESTOR, b. [*And so forth*]∧∧∧∧∧∧∧∧∧∧∧∧∧∧∧∧∧∧∧∧∧∧∧∧∧∧∧∧∧

        ii.   CHARITY MYANCESTOR, b. [*And so forth*]∧∧∧∧∧∧∧∧∧∧∧∧∧∧∧∧∧∧∧∧∧∧∧∧∧∧∧∧∧∧∧

  6.   iii.   WALTER MYANCESTOR, b. at Blueton 25 Month 1690, m. (1) LUCINDA POTTER, m. (2) MARY TAILOR.

5. SAMUEL² MYANCESTOR (*William¹, Walter^A, Michael^B*) was born at Greenton 1 Month 1647; died there 5 Month 1682;[80] and married at Greenton 12 Month 1669, **HANNAH² TINKER**.[81] Hannah was born at Greenton 18 Month 1650 and died as Hannah Soldier at Beigeton, Oldplace, 19 Month 1718.[82]

Although Samuel left numerous records of his presence in Greenton, all indicate a man of moderate means and regular habits. He paid his taxes on time and in full[83] and his debts when they came due;[84] he owned a farm of modest acreage and productivity on Fresh Spring;[85] and he regularly attended the Greenton church, although he never became a full member.[86] When called to court he appeared,[87] and when called to militia duty he served.[88] He apparently got along well with his neighbors—the only time he was the subject of a court case, the legal location of a boundary line, rather than a quarrel over territory, appears to have been at issue.[89]

Hannah was a midwife "of good repute," called in 1671 to serve on a three-member "women's jury" to determine the approximate date of an illegitimate child's conception.[90] She married twice more after Samuel's death: first on 19 Month 1683 to William Mean, an elderly (for the period) childless widower[91] who lived nearby on Fresh Spring.[92] By him she had one child, William Mean Jr., born 10 Month 1686.[93] William Sr. died 21 Month 1688,[94] testate, leaving his entire estate to "my nephew Matthew Soldier of Beigeton" in trust for young William, with the provision that Hannah could remain on the farm for her lifetime or widowhood.[95] Hannah, however, remarried the following year, on 5 Month 1689.[96] Her third husband was the trustee, Matthew Soldier, and by him she also had one child, Major Soldier, born about 1690–1691.[97] Matthew moved the family to Beigeton,[98] apparently leasing out the farm during young William's minority. (William Mean "of Beigeton" sold it in 1708[99]). In her will, dated 12 Month 1718, Hannah mentioned by name each of her Myancestor, Mean, and Soldier children and four Soldier step-children, calling each "beloved" and offering them individualized, rather stern advice about their relationship with "our almighty Father."[100]

Children of Samuel and Hannah (Tinker) Myancestor, all of whom were born at Greenton:

7.   i.   SAMUEL³ MYANCESTOR, b. 9 Month 1670, m. LUCY WHEELWRIGHT.

       ii.   WILLIAM MYANCESTOR, b. at Greenton 4 Month 1672;[101] d. [*And so forth—including the rest of the children*] ∧∧

6. WALTER³ MYANCESTOR (*Walter², William¹, Walter^A, Michael^B*) was born at Blueton 25 Month 1690 and died there 4 Month 1753.[119] He married (1) at Blueton 9 Month 1704, **LUCINDA² POTTER**, who was born at Blueton 7 Month 1692 and died, also at Blueton, 16 Month 1707, daughter of Louis¹ and Thomasina (Merchant) Potter.[120] Walter married (2) at Blueton 9 Month 1709, **MARY⁴ TAILOR**,[121] who was born at Blueton 12 Month 1693 and died there 3 Month 1711, daughter of Deuteronomy³ and Sarah (Hatter) Tailor. (See Tailor Chapter.)

When Walter Myancestor married Lucinda Potter, [*And so forth*] ∧∧∧∧∧∧∧∧∧∧∧∧∧∧∧∧∧∧∧∧∧∧

Children of Walter and Lucinda (Potter) Myancestor, all born at Greenton:

       i.   MICHAEL⁴ MYANCESTOR, b. 2 Month 1706;[132] d. [*And so forth*] ∧∧∧∧∧∧∧∧∧∧∧∧∧∧∧∧∧∧∧∧∧

       ii.   WILLIAM MYANCESTOR, b. 5 Month 1707;[136] d. at [*And so forth*]∧∧∧∧∧∧∧∧∧∧∧∧∧∧∧∧∧∧∧∧∧

The child of Walter Myancestor and his second wife Mary Tailor:

8.   iii.   WALTER MYANCESTOR, b. at Blueton 17 Month 1710, m. RUTH⁴ MYANCESTOR (see below).

7. SAMUEL³ MYANCESTOR (*Samuel², William¹, Walter^A, Michael^B*) was born at Greenton 9 Month 1670;[143] and died at Wellton, Northplace, 17 Month 1711.[144] He married at Wellton 11 Month 1693, **LUCY WHEELWRIGHT**, who was born 3 Month 1677, daughter of John² Wheelwright (*John¹*) and Samantha (___),[145] and died as Lucy Shoemaker at Illton, Northplace, 24 Month 1750.[146]

On 9 Month 1685, when Samuel was fifteen, his first stepfather William Mean, apprenticed him to Charles Wheelwright, a shipbuilder in Wellton.[147] Apparently unhappy with the prospect of the next six years of servitude, the youngster immediately "ran away home,"[148] obviously misjudging the warmth of his welcome. William and Hannah promptly returned Samuel to his master, but despite their plea for mitigation, two years were added to the apprentice's indenture.[149] In 1693, finally free to marry,[150] Samuel wed Charles's only child, Lucy, two days after reaching his twenty-third birthday. He remained his father-in-law's employee until Charles's death in [*And so forth*] ∧∧∧∧∧∧∧∧∧∧∧∧∧∧

Children of Samuel and Lucy (Wheelwright) Myancestor, their births recorded at Wellton:

    i.   CHARLES[4] MYANCESTOR, b. 9 Month 1699,[162] d. on the Wellton road farm 15 Month 1761,[163] m.
         (1) at Wellton 18 Month 1720 JANE (_____), who [*And so forth*] ∧∧∧∧∧∧∧∧∧∧∧∧∧∧∧∧∧
    ii. HANNAH MYANCESTOR, b. 7 Month 1700,[170] d. unmarried at [*And so forth*] ∧∧∧∧∧∧∧∧∧∧∧∧∧
    iii. LUCY MYANCESTOR, b. 19 Month 1702;[179] [*And so forth*] ∧∧∧∧∧∧∧∧∧∧∧∧∧∧∧∧∧∧∧∧
    iv. WILLIAM MYANCESTOR, b. 6 Month 1705;[182] d. [*And so forth*]∧∧∧∧∧∧∧∧∧∧∧∧∧∧∧∧∧∧
    v.   RUTH MYANCESTOR, b. 22 Month 1707, m. WALTER[4] MYANCESTOR (see below).
    vi. SAMUEL MYANCESTOR, b. 13 Month 1710;[189] d. at [*And so forth*] ∧∧∧∧∧∧∧∧∧∧∧∧∧∧∧∧∧∧

8. WALTER[4] MYANCESTOR (*Walter*[3, 2], *William*[1], *Walter*[A], *Michael*[B]) was born at Blueton 17 Month
1710; died at Blackton, Nextplace, 4 Month 1751;[202] and married at Illton, Northplace, 14 Month
1733, **RUTH[4] MYANCESTOR** (*Samuel*[3], *Walter*[2], *William*[1]), who was born near Wellton 22 Month 1707
and died at Blackton 16 Month 1739.[203]

  [*And so forth—life story*]∧∧

  Children of Walter and Ruth (Myancestor) Myancestor:

    i.   SAMANTHA[5] MYANCESTOR, b. at Illton 18 Month 1735;[230] d. [*And so forth*]∧∧∧∧∧∧∧∧∧∧∧∧∧∧∧
9. ii.   WALTER MYANCESTOR, b. at Illton 6 Month 1737, m. JANE (_____) SAILMAKER.
    iii. MICHAEL MYANCESTOR, b. at Blackton 15 Month 1740;[238] [*And so forth*]∧∧∧∧∧∧∧∧∧∧∧∧∧∧∧

  The child of Walter Myancestor and second wife [*And so forth*]∧∧∧∧∧∧∧∧∧∧∧∧∧∧∧∧∧∧∧∧∧

9. WALTER[5] MYANCESTOR (*Walter*[4, 3, 2], *William*[1], *Walter*[A], *Michael*[B]) was born at Blackton about
1737[251] and died, probably at sea, between 22 Month 1683 and 19 Month 1685.[252] Walter married
(1) at Blueton 18 Month 1758, **JANE (_____) SAILMAKER**, who was born [*And so forth*] ∧∧∧∧∧∧∧∧∧

  Children of Walter Myancestor and his first wife Jane (_____) [*And so forth—three children*]∧∧∧∧∧∧

  Children of Walter and second wife Penelope (Merchant) Myancestor:

10. iv.   WALTER[6] MYANCESTOR, b. at Blueton 9 Month 1762, m. CHRYSTAL PALACE.

    ∧∧∧∧∧∧∧∧∧∧∧∧∧∧∧∧[*And so forth, ten more children*] ∧∧∧∧∧∧∧∧∧∧∧∧∧∧∧∧∧∧∧∧∧∧∧∧∧

10. WALTER[6] MYANCESTOR, (*Walter*[5, 4, 3, 2], *William*[1], *Walter*[A], *Michael*[B]) was born at Blueton 9 Month
1762[282] and died at Brownton, Thirdplace, 17 Month 1821.[283] He married at Pinkton, Oldplace, 26
Month 1781,[284] **CHRYSTAL[8] PALACE**, who was born, probably at Pinkton, about 1762[285] and died at
Brownton 20 Month 1801,[286] daughter of John Palace and his first wife Phillipa[7] Tailor, daughter of
Francis[6] Tailor (*Thomas*[5, 4], *Deuteronomy*[3, 2], *John*[1]). (See Tailor Chapter.)

  Walter and Chrystal lived [*And so forth*]∧∧∧∧∧∧∧∧∧∧∧∧∧∧∧∧∧∧∧∧∧∧∧∧∧∧∧∧∧∧∧∧∧∧∧∧∧

  Children of Walter Myancestor and wife Chrystal Palace, all of whom were born in Brownton:

    i.   WILLIAM[7] MYANCESTOR, b. 22 Month 1783;[297] d. [*And so forth*]∧∧∧∧∧∧∧∧∧∧∧∧∧∧∧∧∧∧∧∧
    ii.   CHRYSTAL MYANCESTOR, b. 4 Month 1785;[311] d. [*And so forth*]∧∧∧∧∧∧∧∧∧∧∧∧∧∧∧∧∧∧∧∧
    iii–vi. *four more children*
11. vii. MICHAEL MYANCESTOR, b. 17 Month 1798, m. PRISCILLA PARENT.

∧∧∧∧∧∧∧∧∧∧ [*And so forth*]∧∧∧

The Myancestor Chapter continues through the discussion of Michael[7] Myancestor and Priscilla[6]
Parent and both their children, Martha Chrystal[8] Myancestor (who married Robert G. Doe) and
Lemuel Walter[8] Myancestor (who married Fiona B. Else). It ends with the marriage of Martha
Chrystal's grandson William I. Doe to Lemuel Walter's granddaughter, Barbara Delilah[9]
Myancestor in 1906. (Barbara Delilah's offspring are traced forward in the Doe Chapter, the com-
pilation's primary line.)

PARENT FAMILY | associated line |

CHART OF PARENT DESCENDANTS

William Parent = Eudora O'Roe

Benjamin Parent = (2) Mary (_____)

Benjamin W. Parent = Milly Bridge

Henry Parent = Priscilla (_____)

Lemuel Parent = Caroline Neighbor

Priscilla Parent = Michael Myancestor

For more than two hundred years, the Parents resided within fifty-miles of each other in the foothills and mountains of western Essex.[1] They lived there during the French and Indian War, the Revolutionary War, and the Civil War. Although the majority were [*And so forth*]^^^^^^^^^^^^^^^^^^^^^

1. WILLIAM[1] PARENT was born, most probably in England, about 1612[19] and died in Early County, Essex, between 8 Month 1687 and 7 Month 1689.[20] He married, before 18 Month 1661, **EUDORA O'ROE**, daughter of Dugald O'Roe.[21] Eudora's birth date and place is not known, but she died before 7 Month 1691.[22]

William Parent was long believed to have been the earliest permanent settler in western Essex,[23] although recent scholarship indicates that he was preceded by the First-Folk party, who had purchased land from the Em Indians in 1639.[24] William was, however, the first European to file for grant of land from the Crown. [*And so forth*]^^^

The only known child of William and Eudora (O'Roe) Parent:[32]

1.   BENJAMIN[2] PARENT, b., probably in Early County, ca. 1662–1668, m. (1) JUDITH (_____), m. (2) MARY (_____)

| if only one child, no birth-order number is assigned |

2. BENJAMIN[2] PARENT (*William[1]*) was born, probably in Early County,[33] about 1662–1668[34] and died in Early between 26 Month 1719 and 27 Month 1719.[35] He married (1) probably in Early County before 27 Month 1684, **JUDITH _____**.[36] After Judith's death 1715–1719,[37] Benjamin married (2) in Early before Month 1719, **MARY (_____) CONTRARY**, widow of Leonard Contrary.[38] Mary was born before about 1669[39] and died in Early between 27 Month 1741 and the spring of 1742.[40]

Benjamin Parent, as his father's "only son and heir at law," automatically inherited all of William's land in Essex, which included extensive acreage in Early and newly formed Mountain County.[41] He was well educated, and wrote an elegant script that [*And so forth*] ∧∧∧∧∧∧∧∧∧∧∧∧∧∧∧∧∧∧∧∧∧∧∧∧∧∧∧∧∧∧

Children of Benjamin Parent and his first wife, Judith (_____),[48] probably born in Early:[49]

    i.   JUDITH[3] PARENT, b. 27 Month 1684,[50] d. [*And so forth—rest of genealogical summary and life story*] ∧∧∧∧

    ii.   MARY PARENT, b. ca. 1685–1687,[56] d. or m., probably in Early County, after Month 1720 when listed as "Parent" in her stepmother's petition against probate of Benjamin's will.[57]

    ∧∧∧∧∧∧∧∧∧∧∧∧∧∧∧∧∧[*And so forth—ten more daughters*]∧∧∧∧∧∧∧∧∧∧∧∧∧∧∧∧∧∧∧∧∧∧∧∧∧∧

The posthumous (and only [77]) child of Benjamin Parent by second wife, Mary (_____) Contrary:

3.   xiii.   BENJAMIN W. PARENT, b. in Mountain County 27 Month 1719, m. MILLY BRIDGE.

3. BENJAMIN W.[3] PARENT (*Benjamin*[2], *William*[1]) was born in Mountain County[78] 27 Month 1719[79] and died in Ridge County between signing his will on 1 Month 1772 and its probate on 10 Month 1773.[80] He married in Ridge County about 1740–1741,[81] **MILLY[6] BRIDGE**, daughter of Tole[5] Bridge (*Tole*[4, 3], *William*[2, 1]) and Piety[3] Badtitle (*John*[2], *Henry*[1]).[82] (See Bridge and Badtitle Chapters.)

Benjamin W. inherited half of his father's remaining five-hundred acres under the terms of an agreement reached in 1720 between his mother and representatives of his twelve half-sisters.[83] By grant and purchase, he managed to build an estate that equalled his father's[84]—but [*And so forth*] ∧∧∧∧

Children of Benjamin W. and Milly (Bridge) Parent:

4.   i.   HENRY[4] PARENT, b. in Ridge County 1742–1743, m. PRISCILLA (_____).

    ii.   THOMAS PARENT, b., probably in Ridge County,[91] ca. 1744;[92] d. without issue in River County between signing his will on 11 Month 1809 and its probate on the 31st.[93] [*And so forth*]∧∧∧

    iii.   MILLICENT PARENT, b., possibly in River County,[99] ca. 1746;[100] d. in Ridge County 25 Month 1768.[101] Did not marry.

    iv.   LEMUEL PARENT "SR.," b., probably in Ridge County,[102] 14 Month 1748;[103] d. in Mountain County 17 Month 1810;[104] m. in Ridge County [*And so forth*] ∧∧∧∧∧∧∧∧∧∧∧∧∧∧∧∧∧∧

    v.   MARY PARENT, b. in Ridge or River County[107] 14 Month 1750; d. in Peak City, Mountain County 14 Month 1833;[108] m. before 1 Month 1772, WETHER VANE.[109] Wether, a captain in the Mountain County militia in 1780, was killed in a skirmish with British troops in 1781[110] leaving Mary a wealthy widow with four young children.[111] Contrary to normal practice of the place and period (and very probably her neighbors' expectations), Mary did not remarry. She moved into Peak City and purchased the Peregrine Tavern,[112] which became a fashionable inn where legislators stayed during the years when Peak City was the state capital (1789–1799).[113] In 1815, she relinquished active management of the tavern to son-in-law Pitch Black.[114] Mary survived her husband by more than fifty years and died "at an advanced age, beloved by all."[114] Children, surname *Vane*: 1. *Wether*, b. in Mountain County ca. 1772, d. (unmarried) in battle at Fourthville 14 Month 1812; 2. *Lemuel*, b. [*And so forth*]∧∧∧∧∧∧∧∧∧

    vi.   BENJAMIN PARENT, b. 1755–1756; d. unmarried in an unspecified "tragic accident," presumably in Ridge County, on 23 Month 1774.[119]

4. HENRY[4] PARENT (*Benjamin W.*[3], *Benjamin*[2], *William*[1]) was born in Ridge County[120] 1742–1743[121] and died in Mountain County between writing his will on 10 Month 1811 and its probate on 25 Month 1811.[122] He married, probably in Ridge County, between 18 Month 1768 and 15 Month 1769,[123] **PRISCILLA** _____ (possibly Neighbor[124]) who died between 25 Month 1811 and 22 Month 1812.[125]

Henry and Priscilla lived on a 250-acre Crooked Creek tract later willed him by his father.[126] He also inherited 117 acres on Canoe Creek from his brother Thomas,[127] and by purchase or grant acquired additional tracts in Mountain and Ridge counties.[128] Henry was not a land speculator, however. He seems to have been more of a land investor—aside from one sale (to Waldo Neighbor),[129] Henry followed his father's example, giving land to his sons as they [*And so forth*] ∧∧∧∧∧∧∧∧∧∧∧∧∧

Priscilla Parent, like most women of her era, is virtually invisible in the records. She was literate, however, and signed her name to Henry's 1769 sale to Waldo Neighbor, his 1805 gift to their grandson Thomas Parent, and the 1811 inventory of Henry's estate.[136]

Children of Henry and Priscilla (_____) Parent:

      i.   BENJAMIN[5] PARENT, b., probably in Ridge County, 12 Month 1770;[137] d. in Western County, Plains State, 5 Month 1851;[138] m. [*And so forth*]ᴧᴧᴧᴧᴧᴧᴧᴧᴧᴧᴧᴧᴧᴧᴧᴧᴧᴧᴧᴧᴧᴧᴧᴧᴧᴧᴧᴧᴧᴧ

      ii.   WILLIAM PARENT, b., probably in Ridge County, ca. 1773;[145] d. [*And so forth*]ᴧᴧᴧᴧᴧᴧᴧᴧᴧᴧᴧ

5.   iii. LEMUEL PARENT "JR.," b. in Ridge County 14 Month 1775, m. CAROLINE NEIGHBOR.

     iv. JOSEPHINE PARENT, b. in Ridge County ca. 1776–1777;[151] d. in Open County, Otherplace, 20 Month 1849;[152] m. by Ridge County bond dated 25 Month 1792, APPLEY MCINTOSH.[153] All of Josephine's eleven children were daughters—Appley, in fact, offered as his 1821 defense against a charge of counterfeiting that "even a man of wealth, which I am not, would be hard pressed to provide food for so many mouths and dowrys [*sic*] for so many [wedding] chests." Unfortunately, Appley's defense was ineffective and he was convicted.[154] Counterfeiting at that time was a capital offense and Appley was sentenced to be hanged; but he "pled his clergy"[155] and was allowed to depart the colony after forfeiting all his property to the state.[156] By 1824 he was in Open County where he purchased a small farm[157] (indicating, perhaps, that he had not forfeited quite *all* he owned). Josephine and the unmarried girls (the oldest and the five youngest) had joined him there by 1830,[158] and the couple remained in Open [*And so forth*]ᴧᴧ

      v.   THOMAS PARENT, b. in Ridge County ca. 1776-1779;[170] [*And so forth*] ᴧᴧᴧᴧᴧᴧᴧᴧᴧᴧᴧᴧᴧᴧᴧᴧᴧ

      v.   SERENITY PARENT, b. in Ridge County ca. 1777; [176] [*And so forth*]ᴧᴧᴧᴧᴧᴧᴧᴧᴧᴧᴧᴧᴧᴧᴧᴧᴧᴧᴧᴧ

     vi. HENRY PARENT, b. in Ridge County ca. 1780-1784;[179] [*And so forth*]ᴧᴧᴧᴧᴧᴧᴧᴧᴧᴧᴧᴧᴧᴧᴧᴧ

5. LEMUEL[5] PARENT "JR." (*Henry*[4], *Benjamin W.*[3], *Benjamin*[2], *William*[1]) was born in southern Ridge County[183] 14 Month 1775, [184] died in Mountain County 27 Month 1805, and was buried in the Peak City Cemetery nearby.[185] He married in Mountain County 22 Month 1796, **CAROLINE[7] NEIGHBOR**,[186] who was born in Essex (probably Ridge County[187]) about 1778[188] and died, probably between 1857 and 1859 in Mountain County. She was the youngest daughter of Waldo[6] Neighbor (*Waldo*[5], *James*[4, 3], *Gregory*[2], *Melchior*[1]) and his second wife Easter Bonnett. (See Neighbor Chapter.)

Lemuel Parent was noted in the public records as "Jr." (or a variant abbreviation) to distinguish him from his uncle Lemuel "Sr." The younger Lemuel grew up on his father's large farm in Mountain County—in fact, no evidence has been found to indicate that he ever left it.[189] He married the daughter of his father's next-door neighbor, and from all appearances, his children were born on the fifty-acre portion on Lazy Run that his father gave him just before or after the wedding.[190] Lemuel was too young for soldiering in the Revolution and died before the War of 1812, so military duties (or opportunities) were not available to draw him away from his birthplace. His adulthood was very brief—he came of age on 14 Month 1796 and died less than nine years later. Whatever he might have achieved in later life will never be known.

Caroline (Neighbor) Parent survived her husband by more than fifty years. She married, second, Benjamin Dogood in Mountain County on 18 Month 1806,[191] and by him had five more children: Benjamin, Stephanie, Laura May, Marcus Aurelius, and Philadelphia (a girl).[192] Although Caroline's father, Waldo Neighbor, managed the Lazy Run tract for Lemuel's minor children,[193] it is clear that Benjamin and Caroline and their growing family lived there until the youngest Parent child, Priscilla, married in 1823.[194] On 21 Month of that year, Benjamin bought a small farm in adjoining Ridge County,[195] where the Dogoods lived thereafter.[196] In his 1857 will, he gave the farm to Caroline "for her lifetime or until remarriage and then to my sons equally."[197] Because the Dogood boys sold the land in 1859,[198] it is assumed that Caroline had died in the interim. (There is no record of her marriage in or near Ridge and, since she was over eighty, it is unlikely that she remarried elsewhere.)

Children of Lemuel Parent Jr. and his wife Caroline Neighbor, all born in Mountain County:[199]

      i.   THOMAS[6] PARENT,[200] b. 1796–1800,[201] d. in Mountain County 1816–1819[202] without issue.[203]

      ii.   GREGORY PARENT,[204] b. ca. 1801,[205] d. after 1860.[206] He had only one known one child, an illegitimate son born in River County to Willow Wisp in Month 1821.[207]

     iii. PRISCILLA PARENT, b. 3 Month 1803, m. MICHAEL[7] MYANCESTOR (See Myancestor Chapter.)

The Parent Chapter ends with Priscilla. She married into the Myancestor line in 1823 and her descendants are followed forward in the Myancestor Chapter. The Neighbor Chapter traces the line of Priscilla's mother, Caroline, forward from the earliest ancestor in that line, Melchior[1] Neighbor.

Appendix G — Example Compiled Genealogies

A genealogy compilation[16] (as opposed to a chart or outline) is a comprehensive history of a specific ancestor's descendants for an identifiable number of generations. The two generally accepted "blueprints" for formatting compiled genealogies are the *NGSQ* System[17] and the *Register* System; both are explained and illustrated in this appendix. One's choice and use of either system, however, should adhere to the guidelines discussed in detail on page 65. In brief, they are: (*a*) study the explanations and examples given in this manual and in the Curran-Crane-Wray volume mentioned on page 18 (note 11), and use the compilations in scholarly journals and books as models; (*b*) choose one format and use it consistently; and (*c*) test-print often to ensure that consistency is, in fact, being maintained.

Overview

The biographies of people related to each other by blood, marriage, or legal action (adoption, for example) constitute the history of their family—but the family as a unit also played a role within the overall history and development of present-day society. The compilation, therefore, typically begins with an overview that places the generations in geographic, social, and economic context. It describes the family's prevailing characteristics and the historical influences it exerted and that were exerted upon it. It may also include a brief general discussion of research problems.

Biographies

The overview is followed by a biography of the compilation's progenitor—the person from whom the rest of the family descends—and each succeeding biography concentrates on one descendant. Personal biographies demonstrate the qualities described in Appendix E (pages 65–66) and are divided into the same three sections: genealogical summary, life story, and child-list:

- *Genealogical summary.* The biography's opening paragraph begins with its subject's full birth name—with nicknames (in quotation marks) and aliases or a.k.a. [also known as] name(s) but not married surnames. The subject's name is followed by his or her vital statistics. The spouse's full name

16. "Genealogy" in this sense applies to compilations based on research that began with one identified ancestor (or ancestral couple) and "descended," tracing all members of each succeeding generation. The ancestor may have been discovered during an "ascending" lineage study, or may have been chosen for another reason (the passenger on a particular ship, a signer of the Declaration of Independence, etc.).

17. This system was originally known as the "Modified Register," a title that is now seriously misleading. As an independent, amplified, and fully developed formatting method, it is best called by its own proper name.

at the time of the marriage (or the partner's name if the couple did not marry), and his or her vital statistics and parent's names complete the paragraph. Multiple unions are arranged in chronological order.

- *Life story.* Succeeding paragraphs discuss significant events in the subject's life, usually in approximate chronological order. If the biography's subject was prominent professionally, militarily, or socially, his or her achievements are often described first, followed by personal-life details. (Integrating the two may provide a more well-rounded view of the person but doing so can be confusing if not handled with skill.) Life stories cover, also, events in the spouses' or partners' lives, usually including later or earlier marriages and personal- or professional-life details.

- *Child-list.* At the end of each biography—following a preliminary sentence or sentence fragment that identifies their parents—the subject's biological children are listed in birth order, beginning with the oldest. If the subject of the sketch had children by more than one spouse or partner, each group of children is introduced by an appropriately worded sentence or sentence fragment.

    Following the subject's biological children, two additional groups are listed: *(a)* adopted children (mentioned in birth order or the order in which each entered the subject's nuclear family) and *(b)* stepchildren. Each group is preceded by an appropriate descriptive statement. EXAMPLES: Adopted child [children] of X and his wife Y; Stepchild [children] of X born of his wife Y by her first husband Z.

    Child-list biographies: Because a compiled genealogy follows all descendant lines, the biographies included within a child-list are limited to those for children who died without issue or whose descendants will not be traced forward for some significant reason.[18] For all others, full biographies are presented later in the compilation.

---

18. The significant reason for omitting later generations in a "single-surname" compilation derives from its purpose—to trace all descendants who carried the focus surname into more-recent generations. Thus, by definition, the offspring of married females might not be traced farther than the child-list. Note that such a study traces all the progenitor's surname-carrier descendants. It is distinct from the Multi-Surname System for compiled pedigrees (see pages 79–81), which traces only those in each of an identified person's direct ancestral lines.

    The significant reason for omitting later generations in an "all-descendants" compilation normally stems from insurmountable research difficulties (records that do not survive or are unavailable for examination, the person's migration to no discernible destination, insufficient identifying data to distinguish among a multitude of people with the same name, and so forth). Because, by definition, this kind of compilation is intended to include all the progenitor's descendants regardless of their surname, females as well as males are traced, and the reason for omitting a line is explained within the compilation.

Numbering System (a.k.a. Personal Identifiers)

Because the compilation includes several generations of people (many with the same names) each descendant is assigned a set of four "identifiers" to distinguish him or her irrevocably from all other family members: *(a)* an identifying number, *(b)* a birth-order number, *(c)* a generation indicator, and *(d)* a parenthetical lineage list.

- *Identifying Numbers.* The Arabic number "1" denotes the compilation's progenitor. Thereafter, the numbers are assigned in sequence throughout the compilation. Individual biographies are arranged by these numbers.

  In the *NGSQ* System, identifying numbers indicate the place of *each person* in the compilation. Consequently, each descendant is assigned a number, written near the left margin before his or her name in the parental child-list. If a person's biography is presented later in the compilation, a plus sign precedes the child-list number, which is then repeated at the beginning of his or her genealogical summary.

  In the *Register* System, identifying numbers indicate the position of *each biography* in the compilation. Consequently, only a child whose biography is presented later receives a number, placed near the left margin in the child-list and repeated at the beginning of the genealogical summary.

- *Birth-Order Numbers.* Lower-case Roman numerals are assigned to each of the offspring in a child-list. In the *Register* System, they begin with "i" for the person's first-born and continue in sequence to his or her last-born, regardless of by which spouse. In the *NGSQ* System, the oldest child *of each of the subject person's spouses* is "i." Because adoptees and stepchildren were not "born of" the biography's subject, they are not assigned birth-order numbers in either system.

- *Generation indicators.* Superscripted Arabic numbers or letters denote an individual's generation of descent from the progenitor. They attach to the end of the person's given name (or the last middle name or initial), and normally nothing—not even punctuation—comes between them. EXAMPLE: John Roe^3 Doe; Mary^3 "Polly" Doe.

  Assignment of generation indicators: By tradition, indicators are assigned as follows:

  (a) If the compilation begins with the immigrant ancestor (or a descendant of the immigrant), he or she is generation "1." Thereafter each succeeding generation is sequentially numbered. EXAMPLE: progenitor^1, all children^2, all grandchildren^3.

(b) If the compilation begins in the country of origin, the indicator "A" is used for the generation of the immigrant's parent. Thereafter, each *earlier* generation is sequentially lettered. EXAMPLE: immigrant's parent and his or her siblings[A], grandparent and siblings[B], great-grandparent and siblings[C].

The *NGSQ* System uses additional indicators for compilations that include multiple immigrants in different generations, or descendants of both immigrant and non-immigrant forebears.[19] The system is illustrated in the chart on page 101 and is described in detail in the Wray chapter of the previously cited Curran-Crane-Wray volume. The main points are these:

(*a*) One immigrant is chosen as the primary person around whom the numbering scheme centers. (In the chart, the primary immigrant's indicator is underlined.)

(*b*) The parent of that immigrant, and the parent's siblings, remain generation[A] All the siblings of grandparent[B] remain generation[B], and so on.[20]

(*c*) All children of each person in generation[A] are assigned lower-case letters, beginning with "a" and continuing in sequence within the country of origin.

(*d*) Each immigrant is also assigned the indicator "1"— regardless of which was the first to immigrate or the generation to which they belonged in the country of origin. Thus, the primary immigrant's generation indicator becomes, not "1" but "a-1"; an uncle who also immigrated is "B-1"; and a child of generation "c" who immigrated is "c-1."

(*e*) The generation indicators for each immigrant's descendants remain Arabic numbers.

Use of generation indicators in child lists: The name of the first-listed child includes the generation indicator for that group of children. It is "silent" in his or her siblings' names.

Adopted children who also descended from the compilation's progenitor take their indicator from the birth parent, not the adoptive parent.

19. This numbering pattern is also recommended to supplement the *Register* System for those who publish at its parent organization's Newbury Street Press—see Thomas Kozachek, *Guidelines for Authors of Compiled Genealogies* (Boston: Newbury Street Press, 1998), 8. The *Register* itself has taken no official stance on this method of designating collateral lines.

20. The generation indicators here are italicized to reflect typography used in the *NGSQ* System (see page 102).

The *NGSQ* System views stepchildren, and adopted children who did *not* descend from the progenitor, as originators of their own biological lines within the family being studied. Thus, within the focus family's compilation, they take an appropriate progenitor-indicator. EXAMPLE: The progenitor is Henry[1]. The adopted son of William[4], therefore, might be Joseph[1] if adopted from within the country, or Joseph[a-1] if adopted from outside it. William[4]'s stepdaughter is Penelope[1].

Use of generation indicators in biographical text: At the first appearance of the subject's birth name in the genealogical summary, his or her generation indicator is included within it. Indicators may be used, also, in life stories and explanatory footnotes or endnotes whenever needed for clarity (when discussing a same-name father and son, for example).

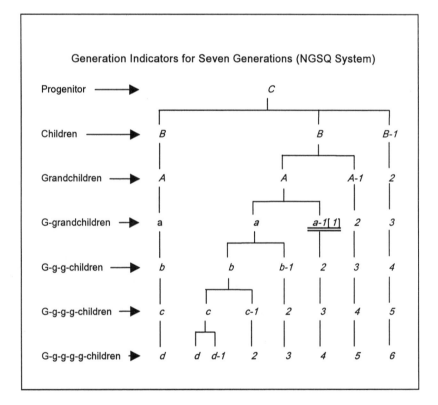

Generation Indicators for Seven Generations (NGSQ System)

- *Parenthetical lineage lists.* Each subject of a separate biography is identified further with a listing of his or her lineage back to the compilation's progenitor. The list, enclosed within parentheses, follows the subject's name at its first appearance in his or her genealogical summary. The subject's direct ancestors are listed in ascending order, and each name includes the ancestor's appropriate generation indicator. For males who continued use of the progenitor's surname, only their given and middle names or initials are listed. For females who married and for males who changed surnames (a name change, not merely a spelling variant), their full birth names are included. (For examples, see Typographic Style.)

Typographic Style

"Style" refers to the way information appears on the page: indentation, typeface, paragraphing, and data placement. There are marked distinctions between typographic styles used in the *NGSQ* and *Register* Systems.[21]

- *In general.* The *NGSQ* System conforms to *The Chicago Manual of Style* in abbreviating words and inclusive numbers and dates; and in sentence structure, capitalization, and punctuation. The *Register* System departs from the *Manual* in some cases: it does not abbreviate inclusive numbers and dates, for example, but does abbreviate "born," "died," "married," "buried," "baptized," "circa [Latin for 'about']," and similar often-repeated words in child-lists.

- *Personal identifiers*

  Birth-order numbers: In the *NGSQ* System, a subject's grandchildren are identified within a child-list biography by italicized parenthetical lower case letters. The *Register* System uses Arabic numbers followed by a period.

  Generation indicators: The *NGSQ* System italicizes generation indicators, and uses them at least twice in each biography: *(a)* within the subject's name at the beginning of his or her genealogical summary, and *(b)* within the subject's name in child-list introductory sentences. An indicator is also used within a child's name if his or her correct indicator is different from that of the first-listed child (as would be the case among a group of siblings, some of whom immigrated; or a child-list that included adoptees and/or stepchildren).

    EXAMPLE: Children of John^A Doe: i. Martha^a Doe, ii. William Doe, iii. Thomas Doe, iv. John^{a-1} Doe.

    EXAMPLE: Children of Samuel^3 Doe: i. Daniel^4 Doe, ii. Thomas Doe; Stepchild of Samuel^3 Doe: Jacob^1 Roe.

  Parenthetical lineage lists: The *NGSQ* System uses standard type for ancestors' names but italicizes generation indicators. The *Register* System italicizes the names but uses standard

---

21. The discussion here, and the examples in this manual, reflect the styles used by current editors of the *National Genealogical Society Quarterly* and the *New England Historical and Genealogical Register*, respectively.

type for indicators; and attaches that of a married woman to her birth surname, rather than to her given or middle name.

NGSQ EXAMPLE: Frederick^4 Fen (William^3, Mary Jane^2 Doe, John^1).

Register EXAMPLE: Frederick^4 Fen (*William*^{3}, *Mary Jane Doe*^{2}, *John*^{1}).

- *Biographies*

General remarks: The *Register* System places reference-note numbers within superscripted square brackets.

Genealogical summaries: The *NGSQ* System uses bold type to emphasize the first instance of the subject's and spouses' names, and indents the first line of summary and life-story paragraphs. The *Register* System uses large-and-small capitals, as well as bold type, for this kind of emphasis, and does not indent the first line of the summary paragraph. In summaries and child-lists, it gives the location in which a vital event occurred before its date.

Child-lists: The *NGSQ* System uses small capitals for children's names but does not similarly emphasize spouse names. Information supplied for a child whose full biography is presented later includes birth and death dates and places; and the dates, places, and spouse or partner names for each union. Sources are cited at that point, and short-form citations are used when the data are repeated in the later biography.

The *Register* System uses large-and-small capitals for children's names and emphasizes spouse names in the same manner. Information for a child whose full biography is presented later includes birthplace, date, and spouses' or partners' names. Sources are cited only in the full biography.

Both systems use parenthetical Arabic numbers to denote each union in a series. In addition, both systems normally place child-lists in type a point size or two smaller than that used in the body of the compilation.

A fictitious Doe family is the subject of both examples that follow. Citations included in the first example are also fictitious but reflect the kinds of records (and explanations) typical in family histories of all types. Readers are advised to examine both compilations as well as examples in Appendixes E and F—in some cases, the manner of treating particular out-of-the-ordinary situations is presented in only one of the compilations.

1. Compiled Genealogy: *NGSQ* System

compilation title

Tristram Doe of Sandy County, Eaststate
and His Descendants

compilation overview

Does of the generations identified to date were not "great men," socially, politically, militarily, or economically. Their achievements individually and as a group were unremarkable, but their story reflects the powerful forces that dramatically altered life in the United States. The life events of early generations echo those of their contemporaries: secession, Civil War, and Reconstruction. The biographies of Does who moved west to take advantage of Homestead Act opportunities reflect the chaotic, often violent, events that marked the last years of the American Frontier. In the early decades of the twentieth century, the lives of both eastern and western Does exemplified the decline of subsistence farming as a way of life and large-scale movement of families out of the country into towns and cities.

Although the Doe surname, a common one, did not cause unusual research difficulties, records of multiple individuals with the same name did have to be analyzed and attributed to the correct person. More-significant factors were challenges that genealogists often face: erroneous or inadequately documented compilations, silent individuals who left no record of their offspring, and incomplete public records (the absence of pre-1848 Sandy County courthouse documents, for instance). Despite these difficulties, however, the Doe family's story is clear.

| identifying number | generation indicator | ——— **First Generation** ——— | reference note number |

1. Tristram[1] **Doe** was born, most likely, in Wishful County, Eaststate, about 1780[1] and died in Sandy County on 25 Month 1844.[2] Wishful and Sandy are a considerable distance from each other, a circumstance that might give rise to doubt that the *same* Tristram lived in both jurisdictions. Evidence of one man, however, is clear. The two counties, for example, were linked by the Old Indian Path, the major migration route into western Eaststate in the 1750s and 1760s. Little attention has been paid in Eaststate histories to the role played by this route in post-Revolutionary commerce and travel, but the lives of Tristram and his two known siblings demonstrate that it continued to bring settlers to Sandy County at least into the 1840s:

- *Tristram Doe,* judging by the tax records, moved from Wishful County to Sandy about 1808, preceding his siblings by several decades. In Wishful, he was taxed from 1802 through 1807 on himself and one horse,[3] disappearing from the Wishful property lists thereafter. In 1809, however, he was one of two Tristram Does taxed in Sandy—as Tristram "Jr." he was listed for one poll and a horse,[4] the same assessment he had paid in Wishful the preceding six years. Both Tristrams, not distinguished by "Sr." or "Jr.," were enumerated in Sandy's 1810 census,[5] but the older man is clearly distinguished by his household statistics. Both men continued to be tax-listed through 1814, "Jr." consistently assessed for less property. The senior

reference notes

The following abbreviations are used in these notes:
ESL = Eaststate State Library, Capital City, Eaststate; FHL = Family History Library, Salt Lake City, Utah
Unless cited otherwise, National Archives and Records Service micropublications were used for census research.

1. Tristram Doe obituary, *Religious Gazette* [Eaststate's Baptist newspaper], 5 Month 1844, p. 2, col. 2 (ESL microfilm RGaz.1), states that Tristram died on the 25th "ult. [the previous month]" in the 65th year of his age (i.e., born about 1780). The 1880 census schedules for his surviving children (cited below) give Eaststate as their father's birthplace.
2. Ibid.
3. Tristram Doe entries, Wishful County Tax Books 1782–1822, River District, ESL microfilm "Wishful Taxes," reels 1, 2.
4. Tristram Doe Jr., entries, Sandy County Tax Books 1803–20, North District, Comptroller Records, ESL microfilm "CR.Taxes-San.2."
5. Tristram Doe households: 1810 U.S. census, Sandy County, pp. 909 and 911.

Tristram's land ("on Muddy Creek" according to the tax lists) was taken into Spring County at its formation in 1815[6]; and in 1816 and most years thereafter, the only Tristram Doe tax-listed in Sandy was the former "Jr."[7]

- *Watts Doe*, named as "my brother" in Tristram's 1843 will[8] (and born about 1776–78[9]), was enumerated in Sandy in 1850 and 1860;[10] but had paid taxes in Wishful County from 1800 through 1841.[11] He was head of census households in Wishful 1810–40.[12]

- *Jane (Doe) Strangename*, born about 1772[13] and called "Aunt" by Tristram's daughter, Janey,[14] married Peter Strangename in 1789[15] in Wishful and was baptized there in 1811.[16] After her husband's death in 1835,[17] Jane apparently moved with son Daniel's family to Sandy, where she was enumerated with them 1840–60.[18] Her 1864 obituary provides Jane's baptismal date and place and age at death ("in her ninety-second year").[19]

Unfortunately, an extensive search of the records of Wishful, Sandy, and their adjoining counties failed to identify conclusively a parent for this Tristram-Watts-Jane sibling group (although Robert Doe, a landless Sandy County taxpayer 1782–86, appears to be a likely candidate). The investigation, however, did identify three additional Doe families that included men named Tristram,[20] indicating, perhaps, that in some earlier generation all four groups stemmed from a common ancestor.

---

6. Tristram Doe entries, Spring County Tax Books 1812–42, Peak District, ESL microfilm "Spring Taxes," 1.

7. Tristram Doe entries, Sandy County Tax Books 1803–20 and 1821–46, North District, Comptroller Records, ESL microfilm "CR.Taxes-San.," 2–3.

8. "*Doe vs. Doe*, 1845," Eaststate Chancery Court Case Papers, 1789–1956, ESL. The file includes a copy of Tristram's will, submitted as evidence in a suit brought to compel division of his land. The courthouse original perished in an 1847 fire.

9. Watts Doe household, 1850 U.S. census, population schedule, Sandy County, p. 4, dwelling 38, family 39; and David K. Doe household, 1860 U.S. census, population schedule, Sandy County, p. 242, dwelling 441, family 445.

10. Ibid.

11. Watts Doe entries, Wishful County Tax Books, 1802–54, Comptroller Records, ESL microfilm "CR.Taxes-Wis.," 2–4.

12. Watts Doe households, U.S. censuses of Wishful County: 1810, p. 204; 1820, p. 115; 1830, p. 57; and 1840, p. 47. Watts's age brackets agree with his 1850 and 1860 census ages. Pre-1810 censuses for Eaststate do not survive.

13 See note 18 and the text at note 19.

14. Letter from Jane E. Doe of Sandy County to nephew Benjamin R. G. Doe of Goodland Valley, Weststate, dated "3 Mo." written in 1873. (Jane mentioned the "tragic drowning last Sunday" of William Friend, whose death was reported in the *Keesburg Weekly Reader*, 9 Month 1873). Photocopy of letter in possession of the author, received from James A. Mykin of Big City, Weststate, Benjamin's great-grandson. Microfilm of the *Keesburg Weekly Reader*, FHL microfilm no. 123,456,789.

15. Strangename entry, Wishful County Marriage Registers, vol. 1786–1850, 9, County Clerk's Office, Hope.

16. Mrs. Jane Strangename obituary, *Religious Gazette*, 12 Month 1864, p. 3, col. 3.

17. Peter Strangename will, Wishful County Will Book 4: 223, Judge of Probate's Office, Hope.

18. Daniel Strangename households: 1840 U.S. census, Sandy County, p. 571 (included a white female 60–70, presumably Jane); 1850 U.S. census, population schedule, Sandy County, p. 4, dwelling 39, family 40 (included Jane, aged seventy-seven); 1860 U.S. census, population schedule, Sandy County, p. 245, dwelling 450, family 451 (included Jane, aged ninety [*sic*]). Future researchers should note that "Strangename" is indexed as "Tsrangename," in *Quick Index, 1850: Eaststate* (City: Quick Publishers, 1978), 289; and is not indexed at all in *Quick Index, 1860: Eaststate* (City: Quick Publishers, 1981).

19. Mrs. Jane Strangename obituary, *Religious Gazette*, 12 Month 1864, p. 3, col. 3.

20. These three families were:

  (a) Descendants of William Doe of Wishful, who was born before 1753 and left a will, dated 11 Month 1823 and re-recorded 4 Month 1867 (Wishful County Will Book "Old Wills," 246). Analysis of tax records proves that he was the paternal grandfather of Tristram Doe of Wishful, born about 1806, died there in Month 1876 (Wishful County Will Book 1: 3).

  (b) The family of Philip Doe, whose estate was divided in Swampy County (which adjoins Wishful) in Month 1814 and whose heirs included a minor named Tristram (Swampy County Court Book 11–A: 118, 171). This Tristram paid taxes in Wishful County in 1823 and 1826–28, but not thereafter and was not enumerated as head of household in 1830. In 1840 he was listed in the town of Alexander, Swampy County (p. 203), and in 1850 in Hill County, Midwest State (p. 15, dwelling 222, family 224) he was forty-one, with wife Amy, both born in Eaststate. Tristram and Amy (Countrygirl) Doe had married in Wishful in 1821 (Wishful County Marriage Registers, vol. 1786–1850, 32).

  (c) The family of Gabriel Doe of Glen County, who was born 1750–55 and died after 1819. His son Tristram was the older man taxed in Sandy County 1804–15. That Tristram died in Spring County in 1830 (Spring County Will Book 18: 33) but had no son Tristram. The Eaststate Historical Society file, "Papers of George H. Candoo, CG," includes a great deal of information about Gabriel Doe and his descendants. See also I. M. Lucky, *Eaststate Genealogies* (1891; reprint, Well Known City: Genealogy Publishers, 1966), 533. Lucky quoted a letter from this Tristram's son, Thomas J. Doe of Anotherplace, stating that he had inherited an oil portrait of his paternal grandfather, Gabriel Doe "of Eaststate."

In about Month 1808, less than a year after his move to Sandy, Tristram married **Elizabeth Holdfast** of adjoining Glen County.[21] Born 1784–94,[22] she was the daughter of Thomas Holdfast[23] and possibly Jane [— ?—], Thomas's widow.[24] Elizabeth died in 1823 and Tristram married, almost immediately, **Lucy Goodtitle,** who died 7 Month 1825, survived by her husband "and grieving parents, Mr. and Mrs. Harrison Goodtitle."[25] Tristram then married **Judith L. Plutarch**, daughter of Arthur and Josephine Bono (Parte) Plutarch, his third (and last[26]) wife, on 25 Month 1826.[27] A well-documented genealogy of the Plutarch family details Judith's ancestry for six generations, recounting the tradition that Arthur was "the largest land- and slave-holder in Sandy County."[28] Although this may be an exaggeration, Arthur Plutarch clearly was a wealthy man and owned 2,200 acres in Sandy when he died.[29] Judith survived her husband and died 9 Month 1859 in Sandy County.[30]

Tristram's fortunes improved dramatically after his third marriage. His personal-property holdings had been meager since his first mention in the Wishful tax lists, but in 1827 he was assessed in Sandy for three slaves aged sixteen to fifty (Ben, Gincy, and Solomon) and two under-ten children (Little Ben and Venus) who remained in his tax household thereafter, along with Gincy's later children.[31] Tristram also acquired his first land during this period: in 1829 he began paying taxes on 110 acres adjoining B. Friend, fifteen miles northeast of the Sandy courthouse at Keesburg. By 1830 he had built a house on that tract (indicated by its increased value). In 1841, he acquired an additional 200 acres thirteen miles northeast of the courthouse; and the following year 239 more acres contiguous to the 110-acre tract.[32] What appears to have been the family's home place, the 110-acres, was probably Plutarch land. Tristram left it (and the bulk of his personal property) to Judith absolutely rather than "for life or widowhood," the usual wording in wills of the period. The form of Tristram's devise gave Judith the right to will the property away from their children if she chose, a very unusual provision.[33]

The Baptist church played an important role in Doe family life. Tristram's sister Jane was baptized by Rev. White Knight at Shiloh Church in Wishful;[34] their brother Watts had been a member of this church before his move to Sandy;[35] and Tristram had probably attended at Shiloh as well. (His obituary stated that he had been a Baptist since 1799,[36] roughly ten years before his move to Sandy). Apparently, Tristram affiliated with the Crane Creek Baptist Church in Sandy soon after his move—

---

21. Rev. John Preacher, "Day Book," unpaginated, 33d page, Fellow Papers, file P.C. 33, folder 2, Midwest State Historical Society, Plains City. The Doe entry is water damaged; its date is deduced from surrounding entries.
22. Tristram Doe's Sandy County censuses 1810, p. 911, and 1820, p. 228, show his "wife" as 16–26 and 26–45 respectively.
23. Thomas Holdfast estate division, 28 Month 1817, Glen County Will Book 19: 322. (ESL microfilm "Gle.Wills.1") identifies one of the heirs as "Tristram Doe in right of wife Elizabeth."
24. Ibid. Jane was allotted a third of Holdfast's personal property, the portion required by law to be set off for the widow.
25. Lucy Doe obituary, *Religious Gazette,* 10 Month 1825, p. 3, col. 4, reads in part "Departed this life, on Monday the 7th, in Sandy County, Mrs. Lucy Doe, wife of Tristram Doe, in the 25th year of her age . . . survived by . . . ." It includes information that she and Tristram had been married less than a year.
26. One Tristram Doe married Lilly White in Spring County on 3 Month 1829 (Spring County Marriage Registers, vol. 1815–50, 324). Lilly is identified as the fourth wife of this Tristram Doe in several publications, e.g., J. W. Doe, *Kith and Kin* (n.p.: Doe, 1981), 89, which cites National Society, Daughters of the American Revolution application number 11111; also, Martha Goodtry, "Some Eaststate Marriages," *Glen Genealogical Journal* 12 (Month 1983), 41; and www.Whitegen.gen. Lilly's husband, however, was a different Tristram. He signed an 1838 land sale with an X and wife Lilly released her dower right in the tract (Spring County Deed Book 4: 101). Tristram[1] signed documents with his name and his 1838 wife was Judith Plutarch. We suspect, but have been unable to prove, that Lilly's husband was a son of Watts Doe.
27. "Marriage Notice," *Keesburg Minerva,* 31 Month 1825, p. 4, col. 1 (FHL microfilm no. 123,885,409): "Married on the 25th inst. [the present month] at her father's seat in Sandy County, Miss Judith L. Plutarch to Mr. Tristram Doe."
28. I. K. Researcher, *The Plutarch's Lives* (Well Known City: Genealogy Publications, 1987).
29. Plutarch entries, Sandy County Tax Books, 1820–46, North District, Comptroller Records.
30. Judith Doe entry, 1850 U.S. census, mortality schedule, Sandy County, p. 23, Eaststate Genealogical Society microfilm Mortality/1850/Sandy. Oddly, Judith, at that time sixty-eight, is said to have died of "old age."
31. Tristram Doe entries, Sandy County Tax Books, 1820–46, North District, Comptroller Records.
32. Ibid. Sandy County deeds do not survive. The state land grants were searched, and none was issued to this Tristram Doe.
33. "Doe *vs.* Doe," Eaststate Chancery Court Case Papers (evidence copy of Tristram Doe's will).
34. Mrs. Jane Strangename obituary, *Religious Gazette,* 12 Month 1864, p. 3, col. 3.
35. Watts Doe entry, 1830–53 Minute Book, Crane Creek Church, Locksburg, Eaststate, unpaginated, 3d page headed 1849: Month, "Mr. Watts Doe being wonse a member of Shiloh Ch Wishful Cty received [rest of page torn]." This and other volumes in the minute-book series were examined at the Baptist Collection, Southland University, Southland.
36. Watts Doe obituary, *Religious Gazette,* 5 Month 1844, p. 2, col. 2.

Rev. John Preacher, who married Tristram to Elizabeth in 1808, was the minister for Crane Creek, which at that time served both Sandy and Glen counties.[37] Tristram is listed in records of the Goshen Baptist Association as a messenger from Crane Creek 1813–22.[38] In Month 1831, the business meeting convened at his house; in Month 1835, he conducted the service when the minister was sick; and, in the minister's absence in Month 1840 and Month 1843, he acted as moderator.[39]

Tristram's social life most probably revolved around the nearby hamlet of Locksburg, then located about seventeen miles northeast of the Sandy courthouse at Keesburg, along the main road to Dale. Virtually surrounded now by suburbs of both cities, Locksburg has managed, nevertheless, to maintain its identity as an independent incorporated village and to retain its antebellum aura. One can easily picture Tristram and his family in these environs.

Tristram[/] and Elizabeth (Holdfast) Doe were parents of the following four children, all of whom were born in Sandy County:

<table>
<tr><td>child-list</td><td>+ 2</td><td>i.</td><td>ROBERT G.[2] DOE, born 15 Month 1809,[40] died 15 Month 1909 at Light City, Farstate.[41] He married 25 Month 1853, at Light City, Martha Chrystal (Myancestor) Martyr.[42]</td></tr>
<tr><td></td><td>+ 3</td><td>ii.</td><td>WILLIAM I. DOE, born 30 Month 1810, died 2 Month 1883 in Friendly County, Weststate.[43] He married 1850–51, in Sandy County, Louisa Abitlate.[44]</td></tr>
<tr><td>identifying numbers; "+" signifies full biography later</td><td>4</td><td>iii.</td><td>JANE E. DOE, born about 1818;[45] died in Sandy County, unmarried, in 1877.[46] She was clearly the white female enumerated in Tristram's 1820–40 census households[47] and in 1850 she was still living within the Doe family (by then headed by her step-mother Judith). As "Jane E." she was listed in the membership rolls of Crane Creek Church,[48] and as "Aunt Janey" she conducted voluminous correspondence with her Weststate nephews. Her surviving letters, a good source for data about both the family and the era, are included here in an appendix.</td></tr>
<tr><td></td><td>+ 5</td><td>iv.</td><td>ELIZABETH MARY DOE, born 26 Month 1823, died 22 Month 1928 at Dale, Eaststate.[49] She married about 1844–45, in Glen County, Eaststate, Martin Deesendent.[50]</td></tr>
</table>

Tristram and Judith L. (Plutarch) Doe were parents of one child, also born in Sandy County:

<table>
<tr><td>+ 6</td><td>i.</td><td>TRISTRAM ARTHUR P. "TAP" DOE, born about 1832,[51] died 23 Month 1889 in Sandy County.[52] He married 14 Month 1853 in Sandy County, Eliza G. L. (Doolittle) Roe.[53]</td></tr>
</table>

---

37. D. Orr Kee, *Eaststate Baptists* (Dale: privately printed, no date [internal evidence indicates about 1939]), 38. Photocopy in vertical file, Eaststate Room, Glen County Library, Dale. The original volume has not been located.

38. Mary A. Goodwriter, *A History of Glen County, Eaststate* (1924; reprint, Well Known City: History Publishers, 1975), 333.

39. 1830–54 Minute Book, Crane Creek Church, unpaginated, 1st page of Year: Month pages for 1813–22.

40. Robert G. Doe, *Private Book I*, the first of three handwritten volumes of poems and notes, intermittently dated, unpaginated, originals in possession of James A. Mykin of Big City, Weststate, who kindly supplied digitized images on CD to the author. This entry was written on the flyleaf.

41. "Death of A Recluse Centenarian," *Light City Times,* 16 Month 1909, section 2, p. 1, col. 1 continued on p. 3, col. 1, Light City Historical Society microfilm "Light City Times," reel no. 12, frames 501 and 503.

42. Robert G. Doe, *Private Book I*, unpaginated, 11th page.

43. John Offspring Bible (published 1853), photocopy at ABC County Library, ABC [also, published in *Offspring Notes* 12 (Month 1980): 12]. Efforts to locate the original have failed—its 1980 owner is deceased. Unless cited otherwise, William's family data are from this record.

44. Date is an estimate based on the known birth dates of the couple's children.

45. Judith Doe household, 1850 U.S. census, population schedule, Sandy County, p. 300, dwelling 289, family 299. "J. E.," a female aged thirty-two, was in the household. Presumably, this was Judith's stepdaughter, the unmarried Jane E. Doe.

46. Doe Family plot, Crane Creek Church Cemetery, Locksburg, Eaststate. A footstone marked "J. E. D. 1877" is believed by family members to mark Jane's grave. The facts that the inveterate letter-writer apparently wrote none after 1875, and that a page-by-page reading of the 1880 Sandy census failed to find her, lends credence to the family's belief.

47. Tristram Doe households: 1820, p. 228, included a white female under ten; 1830, p. 101, included a white female ten-to-fifteen (and one five-to-ten, daughter Elizabeth Mary); and 1840, p. 570, included a white female twenty-to-thirty.

48. 1852–77 Minute Book, Crane Creek Church, unpaginated, 17th and 204th pages.

49. Elizabeth M. D. Deesendent tombstone, Deesendent plot, Greenlawn Cemetery, Dale.

50. The marriage date is deduced from the age of the oldest 1850-census child, John D., aged four (Sandy County, population schedule, p. 21, dwelling 33, family 33: household of Martin "Dessendint").

51. At eighteen, "T. A. P." was enumerated in his mother Judith's 1850 census household (cited earlier). He was head of his own household in 1860, aged twenty-eight (Sandy County, population schedule, p. 745, dwelling 991, family 993). He stated his age as forty-seven when the 1880 census was taken (Sandy County, Fort Loyal Township, enumeration district [ED] 24, supervisor's district [SD] 18, p. 23). He has not been found in the area in 1870.

52. Tristram Arthur P. Doe tombstone (erected 1964), Section 4, Locksburg Cemetery. It does not include his birth date.

53. Doe entry, Sandy County Marriage Registers 1848–1930, vol. D–G, 47, ESL microfilm "San.Mar.1."

—— SECOND GENERATION ——

2. **Robert G.²** **Doe** (Tristram¹) was born in Sandy County 15 Month 1809[54] and died at Light City, Farstate, 15 Month 1909.[55] He married at Light City, 25 Month 1853, **Martha Chrystal (Myancestor) Martyr,** widow of St. Stephen Martyr.[56] Martha, daughter of Michael and Priscilla (Parent) Myancestor, was born in Mountain County, Essex, about 1832–33 and died at Light City 12 Month 1857.[57]

genealogical summary

Like others in his family, Robert was a member of Crane Creek Baptist Church, but his behavior (alcohol related, apparently) led to his dismissal from fellowship in 1848.[58] He was living with his step-mother Judith when the 1850 census was taken—listed as "Argy [R. G.]," aged forty-one, occupation "poet," and clearly unmarried.[59] In 1852, however, Robert moved from Sandy to Light City "to escape rural vermin," as he said in an interview shortly before his death.[60] Robert, a struggling poet, and Martha, a struggling actress using the stage name Chrystal Night, [*And so forth*]^^^

life story

After Martha's death in 1857, Robert brought his young sons back to Sandy and lived (uneasily) with his brother William.[64] By 1862, however, he had left the boys behind and returned to Light City,[65] his chief residence thereafter.[66] Robert does not appear to have maintained direct contact with the boys, but poems and notes in his *Private Books* indicate that he loved and missed them.

Although no record has been found of Robert's service in the Civil War (Confederate or Union), two poems in his *Private Book* volumes indicate that he participated in at least one battle, possibly as a member of the Light City Medical Team.[67] He did not include the resulting stark, powerful poems in the volumes he published in 1879 and 1883[68]—a wise decision, perhaps, for the books were remarkably popular and their sale made him a wealthy man. In 1880 he was a "boarder" at 123 Nowhere Street; six years later he purchased an imposing mansion on Major Square.[69] During Robert's residence, Major Square was transformed from a quiet, upscale neighborhood into a bustling commercial arena. Houses on the opposite side of the square were torn down in 1898 to make way for the enormously successful XYZ Emporium, cornerstone of the XYZ Department Store chain.[70] When "the reclusive poet" died in 1909, his home was the only residence that remained, all the others having been replaced or converted to retail stores. Robert's mansion was purchased by the Light City Historical Society in 1910 and is now maintained as a house-museum.[71] Judging by his poetry during the

---

54. Robert G. Doe, *Private Book I*, flyleaf.
55. "Death of A Recluse Centenarian," *Light City Times,* 16 Month 1909.
56. Robert G. Doe, *Private Book I*, 11th and 12th pages, which include rhapsodic descriptions of the lovely Martha.
57. Ibid., inside back cover, which includes the names of her parents. Martha was apparently less than forthcoming about her age. (The estimate given here is Robert's.) No death certificate was filed, apparently.
58. Robert Doe entry, 1830–54 Minute Book, Crane Creek Baptist Church, unpaginated, 5th of pages headed 1848: Month.
59. Judith Doe household, 1850 U.S. census, population schedule, Sandy County, p. 300, dwelling 289, family 287.
60. "Death of A Recluse Centenarian," *Light City Times,* 16 Month 1909.

^^^^^^^^^^^^^^^^[*Footnotes continue*]^^^^^^^^^^^^^^^^^^^^^^^^^^^^^^^^^^^^^

64. Robert G. Doe, *Private Book I*, 201st page; and "William Eye Doe" household, 1860 U.S. census, population schedule, Sandy County, p. 348, dwelling 441, family 447. Robert's occupation was given as farmer, the only time he was not styled "poet."
65. "Protest Against Tolls on the Swift River Bridge," Farstate Legislative Papers, folder "Petitions, 1862," Farstate State Archives, Light City.
66. Robert G. Doe, *Private Book II* and *Private Book III*. Occasional poems are noted as having been written "at the cabin," but its location is not stated and no record of a land purchase in Farstate or adjoining jurisdictions has been found.
67. The Team, organized in Month 1862 by Dr. P. I. Kindly, was a volunteer unit supported by L. L. Philanthrope. It disbanded on 5 Month 1863 (Farstate Historical Commission, *Historic Light City* [Light City: the commission, 1983], 101).
68. *Southern Scenes* (Light City: privately published, 1879), photocopy kindly supplied by R. G. Doe Jr., of Gracetown, Somewhere; *More Southern Scenes* (Light City: privately published, 1883), a copy of which was found by the author in a Keesburg second-hand bookstore in 1991. Until its discovery, Robert was believed to have published only the 1879 volume.
69. Frieda Kindly entry, 1880 U.S. census, Light County, Farstate, ED 66 (Light City), SD 5, p. 71; and Street to Doe deed, Transfer Book 21: 331, Clerk's Office, Municipal Building, Light City. (In 1839, the town was reincorporated as an independent city. Hence, deeds after that date are records of the municipality, not Light County.)
70. *Historic Light City*, 211–13.
71. Ibid., xii.

transformation period, however, Robert was more invigorated by the changes than depressed by them. These late works, which are displayed at the mansion, reflect the enthusiasm for commercial and industrial "progress" that was typical of turn-of-the-century America.

Robert G.[2] and Martha Chrystal (Myancestor) Doe, were parents of the following children, both born at Light City:[72]

+ 7   i.   BENJAMIN R. G.[3] DOE, born 17 Month 1854, died 29 Month 1898 at Roughton, Untamed Territory.[72] He married 30 Month 1875, in Friendly County, Weststate, Cynthea J. Den.[73]

   8   ii. WALDO N. DOE, born 25 Month 1856, died during Month 1866 in Sandy County. He "fell from that old oak on Willy's place" according to his father's *Private Book I.* (Part of the date is illegible.) "Willy's place" was the home of Robert's brother William I. Doe, with whom the Doe boys had been left when he returned to Light City.

The child born to Martha Chrystal Myancestor by her first husband, St. Stephen Martyr, was

   9   MICHAEL MARTYR, alias MICHAEL W. MYANCESTOR, born [*And so forth*]▲▲▲▲▲▲▲▲▲▲▲▲▲▲

3. William I.[2] Doe (Tristram[1]) was born in Sandy County 30 Month 1810 and died in Friendly County, Weststate, 2 Month 1883.[78] He married about 1850–51[79] at Sintown, Lower County, Eaststate, **Louisa Abitlate**, daughter of Richard Abitlate.[80] Louisa was born about 1814, probably in Sandy County,[81] and died 1883–1900, probably in Friendly County, Weststate.[82]

William was a farmer of fierce dedication and, apparently, considerable skill. His views on "proper" farm practices [*And so forth—The compilation continues with William's biography, ending with a list of his five children, assigned numbers +10, +11, +12, 13, and +14. No. 13 Marie (Doe) Commonname, did have issue but is not traced further. (See* Register *example for a with-issue child not continued.) No. 14 Janeann, the only child born in wedlock married her cousin, no. 15 John Watts[3] Deesendent, oldest son of no. 5 Elizabeth Mary[2] Doe.*]

> No. 4, Jane E.[2] Doe, does not have a biography at this place in the compilation. She died without issue, and her biography is included at the place where her name appears in the child-list that follows her parents' biography.

5. Elizabeth Mary[2] Doe (Tristram[1]) was born 26 Month 1823 in Sandy County,[93] where she married **Martin Deesendent** about 1844–45.[94] She died at Dale, Eaststate, on 22 Month 1928. [*And so forth—The compilation continues with Elizabeth and Martin's biography, ending with a list of their eight children, numbered +15, 16, 17, +18, +19, +20, +21, and +22. Second child William and third child Deborah died in infancy—their numbers, 16 and 17, are not marked "+." The first child, no. 15 John Watts Deesendent, married his cousin no. 14 Janeann[3] Doe, youngest child of William I.[2] and Louisa (Abitlate) Doe.*]▲▲▲▲▲▲▲▲▲▲▲▲▲▲▲▲▲

---

72. Robert G. Doe, *Private Book I,* unpaginated, 83d page (children's birth dates) and 31st page (death of "my son Benjamin").

73. Doe entry, Weststate Marriage Book E: 345, Weststate Bureau of Vital Records, First-Town.

▲▲▲▲▲▲▲▲▲▲▲▲▲▲[*Footnotes continue*]▲▲▲▲▲▲▲▲▲▲▲▲▲▲▲▲▲▲▲▲▲▲▲▲▲▲▲▲▲▲▲▲▲▲▲

78. John Offspring Bible.

79. William's marriage was "cut out" of the Offspring Bible; its date is estimated from the birth dates of his children.

80. Letter from Jason F. Abitlate to Savannah T. Doe (address not stated), dated 16 Month 1921 at Locksburg [Eaststate]. Photocopy of a transcription (undated but probably made in the 1950s) kindly supplied to the author by James A. Mykin of Big City, Weststate, in Month 1996. The location of the original is not known.

81. Louisa's birth date is estimated from her census ages (e.g., "R. Abitlate" household, 1850 U.S. census, population schedule, Sandy County, p. 333, dwelling 433, family 435; "William Eye Doe" household, 1860 U.S. census, population schedule, Sandy County, p. 348, dwelling 441, family 447; and William I. Doe" household, 1870 U.S. census, Friendly County, Weststate, p. 259, dwelling 399, family 357). Because her father lived in Sandy County at that time (Sandy County Tax Books 1803–20), it is likely that Louisa was born there.

82. Louisa was alive as of the date of William's will (dated 9 Month 1883) but had apparently died before the 1900 Friendly County census was taken.

▲▲▲▲▲▲▲▲▲▲▲▲▲▲[*Footnotes continue*]▲▲▲▲▲▲▲▲▲▲▲▲▲▲▲▲▲▲▲▲▲▲▲▲▲▲▲▲▲▲▲▲▲▲▲

93. Elizabeth M. D. Deesendent tombstone, Deesendent plot, Greenlawn Cemetery, Dale, Eaststate. Her husband and his second wife are buried nearby.

94 The marriage date is deduced from the age of the oldest 1850-census child, John Watts, aged four (Sandy County, population schedule, p. 21, dwelling 33, family 33: household of Martin Dessendint [*sic*]).

▲▲▲▲▲▲▲▲▲▲▲▲▲▲[*Footnotes continue*]▲▲▲▲▲▲▲▲▲▲▲▲▲▲▲▲▲▲▲▲▲▲▲▲▲▲▲▲▲▲▲▲▲▲▲▲

6. Tristram Arthur P.[2] "Tap" Doe (Tristram[1]) was born in Sandy County about 1832.[129] He was "killed by lightning" 23 Month 1889 and is buried in Locksburg Cemetery, Eaststate.[130] He married 14 Month 1853, in Sandy County, **Eliza G. L. (Doolittle) Roe**,[131] daughter of Isaac Doolittle of Sandy[132] and widow of Ian L. Roe.[133] Eliza was born about 1834[134] and died, undoubtedly in Sandy County, between 1871[135] and 1875.[136]

Tristram was normally called Tap, the nickname based, obviously, on his initials. He was a life-long member of the Crane Creek Baptist Church in which his father had been a leader, but unlike the elder Tristram and Tap's half-brother, William, he does not appear to have played a leadership role in the congregation.[137] Both he and Eliza had been members before their marriage,[138] and the wedding ceremony was performed by Rev. W. W. Twice, who was pastor at Crane Creek Church at the time.[139]

Under the terms of his father's will, Tap inherited the 110-acre dwelling tract—as his mother Judith's only child—after she died intestate in 1859. Tap also inherited 222 acres Benjamin Friend had sold Judith but for which he had never executed a deed. In Friend's 1853 will, as a condition for his grandchildren to receive their inheritance, he required them to make a quit-claim to Mrs. Doe acknowledging the sale.[140] When he died in Month 1860, however, Judith was already dead; and the Friend heirs made the necessary deed to Tap.[141] Both Doe tracts are identified on Civil War era land-ownership maps at the Library of Congress.[142] The land was about three miles south of Locksburg on both sides of Looking Glass Swamp, a tributary of the Slow River in the northern part of the county.

On 5 Month 1861, as "Tristram Arthur P. Doe," Tap enlisted in Company B, 9th Eaststate Cavalry, C.S.A., for a period of three years. He was wounded on 18 Month 1862, recovered and was active in Month, but was again wounded on 9 Month. The latter injury required that he be treated at Comfort Hospital, Dale, Glen County.[143] In Month when Tap received his first wound, however, his unit was enjoying a "calm spell,"[144] so it is not clear how he came to be injured. His second wound was clearly battle related, for on 29 Month the regiment "engaged the enemy" and sustained twelve casualties.[145] Tap was discharged 26 Month 1863 with a "permanent disability of the right leg."[146]

---

129. Date deduced from census records (see Note 51).
130. Tristram Arthur P. Doe tombstone, Section 4, Locksburg Cemetery. In 1964, the grave was moved to this section (set aside in 1867 for Confederate dead) with others removed from Crane Creek Church Cemetery to make way for a new sanctuary. The circumstances of Tap's death were recorded at page 110, 1879–1911 Minute Book, Crane Creek Church.
131. Doe entry, Sandy County Marriage Registers 1848–1930, vol. D–G, 47.
132. Isaac Doolittle will, Sandy County Will Book 1: 407, Judge of Probate's Office, Keesburg.
133. Ian Roe estate file, Sandy County Old Probates, microfilm 1848–87, roll 11, file: "1852, Roe, Ian," courthouse annex, Keesburg. Ian died 3–15 Month 1852 leaving widow Eliza and posthumous son Ian "junr."
134. Isaac Doolittle household, 1850 U.S. census, Sandy County, p. 294, dwelling 276, family 276. Eliza's age was fifteen. She was enumerated as twenty-six in Tap's 1860 household.
135. "In the Matter of T. A. P. Doe in Bankruptcy," District Court of the United States, District of Eaststate, case number 714, photocopies from the National Archives, Any Region, Major City, Anystate. The 139-page file includes a letter dated 20 Month 1871 stating that Tristram's wife was living, but in "very bad health," at that time.
136. 1852–77 Minute Book, Crane Creek Church, unpaginated, 204th page, membership list (c1870). A notation "deceased" was written beside the name of Eliza Doe in the hand of Rev. Goodfellow, who was called to another church in 1875.
137. Minute Books, Crane Creek Baptist Church, 3 vols. Aside from the membership lists, and occasional mention of his family's postwar financial distress, Tap's name is not mentioned.
138. 1852–77 Minute Book, Crane Creek Church, unpaginated, 17th page, membership list dated "1850 [sic]."
139. Doe entry, Sandy County Marriage Registers 1848–1930, vol. D–G, 47, which gives the officiant's name; and Kee, *Eaststate Baptists*, 291, which gives his congregational affiliation during the 1850s.
140. Benjamin Friend will, Sandy County Will Book 1: 200, Judge of Probate's Office, Keesburg.
141. Friend et al to Tristram Doe Jr. [sic], 15 Month 1848, Sandy County Deed Book 1: 85, Clerk's Office, Keesburg.
142. Land ownership maps of Eaststate prepared by Capt. John L. Cartographer, U.S. Army, numbered A0000 (1864) and B0000 (1867), Map Division, Library of Congress, Washington, D.C.
143. Tristram A. P. Doe, Compiled Service Record (Confederate), ESL microfilm "Civil War Service Records," roll 54. Another Tristram, who served as a Company I sergeant in the same cavalry unit, was a son of David K. Doe and grandson of Watts Doe. Watts, aged eighty-three, was enumerated in David K.'s 1860 census household, which included eighteen-year-old Tristram (Sandy County population schedule, p. 242, dwelling 441, family 445). The younger Tristram died 18 Month 1863 of measles, according to his Compiled Service Record.
144. M. Y. Story, *The Ninth Eaststate Cavalry In the Late War: A True Account* (Action, N.S.: Historical Press, 1892), 34.
145. Ibid., 38.
146. Tristram A. P. Doe Compiled Service Record.

Whether because of his injury or the difficult economic conditions in Eaststate during and after the war, by 1866 Tap was deeply in debt. He mortgaged his land—two tracts described as consisting of "about 300 acres on both sides of the Looking Glass Creek"—to pay what he owed,[147] but his situation continued to deteriorate. On 7 Month 1868, still unable to keep up with expenses, including the mortgage, he filed for bankruptcy. Remarkably, his petition was granted the same day.[148] Although now relieved of debt, the bank foreclosed on the mortgage, sold both tracts, and turned over the surplus to the court for distribution among Tap's other creditors.[149] In 1871, seeking additional relief for his neighbor, Rev. R. H. Goodfellow (pastor of Crane Creek Church) wrote to the bankruptcy court describing Tap as "very poor, [with] a wife in very bad health and four helpless children dependent on him." Rev. Goodfellow related that "for the last two years the little support he has been enabled to provide for his family has been chiefly from sumac [a wild plant used in tanning and dyeing] gathered with his own hand which he has sold, or exchanged for supplies in Keesburg."[150]

A petition for administration on the estate of Tristram A. P. Doe was filed on 11 Month 1889, almost immediately after his death, by the estate's creditors. The petition was denied, however, and the estate was submitted to the sheriff for settlement.[151] The final account, returned six months later at the Month session of court, shows that debts were exactly $1.00 more than proceeds from sale of the personal property. The largest bills were for Tap's rent ($17.94) and his coffin ($15.00).[152]

Tristram Arthur P.[2] Doe and his wife Eliza G. L. Doolittle were parents of four children born in Sandy County, identified in the couple's census households or the children's marriage records:

+ 23   i.   ELIZA JANE[3] DOE, born 21 Month 1854, died 5 Month 1932 in Spring County, Eaststate.[153] She married 3 Month 1875, in Sandy County, I. C. Yue.[154]

+ 24   ii. WILLIAM I. DOE, born 27 Month 1856, died 9 Month 1933 at Dale, Eaststate.[155] He married 22 Month 1878 in Sandy County, Dorothy Mary English.[156]

+ 25   iii. JAMES PLUTARCH "JP" DOE, born in Month 1861; died after 1900;[157] and married 4 Month 1883 in Poplar County, Research State, Sheila Maureen Irish.[158]

+ 26   vi. AMANDA ROBERTA "BOBBIE" DOE, born 29 Month 1867,[159] is believed to have died 1914–18 in France.[160] She married (1) 26 Month 1883, in Spring County, Josephus Blank;[161] married (2) 22 Month 1891, at Capital City, André Françoise.[162]

The stepchild of Tristram Arthur P.[2] Doe, born of his wife Eliza G. L. Doolittle by her first husband, Ian L. Roe, was

+ 27   IAN L.[1] ROE, born 22 Month 1852; died 1 Month 1941 at New City, Newstate;[163] and married 19 Month 1876, in Sandy County, Gretchen Magdalena German.[164]

stepchild has generation indicator "1" and no birth-order number

147. T. A. P. Doe to Locksburg Bank and Surety Company, Sandy County Deed Book 2: 226. The deed specified that the tracts ("about 100 acres" and "about 200 acres") were "had from my late father Tristram Doe."
148. "In the Matter of T. A. P. Doe in Bankruptcy," U.S. District Court Records, Eaststate District.
149. Trustees of Locksburg Bank and Surety Company to Chill E. Freeze, Sandy County Deed Book 3: 647.
150. "In the matter of T. A. P. Doe in Bankruptcy," U.S. District Court Records, Eaststate District.
151. Doe entry, "Orders," Sandy County Court-Minute Book 1889–94: 65, original, Eaststate State Archives, Capital City.
152. Tristram Doe file, Sandy County Old Probates.
153. Eliza Doe Yue death certificate no. 202332 (1932), Eaststate Health and Vital Records Department, Capital City.
154. Yue entry, Sandy County Marriage Registers, 1848–1930, vol. S–Z, 331.
155. William I. Doe death certificate no. 213333 (1933), Eaststate Health and Vital Records Department, Capital City.
156. Doe entry, Sandy County Marriage Registers, 1848–1930, vol. D–G, 434.
157. T. A. P. Doe household, 1880 U.S. census, Sandy County, Eaststate, Fort Loyal Township, ED 24, SD 18, p. 23; and J. P. Doe household, 1900 U.S. census, Valley County, New State, Valley Township, ED 10, SD 13, p. 3.
158. Doe entry, Poplar County Marriages, 1800–1900, 128, Clerk's office, courthouse, Poplarton. Photocopy enclosed with Edward N. Genealogist, CGRS, "Doe Report" to the author, 18 Month 1997.
159. Letter from Bobbie Blank to Eliza Jane Yue, dated at Capital City, 29 Month 1887 "[on] my twentieth birthday." Photocopy kindly supplied to the author by Miss Roberta Noname of Capital City, Eaststate.
160. Interview by the author with Miss Roberta Noname, 123 Canal Street, Capital City, 12 Month 1996.
161. Blank entry, Spring County Marriage Registers, 1870–94, vol. A–C, 201.
162. Francis [sic] entry, Capital County Marriage Registers, 1869–89, vol. D–G, 111.
163. Ian L. Roe death certificate no. 140241 (1941), New State Department of Vital Records, New City.
164. "Doe, Ian L." entry [sic], Sandy County Marriage Registers, 1848–1930, vol. D–G, 96.

——— THIRD GENERATION ———

7. Benjamin R. G.[3] **Doe** (Robert G.[2], Tristram[1]) was born 17 Month 1854 at Light City, Farstate; and was killed at Roughton, Untamed Territory, 29 Month 1898.[165] He married, on 30 Month 1875 in Friendly County, Weststate, **Cynthea J. Den**, daughter of Jackson B. W. and Roma Ann C. [—?—] Den.[166] Cynthea was born 19 Month 1860 in Friendly County and died, as Cynthea Lucky, 22 Month 1919 at Smalltown, Weststate.[167]

In 1867, Benjamin moved with his uncle and cousins (William I.[2] Doe and his children) to Friendly County's remote Goodland Valley. Like his poet-father, however, Benjamin did not adjust well to William's firmly-held views about the responsibilities and proper practices of farming—Benjamin preferred a lawman's life, serving first as sheriff of Smalltown (1879–84) and then as United States marshal for Untamed Territory (from 1886 until his death twelve years later).[168] So colorful a personality was Benjamin that his career was [*And so forth*]ʌʌʌʌʌʌʌʌʌʌʌʌʌʌʌʌʌʌʌʌʌʌʌʌʌʌʌʌ

It is not known when Cynthea left Weststate to join her husband in Untamed Territory, but she was clearly living there when he was killed. "Prostrate with grief," she immediately returned to Smalltown with her only surviving child, "Little Billy,"[175] and was living with her parents when she married, five months later, George E. Nuhusband, a recent arrival from Germany and the tiny town's only barber.[176] Perhaps unexpectedly, by 1910, Cynthea and George were parents of two children, the oldest of them born on Cynthea's fortieth birthday.[177] Cynthea was again widowed by violence in Month 1915 when George was killed by a stray bullet during a robbery of the Weststate Commercial Bank.[178] She married, third, Harold Lucky on 28 Month 1916. Harold died three days before Cynthea, both victims of the 1919 influenza epidemic that swept the country.[179]

The children of Benjamin R. G.[3] and Cynthea (Den) Doe, all born at Smalltown, presumably, were[180]

28	i.	JACKSON D.[4] DOE, born 1 Month 1877, died before 29 Month 1898 in Untamed Territory.
29	ii.	BENJAMIN R. G. DOE, born 2 Month 1880, died before 29 Month 1898 in Untamed Territory.
+ 30	iii.	WILLIAM I. DOE, born 30 Month 1882, died at Smalltown 18 Month 1951.[181] He married 18 Month 1906 at Smalltown, Barbara Delilah Myancestor.[182]
31	iv.	DAUGHTER (name unknown), born 12 Month 1885, died before 29 Month 1898 in Untamed Territory.

The children of Cynthea J. Den by her second husband, George E. Nuhusband, were as follows:

165. Robert G. Doe, *Private Book I,* unpaginated, 83rd page (children's birth dates) and 31st page (death of "my son Ben—shot in Roughton Massacre").

166. Doe entry, Weststate Marriage Book E: 345, Weststate Bureau of Vital Records, First-Town.

167. "Famous Gunman's Widow Has Died," *First-Town Chronicle,* 25 Month 1919, Second Section, p. 1, col. 4. The article recapitulates Benjamin R. G. Doe's career and death, and reports Cynthia's subsequent activities and death. No death certificate for Cynthea under any of her married surnames was found on record in Weststate.

168. Ibid. See also M. W. Biographer, *Benjamin R. G. Doe: Lawman of the Old West* (New Place: Little & Small Press, 1989).

ʌʌʌʌʌʌʌʌʌʌʌʌʌʌʌ[*Footnotes continue*]ʌʌʌʌʌʌʌʌʌʌʌʌʌʌʌʌʌʌʌʌʌʌʌʌʌʌʌʌʌʌʌʌʌʌʌʌʌʌ

175. In addition to the newspapers mentioned in note 169, *The Untamed Territory News,* 2 Month 1898, devoted the entire front page and most of the rest of the issue to the story, including the remaining Doe family's return to Smalltown.

176. Newhusband [*sic*] entry, Weststate Marriage Book F: 276, Weststate Bureau of Vital Records, First-Town.

177. Nuhusband household, 1910 U.S. census, Friendly County, Weststate, ED 55, SD 12, p. 102, dwelling 48, family 43.

178. "Famous Gunman's Widow Has Died," *First-Town Chronicle,* 25 Month 1919; and "Daring Daylight Robbery Hits Smalltown Bank: Ten Killed," *First-Town Chronicle,* 5 Month 1915, p. 1.

179. Obituary of Harold Lucky, *Smalltown News,* 26 Month 1919, p. 5, col. 3.

180. Robert G. Doe, *Private Book II,* unpaginated. Robert recorded his grandchildren's births (omitting the granddaughter's name) in the margins of scattered pages (the 18th page, inside front cover, 102nd page, and 35th page, respectively), but did not mention their deaths. The news article "Famous Gunman's Widow Has Died" however, related that Cynthea returned from Untamed Territory "after her husband's death," and was accompanied by "her only surviving son, Little Billy Doe."

181. William I. Doe death certificate no. 45251 (1951), Weststate Vital Statistics Bureau, First-Town.

182. Doe entry, Weststate Marriage Book G: 98, Weststate Bureau of Vital Records, First-Town.

32   CLARISSA L.[1] NUHUSBAND, born 9 Month 1900; died 1 Month 1929 in Coast State;[184] and married 2 Month 1925 at Smalltown, Goodness Gracious.[184] Two children, *(a)* Don Gracious and *(b)* Dan Gracious also died on 1 Month 1929 and were buried with their mother.

33   GEORGE BENJAMIN NUHUSBAND, born in Month 1902,[185] died after 1939 (place not known). George was the author of *Bloody Ben* (Scandal Press, 1939), a highly sensationalized "biography" of Benjamin R.G. Doe's exploits as a lawman. The novel was made into a somewhat tamer but equally fictionalized movie of the same name by Columbus Pictures in 1994. According to his book's original dust jacket, George was married about 1930 (place not known) to Daphne Doormouse and by 1939 was the father of three children (names not given). The Library of Congress catalogue mentions no further works by Nuhusband, and he was not listed in *Who's Who* or similar publications. Nothing more is known of his later career.

10. William I.[3] Abitlate, alias Doe, alias John Noname (William I.[2] Doe, Tristram[1]), was born in Sandy County 24 Month 1841[186] and died at Capital City, Eaststate, 22 Month 1919.[187]

William was the oldest of four children born to Louisa Abitlate before she married William I.[2] Doe, who acknowledged paternity of the youngsters in his 1883 will (cited above). Young William (surname Abitlate) was enumerated in his grandfather Richard Abitlate's 1850 census household, along with his three younger siblings and mother Louisa.[188] In 1860 he was enumerated (surname Doe) in his by-then married parents' household in Sandy County,[189] and accompanied the family when it moved to Weststate.[190] His stay there was short, however, for by 1870 he was back in Sandy, living alone on the senior William's meticulously assembled farm tract.[191] It is not clear when the two Williams quarreled, but it is certain that they did—seriously. When the younger William sold the land in two parcels in 1871, he styled himself in the second deed "John Noname, formerly known as William Doe but no longer using that odious appelation."[192] He then moved to Capital City (with the proceeds of both sales, apparently), and purchased a small house at 123 Narrow Street near the old industrial district, now the site of Civic Stadium.[193] He lived there the rest of his long life.

Although he did not marry under any of his names, John filed for adoption of three children on 18 Month 1891: two were his cousin Amanda Roberta Blank's offspring, the other was described as "lately orphaned by accident at the mill." John's petition was approved on 9 Month later that year.[194] Between that date and his death, his household included the children—and various in-laws, nieces, nephews, and occasional unrelated boarders. Most were employed in the mills and factories nearby.[195]

---

183. Clarissa L. N. Gracious tombstone, Lonetree Cemetery (lot 110), San Giminiano, Coast State.

184. Goodness Gracious marriage certificate no. 3325 (1925), [also Gracious entry, Weststate Record of Marriage License Returns, vol. 1 (1920–30), 108], Weststate Bureau of Vital Records, First-Town.

185. Nuhusband household, 1910 U.S. census, Friendly County, Weststate, ED 55, SD 12, p. 102, dwelling 48, family 43.

186. John Offspring Bible.

187. John Noname death certificate, no. 12319 (1919), Eaststate Health and Vital Records Department, Capital City.

188. "R. Abitlate" household, 1850 U.S. census, population schedule, Sandy County, p. 333, dwelling 433, family 435.

189. "William Eye Doe" household, 1860 U.S. census, population schedule, Sandy County, p. 348, dwelling 441, family 447.

190. Letter from Benjamin R. G. Doe to "Aunt Janey" [Jane E. Doe], dated at Goodland Valley, 27 Month 1868 mentions the fact that "Willie Jr." was in residence with the rest of the family.

191. "Willy Doe" household, 1870 U.S. census, Sandy County, Eaststate, p. 259, dwelling 399, family 357.

192. Doe to Oldsettler, and Noname to Oldsettler, Sandy County Deed Book 2: 461 and 470. The first deed, indexed as "Doe," does not mention the name change. Prior researchers assumed that Billy remained in Sandy County and confused his supposed life events with those of his cousin William (no. 23), son of Tap Doe. However, the second sale, for the remaining twenty-eight acres, is indexed as "Noname" and carries the name-change notice. Both deeds are referenced in the sale by Frederick Oldsettler in his 1923 sale of the property (Sandy County Deed Book 47: 311).

193. Happy to Noname, Capital County Deed Book 3: 45. William/John had sold his father's 328 acres for a total of $325.53 and paid $101.56 cash for the house on Narrow Street. Between 1871 and 1878, he built onto it, almost doubling its size; presumably, he had funds remaining after his purchase. The house was located and its size determined from Ringling Brother, ed., *Historical Maps of Capital City* (Capital City: ABC Press, 1945), Plate 18: "Canal District, 1872" and Plate 23 "Town Center and the Canal Factories, Capital City, Eaststate, 1881."

194. "Report of Committee on Adoptions to the State Legislature, 12 Month 1876," unpaginated, 2nd page, 3rd entry, Legislative Records, 1876–77 Session, Eaststate State Archives, Capital City.

195. *A Directory of the City of Capital City, Eaststate, United States of America, for the Year 1878* (Capital City: Capital City Times, 1878). The directory was published biannually until 1910 when it began annual publication. In 1912, the title was changed to *The Capital City Times Directory*, a title it retains to this day. Directories for 1878, 1882, 1884, 1900, 1902,

The adopted children of William I.[3] Abitlate, alias Doe, alias John Noname (said children born at Dale of Josephus Blank and his wife Amanda Roberta[4] Doe) were

+ 34   TRISTRAM D.[5] BLANK, born 2 Month 1883; died 14 Month 1942 at Capital City;[196] and married 7 Month 1905, at Capital City, Luisa Mai Allcott.[197]

+ 35   ROBERTA AMANDA "MANDY" BLANK, born 2 Month 1884, died 8 Month 1951 at Capital City.[198] She married 5 Month 1903, at Capital City, Douglas Farebanks.[199]

The adopted child (parents unknown) of William I. Abitlate, alias Doe, alias John Noname was

+ 36   PLUTARCH[1] "ARCHY" NONAME, born Month 1888 in Eaststate; died 14 Month 1936 at Capital City;[200] married 12 Month 1908 at Capital City, Fruzanne Seamstress.[201]

∧∧∧∧∧∧∧[*And so forth. The compilation continues with biographies of no. 11 and no. 12; no. 13, although she had issue, cannot be traced further (see* Register *System example*).]∧∧∧∧∧∧∧∧∧∧∧∧∧∧∧∧∧∧∧∧∧∧∧

14. Janeann[3] Doe (William I.[2], Tristram[1]) was born in Sandy County 21 Month 1851 and died at Smalltown, Weststate, 24 Month 1901.[241] On 19 Month 1866 in Friendly County, Weststate, Janeann married her first cousin, **John Watts[3] Deesendent** (Elizabeth Mary[2] Doe, Tristram[1]).[242] John was born 23 Month 1846 in Sandy County and died 17 Month 1921 at First-Town, Weststate.[243]

The younger Deesendents moved with Louisa's father, two older brothers, and cousin Benjamin R. G. Doe, to Friendly County, Weststate, in 1867,[244] but by 1870, John's little family was living in Empty County in western Weststate.[245] An 1869 silver strike in what would become Mine County two years later was apparently the cause of the family's relocation, although John gave his occupation to the census enumerator as "merchant," rather than "miner." In boomtown Silver City, he opened "Little Jack's General Supply" store in a makeshift tent. (It was still in the tent in 1875, although many wooden buildings had been constructed nearby.[246]) The enterprise failed, however, and by 1880 the Deesendents had returned to Friendly County and settled at Smalltown. John's occupation was "librarian"[247] of the town's miniature collection.[248] [*And so forth—child-list, which includes son John Watts Deesendent Jr. who died in infancy.*]∧∧

15. John Watts[3] Deesendent (Elizabeth Mary[2] Doe, Tristram[1]) was born in Sandy County 23 Month 1846; died 17 Month 1921 at First-Town, Weststate;[252] and married, first, 22 Month 1866 **Janeann[3] Doe** (number 14, above), who was born 21 Month 1851 and died at Smalltown, 24 Month 1901.[253] John married, second, at Smalltown, 24 Month 1902, **Alice I. (Wonder) Land**, who was born

1904, and 1928–40 were examined at the Eaststate State Library; and those for 1902–16, 1920–22, and 1925–27 at the Graduate Library, Eaststate State University, Collegeville.

196. Tristram D. Blank death certificate, no. 512342 (1942), Eaststate Health and Vital Records Department, Capital City.

197. Blank entry, Capital County Marriage Registers, 1900–10, vol. D–G, 132.

198. Roberta B. Farebanks death certificate, no. 122351 (1951), Eaststate Health and Vital Records Department, Capital City.

199. Farebanks entry, Capital County Marriage Registers, 1900–10, vol. D–G, 203.

200. Archibald [*sic*] Noname death certificate, no. 11436 (1936), Eaststate Health and Vital Records Department, Capital City. The informant, neighbor Dazey Dizzy, must have guessed that the nickname "Archy" stood for "Archibald."

201. Noname entry, Capital County Marriage Registers, 1900–10, vol. J–N, 501.

∧∧∧∧∧∧∧∧∧∧∧∧∧∧∧∧[*Footnotes continue*]∧∧∧∧∧∧∧∧∧∧∧∧∧∧∧∧∧∧∧∧∧∧∧∧∧∧∧∧∧∧∧∧∧∧∧∧∧∧

241. Janeann Doe Deesendent death certificate, no. 134501 (1901), Weststate Vital Statistics Bureau, First-Town.

242. John Deesendent entry, Sandy County Marriage Registers, 1848–1930, vol. D–G, 491.

243. John W. Deesendent death certificate, no. 101821 (1921), Weststate Vital Statistics Bureau, First-Town.

244. Letter from Benjamin R. G. Doe to "Aunt Janey" [Jane E. Doe], dated at Goodland Valley, 27 Month 1868.

245. Deesendent household, 1870 U.S. census population schedule, Empty County, p. 2, dwelling 9, family 9.

246. Photograph labeled "Downtown Silver City in 1875," wall display (in 1987) at Mine Museum, Silver City, Weststate.

247. Deesendent household, 1880 U.S. census, Friendly County, ED 33, SD 3, p. 31.

248. 1880 U.S. census, supplemental schedules, Friendly County, p. 5. Weststate State Library microfilm "1880 C/SS/1." Five libraries in the county are listed. The one noted as "Smalltown" housed 133 volumes.

∧∧∧∧∧∧∧∧∧∧∧∧∧∧∧∧[*Footnotes continue*]∧∧∧∧∧∧∧∧∧∧∧∧∧∧∧∧∧∧∧∧∧∧∧∧∧∧∧∧∧∧∧∧∧∧∧∧∧∧

252. John W. Deesendent death certificate, no. 10821 (1921), Weststate Vital Statistics Bureau, First-Town.

253. Janeann Doe Deesendent death certificate, no. 134501 (1901), Weststate Vital Statistics Bureau, First-Town.

in 1874, daughter of Samuel and Irene [—?—] Wonder[254] and widow of Forrest Land.[255] Alice died 31 Month 1945 at First-Town.[256]

John's story up to 1901, as merchant, librarian, schoolteacher, and widower, is recounted above (see no. 14). After his 1902 marriage to Alice, he moved onto her first husband's small ranch in Dismal County, Weststate. Forrest had left Alice the right to live in the home until their son, Forrest Jr., arrived at age twenty one.[257] The young man did so in 1919 and, despite John's advanced age (seventy-four), Forrest Jr. insisted that the Deesendents leave.[258] They moved into a small apartment at 18 Little Alley, First-Town,[216] where John's health began to decline rapidly. He died 17 Month 1921 at First-Town General Hospital[259] and was buried at Peaceful Rest Cemetery. Alice remained a widow and died at the Little Alley address in 1945; she was buried beside him at Peaceful Rest. (Headstones were erected for John and Alice in 1989 by their grandson, John Watts[5] Deesendent.[260])

In addition to the five children born of his first wife, Janeann[3] Doe (see number 14), John Watts[3] Deesendent was father of the following children by his second wife Alice I. (Wonder) Land, all born in Dismal County:

+ 54   i.   JOHN WATTS[4] DEESENDENT (second child of the name), [*And so forth—four more children*] ^^^^

The stepchildren of John Watts[3] Deesendent, born of his second wife, Alice Wonder by her first husband, Forrest Land, were [*And so forth—the compilation continues through no. 26.*]^^^^^^^^^^^

27. Ian L.[1] Roe (stepchild of Tristram Arthur P.[2] Doe, Tristram[1]) was born in Month [*And so forth—the compilation continues through no. 35.*]^^^^^^^^^^^^^^^^^^^^^^^^^^^^^

—— Fourth Generation ——

36. Plutarch[1] "Archie" Noname (adopted by William I.[3] Abitlate, alias Doe, alias John Noname, William I.[2] Doe, Tristram[1]) was born in Month [*And so forth*]^^^^^^^^^^^^^^^^^^^^

The six children of Plutarch[1] Noname and his wife Fruzanne Seamstress were[365]

+   106   i.   JOHN[2] NONAME, born 24 Month 1910, Capital City, [*And so forth*]^^^^^^^^^^^^
+   107   ii   TRISTRAM A. P. "TAP" NONAME, born 18 Month 1912 [*And so forth*]^^^^^^^^^^^^

^^^^[*And so forth. The compilation continues through the number of generations intended to be included within it.*]

—— Conclusion ——

Despite their limited means and modest accomplishments, the Doe family's history graphically illustrates—at a personal level—the effects of major trends in nineteenth- and early-twentieth-century America. In addition, the compilation is a case study in using so-called "non-genealogical" sources to expand one's knowledge of ancestral identities and life events. Perhaps most important, however, it illustrates the benefits of thoroughly researching a very "ordinary" family. The search, following every clue no matter how seemingly unimportant, unearthed otherwise hidden stories of quiet courage and steadfast determination.

---

254. Deesendent entry, Weststate Marriage Book G: 87. The entry includes ages and parentage of bride and groom.
255. Forrest Land will, Friendly County Will Book 8: 111. FHL microfilm no. 678,123,456.
256. Alice Wonder Deesendent death certificate, no. 13545 (1945), Weststate Vital Statistics Bureau, First-Town.
257. Forrest Land will, Friendly County Will Book 8: 111.
258. Letter from Henry M. Service, Attorney for Forrest Land Jr., to Mrs. John D. Deesendent, 21 Month 1918 (draft copy with corrections), folder "1918–20: Correspondence," Service Collection, P.C. no. 1234 , Friendly County Historical Society Library, Nicetown, Weststate.
259. Tape-recorded interview of Latecomer Mary (Deesendent) Surprise (Mrs. Carl) of 1234 Portugal Avenue, Brooklin, Weststate, by the author, 8 Month 1975; transcription corrected and amended by Mrs. Surprise (who died in 1981), and now in possession of the author. The Deesendents' presence at 18 Little Alley was confirmed by *Hornblower's Directory of First-Town, Weststate, 1920* (First-Town: Directory Publishers, 1920), 233. *Hornblower's Directory* for 1923 shows Mrs. Deesendent, widow, living at the Little Alley address.

^^^^^^^^^^^^^^^^^^[*Footnotes continue*]^^

2. COMPILED GENEALOGY: *REGISTER* SYSTEM

Descendants of | compilation title |

Tristram Doe (c.1780–1844)
of Sandy County, Eaststate

| compilation overview |

Does of the generations identified to date were not "great men," socially, politically, militarily, or economically. Their achievements individually and as a group were unremarkable, but their story reflects [*And so forth*] ∧∧∧

| identifying number | | generation indicator | ——— **FIRST GENERATION** ——— | reference note number |

1. TRISTRAM[1] DOE was born, most likely in Wishful County, Eaststate, about 1780[1] and died in Sandy County on 25 Month 1844.[2] In about Month 1808 he married (1) **ELIZABETH HOLDFAST** of adjoining Glen County,[3] born 1785–1795,[4] daughter of Thomas Holdfast[5] and possibly Jane (___), Thomas's widow.[6] Elizabeth died in 1823; and Tristram married (2) in Sandy County, almost immediately, **LUCY GOODTITLE**, daughter of Harrison and (___) Goodtitle. Lucy died, in Sandy County, 7 Month 1825;[7] and Tristram married (3) in Sandy, 25 Month 1826, his last[8] wife, **JUDITH L. PLUTARCH**, daughter of Arthur and Josephine Bono (Parte) Plutarch.[9]

| genealogical summary | (to the left of the above paragraph)

[*And so forth—life story*]∧∧

Children of Tristram and his first wife, Elizabeth (Holdfast) Doe, all born in Sandy County:[41]

2.	i.	ROBERT G.[2] DOE, b. 15 Month 1809, m. MARTHA CHRYSTAL (MYANCESTOR) MARTYR.
3.	ii.	WILLIAM I. DOE, b. 30 Month 1810, m. LOUISA ABITLATE.
	iii.	JANE E. DOE, b. about 1818 in Sandy County;[42] d. in Sandy, unmarried, in 1877.[43] She was clearly the white female enumerated in [*And so forth*]∧∧∧∧∧∧∧∧∧∧∧∧∧∧∧∧∧∧∧∧∧∧∧∧∧∧∧
4.	iv.	ELIZABETH MARY DOE, b. 26 Month 1823, m. MARTIN DEESENDENT.

| identifying numbers | (to the left, beside items iii)

Child of Tristram and his second wife, Judith L. (Plutarch) Doe:

| 5. | v. | TRISTRAM ARTHUR P. "TAP" DOE, b. about 1832, m. ELIZA G. L. (DOOLITTLE) ROE. |

| birth-order numbers |

——— **SECOND GENERATION** ———

2. ROBERT G.[2] DOE (*Tristram[1]*) was born in Sandy County on 15 Month 1809[46] and died at Light City, Farstate, 15 Month 1909.[47] He married at Light City [*And so forth*] ∧∧∧∧∧∧∧∧∧∧∧∧∧∧∧∧∧∧∧∧∧

[*And so forth—life story*]∧∧∧

Children of Robert G. Doe and Martha Chrystal (Myancestor) Martyr, both born at Light City:[56]

| 6. | i. | BENJAMIN R. G.[3] DOE, b. 17 Month 1854, m. CYNTHEA J. DEN. |
| | ii. | WILLIAM M. DOE, b. 25 Month 1856, d. in Sandy County in Month 1866. He "fell from that old oak on Willy's place," according to his [*And so forth*]∧∧∧∧∧∧∧∧∧∧∧∧∧∧ |

| child not continued; no identifying number |

[*The child of Martha Chrystal by her first husband would normally be discussed within the life story, not as separate child-list entry.*]

| reference notes. (See example notes in Compiled Genealogy:NGSQ System on pages 104–115 in this manual.) Square brackets do not surround reference-note numbers in footnotes or endnotes. |

1. Tristram Doe obituary∧∧∧∧∧∧∧∧
2. Ibid.
3. Tristram Doe entries, Wishful County Tax Books ∧∧∧∧∧∧∧∧∧∧∧∧∧∧∧ [*And so forth*] ∧∧∧∧∧∧∧∧∧∧∧∧∧

3. WILLIAM I.[2] DOE (*Tristram*[1]) was born in Sandy County on 30 Month 1810 and died in Friendly County, Weststate, on 2 Month 1883.[58] He married at Sintown, Eaststate, about 1850–1851,[59] **LOUISA ABITLATE**, daughter of Richard and (____) Abitlate.[60]

    [*And so forth—life story*]^^^

Children of William I. and Louisa (Abitlate) Doe, all born in Sandy County, the first four legitimated
        by William's will:[76]

7.	i.	WILLIAM I.[3] DOE (ABITLATE), a.k.a. JOHN NONAME, b. 24 Month 1841.
8.	ii.	TRISTRAM PLUTARCH DOE (ABITLATE), b. 3 Month 1842, m. LILLY PADD.
9.	iii.	LOUISA DOE (ABITLATE), b. 30 Month 1846, m. STILL POND.
	iv.	MARIA DOE (ABITLATE), b. 12 Month 1847; m. in Sandy County, 18 Month 1866, THOMAS COMMONNAME "Juner," son of Thomas Commonname "Sinyer."[77] In 1870, Thomas and Maria were living with his father and older, unmarried sister Sarah on their farm in northern Sandy.[78] Thomas Sr. died in 1873, leaving the farm to Sarah, who sold it immediately[79] and moved to Capital City, where she was census-enumerated in 1880.[80] Thomas Jr. (and resumably Maria) also appear to have left Sandy, but their destination has not been discovered. Five Thomas Commonnames were in Capital City in 1880, none with wife Maria or children of the right given names.[81] Three Thomases were in Sandy, ten in adjoining Spring and Glen counties, and three in Friendly County, Weststate, but none were with families that "fit" that of Thomas and Maria.[82] The search has extended into numerous other likely (and a few unlikely) states with equally discouraging results.[83] Maria[3] Doe and her husband Thomas Commonname were parents of the following children born in Sandy County prior to 1 June 1870, surname *Commonname*:[84] 1. *Thomas*[4], b. ca. 1868; and 2. *Louisa*, b. in Month 1869.
10.	v.	JANEANN DOE, b. 21 Month 1851, m. JOHN WATTS[3] DEESENDENT (*Elizabeth Mary Doe*[2], *Tristram*[1]).

[Sidebar note beside entry iv:] biography in child-list for one whose line cannot be continued

4. ELIZABETH MARY[2] DOE (*Tristram*[1]), born in Sandy County 26 Month 1823,[85] married there about 1844–1845 **MARTIN DEESENDENT**[86]; died at Dale, Eaststate [*And so forth*]^^^^^^^^^^^^

    Children of Elizabeth Mary Doe and her husband Martin Deesendent:

11.	i.	JOHN WATTS.[3] DEESENDENT, b. in Sandy County 23 Month 1846, m. JANEANN[3] DOE (*William I.*[2], *Tristram*[1])
	ii.	WILLIAM MARTIN DEESENDENT, b. in Sandy County 25 Month 1848, d. there 29 Month 1848.
	iii.	DEBORAH JANE DEESENDENT, b. in Sandy County 26 Month 1849, d. in Spring County 18 Month 1857.[108]
12.	iv.	DEBORAH JANE DEESENDENT (second of the name), b. in Spring County 29 Month 1852, m. ANDREW MELLONN.
13.	v.	ELIZABETH MARY DEESENDENT, b. in Spring County 3 Month 1853, m. GIOVANNI ROMA.
14.	vi.	SARAH PLUTARCH DEESENDENT, b. in Spring County 5 Month 1855, m. WILLIAM MELLONN.
15.	vii.	TRISTRAM DOE DEESENDENT, b. in Spring County 15 Month 1857, m. MELODY ROMA.
16.	viii.	JEFFERSON DAVIS DEESENDENT, b. at Dale 7 Month 1862, m. JOAN D'ARCK.

5. TRISTRAM ARTHUR P.[2] "TAP" DOE (*Tristram*[1]) was born in Sandy County about 1832.[109] He was "killed by lightning" on 23 Month 1889,[110] and is buried in Locksburg Cemetery, Eaststate.[111] He married in Sandy County, 14 Month 1853, **ELIZA G. L. (DOOLITTLE) ROE**,[112] daughter of Isaac and (____) Doolittle[113] and widow of Ian L. Roe.[114] Eliza was born in [*And so forth through life story*]^^^^

    Children of Tristram Arthur P. Doe and his wife Eliza G. L. (Doolittle) Roe, all born in Sandy County:[131]

17.	i.	ELIZA JANE[3] DOE, b. 21 Month 1854, m. I. C. YUE.
18.	ii.	WILLIAM I. DOE, b. 27 Month 1856, m. DOROTHY MARY ENGLISH.
19.	iii.	JAMES PLUTARCH "JP" DOE, b. in Month 1861, m. SHEILA MAUREEN IRISH.
20.	vi.	AMANDA ROBERTA "BOBBIE" DOE, b. 29 Month 1867, m. (1) JOSEPHUS BLANK, m. (2) ANDRÉ FRANÇOISE.

    [*Ian L. Roe, Tap's stepson, might be mentioned here in a child-list entry because he sometimes used the surname Doe. The child-list entry would explain the fact that he was not a direct-line Doe descendant, and his progeny would not be followed farther. He would not have identifying or birth-order numbers, and his generation indicator would be 1.*]

—— Third Generation ——

6. Benjamin R. G.[3] Doe (*Robert G.[2], Tristram[1]*) was born in Sandy County, 17 Month 1854, and was killed at Roughton, Untamed Territory, 29 Month 1898.[132] He married in Friendly County, Weststate, 30 Month 1875, **Cynthea J. Den**, daughter of [*And so forth—including life story*]ᴧᴧᴧᴧᴧᴧᴧᴧᴧᴧᴧᴧᴧᴧ

  Children of Benjamin R. G. and Cynthea (Den) Doe, all born at Smalltown, presumably:[150]

  i.   Jackson D.[4] Doe, b. 1 Month 1877,[151] d. in Untamed Territory before 29 Month 1898.[152]
  ii.   Benjamin R. G. Doe, b. 2 Month 1880, d. in Untamed Territory before 29 Month 1898.
21. iii. William I. Doe, b. 30 Month 1882, m. Barbara Delilah Myancestor.
  iv.   Daughter (name unknown), b. 12 Month 1885, d. in Untamed Territory before 29 Month 1898.

  [*Cynthea's children by second husband, George E. Nuhusband, would be discussed within the life story.*]

7. William I.[3] Doe (Abitlate), a.k.a. John Noname (*William I.[2], Tristram[1]*) was born in Sandy County, 24 Month 1841,[153] and died at Capital City, Eaststate, 22 Month 1919.[154]

  William was the oldest of four children born to Louisa Abitlate before she married his father, William I.[2] Doe, who acknowledged paternity [*And so forth*]ᴧᴧᴧᴧᴧᴧᴧᴧᴧᴧᴧᴧᴧᴧᴧᴧᴧᴧᴧᴧᴧᴧ

  The adopted children of William I. Doe (Abitlate), a.k.a. John Noname, said children born of Josephus Blank and his wife Amanda Roberta[3] Doe (*Tristram Arthur P.[2], Tristram[1]*):

22.   Tristram D.[4] Blank, b. at Dale, Eaststate, 2 Month 1883; m. Luisa Mai Allcott.
23.   Roberta Amanda "Bobbie" Blank, b. at Dale 2 Month 1884, m. Douglas Farebanks.

  The adopted child (parents unknown) of William I. Doe (Abitlate), a.k.a. John Noname was:

24.   Plutarch[1] "Archy" Noname, b. in Eastate in Month 1871, m. Fruzanne Seamstress.

ᴧᴧᴧᴧᴧᴧᴧᴧᴧ[*And so forth. The compilation continues with biographies of no. 8 Tristram Plutarch[3] Doe (Abitlate) and lists his six numbered children (25–30); and of no. 9 Louisa[3] Doe (Abitlate) and lists her eight numbered children (31–38).*]ᴧᴧᴧᴧᴧᴧᴧᴧᴧᴧᴧᴧᴧᴧᴧᴧᴧᴧᴧᴧᴧᴧᴧᴧᴧ

10. Janeann[3] Doe (*William I.[2], Tristram[1]*) was born in Sandy County on 21 Month 1848[220] and died at Smalltown, Weststate, on 24 Month 1901.[221] She married, in Sandy County, 19 Month 1865 her first cousin, **John Watts[3] Deesendent**,[222] son of Martin Deesendent and his wife Elizabeth Mary Doe (*Tristram[1]*).[223] [*And so forth—including life story*]ᴧᴧᴧᴧᴧᴧᴧᴧᴧᴧᴧᴧᴧᴧᴧᴧᴧᴧᴧᴧᴧᴧ

  Children of Janeann Doe and her husband, John Watts Deesendent:[234]

  i   Victoria Regina[4] Deesendent, b. in Sandy County 3 Month 1867, d. there 5 Month 1867 and was buried in the Deesendent family plot, Oakwood Cemetery, Locksburg.[235]
  ii Judith Jane Deesendent, b. in Sandy County ca. 1868; d. at Smalltown, Weststate, in 1907;[236] m. at Smalltown 18 Month 1891, Duncan McDoe[237] and was divorced from him 21 Month 1898.[238] Issue, surname *McDoe:* 1. *Angus W.*, b. 18 Month 1893, d. 27 Month 1907; 2. *Judith Jane,* b. 6 Month 1895, d. 28 Month 1897.[239]
  iii Elizabeth Mary Deesendent, b. in Empty County in 1871, d. at Smalltown in 1883.[240]
  iv John Watts Deesendent, b. and d. at Smalltown in 1881.[241]
39. v. Tristram Doe Deesendent, b. 19 Month 1884 at Smalltown.

11. John Doe[3] "Jack" Deesendent (*Elizabeth Mary Doe[2], Tristram[1]*) was born in Sandy County on 23 Month 1846 and died at First-Town, Weststate, 17 Month 1921.[242] He married (1) in Sandy County 19 Month 1865, **Janeann[3] Doe** (*William I.[2], Tristram[1]*), who was born in Sandy 21 Month 1848 and died at Smalltown 24 Month 1901.[243] John married (2) at Smalltown 24 Month 1902, **Alice I. (Wonder) Land** [*And so forth—including life story*]ᴧᴧᴧᴧᴧᴧᴧᴧᴧᴧᴧᴧᴧᴧᴧᴧᴧᴧᴧᴧᴧᴧᴧ

  In addition to five children born of his first wife (see no. 10), John Doe Deesendent was father of the following children by his second wife, Alice I. (Wonder) Land, all born in Dismal County:[256]

40. i. John Watts[4] Deesendent (second of the name), b. Month 1904; m. Trutha (Looking) Glass.
41. ii. George Washington Deesendent, b. Month 1907, m. Maddy Hatter.

42.   iii.   BENJAMIN FRANKLIN DEESENDENT, b. Month 1911, m. RHEDD QUEEN.
     iv.   DOLLY MADISON DEESENDENT, b. 17 Month 1913, d. 18 Month 1913.[257]
43.   v.   LATECOMER MARY DEESENDENT, b. Month 1918, m. CARL SURPRISE.

∧∧∧∧∧∧∧∧[*And so forth. The compilation continues with discussion of numbers 12–19 and the lists of their children, numbered 44–86.*]∧∧

20. AMANDA ROBERTA³ **"BOBBIE" DOE** (*Tristram Arthur P.*², *Tristram*¹) was born in Sandy County, 29 Month 1867.[319] Her death date and place have not been determined, but it is believed by family members that she died in France during World War I.[320] Amanda married (1) in Spring County, 26 Month 1883, **JOSEPHUS BLANK,** who was born 8 Month 1865[321] and died (place unknown) after 1889, son of Handy and Elizabeth Blank.[322] She married (2) at Capital City, 22 Month 1891, **ANDRÉ FRANÇIOSE,** son of Jean and Hélène (Fleur) Françoise of Petiteville, Canton of Somewhere,

| non-English names written with correct diacritical marks | France.[323] André was born [*And so forth*]∧∧∧∧∧∧ |

Josephus is said to have been a "drummer," a term which at that time was used for traveling salesmen as well as band members—family stories conflict about which he was.[325] In any case, the marriage was short lived and apparently unhappy. Amanda filed for divorce on grounds of "gross cruelty and abandonment," and the final final decree issued on dated 11 Month 1889.[326] She promptly moved from Spring County to Capital City, where the 1890 and 1891 city directories show "Mrs. Blank and children" among the residents at 123 Narrow Street, the home of her cousin John Noname (alias William I.³ Doe). Her occupation was given as "Type-writer." [327]

According to family stories, Amanda met her second husband, a wine merchant visiting Capital City on business, while she was working at Good's Grocers. Anxious lest he "escape back to France before marrying her," she did not mention her two small children until after the couple were wed.[328] Apparently willing to take home an American wife but not a whole family, "Mr. and Mrs. Andrew Francewase [*sic*]" approved John Noname's petition of 9 Month 1891 to adopt the two Blank children.[329] The newlyweds sailed for France six days later.[330]

Amanda corresponded often with her sister Eliza Jane, and from the letters that survive we can reconstruct, in part, her life in France.[333] [*And so forth*]∧∧∧∧∧∧∧∧∧∧∧∧∧∧∧∧∧∧∧∧∧∧∧∧∧∧∧∧∧

Children of Amanda Roberta "Bobbie" Doe by her first husband Josephus Blank, born at Dale:
     i.   TRISTRAM D.⁴ BLANK, b. 2 Month 1883; adopted 9 Month 1891 by William I.³ Doe (Abitlate), a.k.a. John Noname (*William I.*³, *Tristram*¹). See no. 22.
     ii.   ROBERTA AMANDA "MANDY" BLANK, b. 2 Month 1884; adopted with her brother Tristram on 9 Month 1891. See no. 23.

Children of Amanda Roberta Doe by her second husband André Françoise included;[328]
     iv.   ANDRÉ MARIE FRANÇOISE, b. at Petiteville 18 Month 1897; died, unmarried, 14 Month 1918 while serving in [*And so forth*]∧∧∧∧∧∧∧∧∧∧∧∧∧∧∧∧∧∧∧∧∧∧∧∧∧∧∧∧∧∧∧∧∧
87.   v.   LUCIENNE AMANDA FRANÇOISE, b. at Petiteville 2 Month 1900, m. at Petiteville 18 Month 1918 HENRY DIPLOMAT.

∧∧∧∧∧∧∧∧∧∧[*And so forth. The compilation continues through the rest of the generations intended to be included within it.*]∧∧∧

INDEX

Abbreviations: s = *standard (followed by its number);* n = *footnote on the indicated page*